Praise for
Corporate Creativity

"**Identifies six essential elements** that provide an environment to unleash creativity at every level of the organization."

—John F. Smith, Jr., Chairman, CEO, and President, General Motors

"*Corporate Creativity* **describes in rich detail** how creativity actually happens in companies and what can be done to get more of it. It is truly a joy to read."

—George Rathmann, Cofounder, Amgen, and
Cofounder, Chairman, and CEO, ICOS

"**This is one of the very few books on creativity that is a must-read for executives.** It is chock full of fascinating examples that demystify the creative process."

—Lt. General Walter F. Ulmer, Former Commandant of Cadets at West Point,
and Former President, The Center for Creative Leadership

"**I thought I understood creativity and its processes,** but *Corporate Creativity* gave me a whole new insight. I recommend it for pleasure as well as for serious reading."

—Philip Crosby, author of *Quality is Free* and *The Absolutes of Leadership*

"*Corporate Creativity* **argues persuasively** that great ideas, more than anything else, fuel corporate growth.... The book brims with anecdotes about baggage handlers and part-time accountants whose ideas save companies millions, even hundreds of millions of dollars.... *Corporate Creativity* is worth reading for its fascinating trek through the history of idea-hunting."

—*BusinessWeek*

"**Robinson and Stern, through historical analysis,** squash the long-held belief of many workplace experts that creativity can be planned, or that it can be a quota-driven, by-the-numbers endeavor."

—*The Hartford Courant*

"*Corporate Creativity* **is full of stories** that point out that creative acts come at unlikely times from the least likely sources."

—*Seattle Post-Intelligencer*

CORPORATE CREATIVITY

How Innovation and Improvement Actually Happen

ALAN G. ROBINSON & SAM STERN

Berrett-Koehler Publishers, Inc.
San Francisco

Berrett-Koehler Publishers, Inc.
450 Sansome Street, Suite 1200
San Francisco, CA 94111-3320
Tel: (415) 288-0260   Fax: (415) 362-2512
www.bkpub.com

ORDERING INFORMATION

Individual sales. Berrett-Koehler publications are available through most bookstores. They can also be ordered direct from Berrett-Koehler at the address above.

Quantity sales. Special discounts are available on quantity purchases by corporations, associations, and others. For details, contact the "Special Sales Department" at the Berrett-Koehler address above.

Orders for college textbook/course adoption use. Please contact Berrett-Koehler Publishers at the address above.

Orders by U.S. trade bookstores and wholesalers. Please contact Publishers Group West, 1700 West Fourth Street, Berkeley, CA 94710. Tel: (510) 528-1444; Fax: (510) 528-3444.

Printed in the United States of America
Printed on acid-free and recycled paper that is composed of 85% recycled fiber, including 10% postconsumer waste.

Library of Congress Cataloging-in-Publication Data

Robinson, Alan G.
    Corporate creativity : how innovation and improvement actually
happen / Alan G. Robinson, Sam Stern.
      p.   cm.
    Includes bibliographical references (p.   ) and index.
    ISBN 1–57675–049–3 (paperback: alk. paper)
    ISBN 1–57675–009–4 (hardcover: alk. paper)
    1. Creative ability in business.   2. Technological innovations—
Management.   3. Organizational learning.   I. Stern, Sam.
II. Title.
HD53.R6   1997
658—dc21
                                             97–24838
                                               CIP

First hardcover edition: July 1997
First paperback edition: July 1998

This paperback edition contains the complete text of the original hardcover edition.

98 97   10 9 8 7 6 5 4 3 2 1

Book Production: Pleasant Run Publishing Services
Composition: Classic Typography

To Margaret, Phoebe, and Margot
—AGR

To Kitzie, David, and Jesse
—SS

Contents

— *Acknowledgments*—

Many people played an important role in bringing this book to life. First and foremost, we are grateful to all those from so many different companies around the world who told us their stories. Without them, this book could never have come about. We fondly remember the time we spent with each of them, and we thank them for their generosity and help.

We were also fortunate to have the support of a number of institutions and organizations. Our home institutions, the University of Massachusetts and Oregon State University, gave us wonderful environments in which to work, never failed to back us when we needed it, and made the space for us to carry through on what turned out to be a somewhat longer and different journey than we had expected. When we were in Japan, the Tokyo Institute of Technology, the Japan Management Association, and the Japan Industrial Training Association greatly helped with our research. Special thanks also go to the Athens Laboratory of Business Administration in Greece, whose faculty and students gave us an excellent testing ground for our ideas during their early stages.

We always believed that publishing this book with Berrett-Koehler would make it better than it would otherwise have been. Working with Steven Piersanti and Richard and Barbara Swanson, whose wonderful insights and critical observations greatly sharpened our thinking, made it clear that this was true. We are also grateful to the reviewers, whose comments and suggestions raised the quality of the manuscript to a much higher level. And to Gwen and Alan Robinson, who were with us all the way and taught us so very much, we will always be grateful.

Introduction

THE POWER
of the
UNEXPECTED

Many organizations helped us during the writing of this book and encouraged employees at all levels to spend time with us. Their interest and enthusiasm reflect the general realization that creativity in companies falls far short of what is possible. Most companies are aware that their creative *potential* greatly exceeds their creative *performance*. The problem is that they don't know what to do about it. We believe that this potential cannot be realized until people recognize where it actually lies. Consider this. Most creative acts, as they now occur in companies, are not planned for and come from where they are least expected. It is impossible to predict *what* they will be, *who* will be involved in them, and *when* and *how* they will happen. This is the true nature of corporate creativity, and it is here that a company's creative potential really lies. For corporate creativity, the real power is in the unexpected.

A good example of the power of the unexpected occurred at Japan Railways (JR) East, the largest rail carrier in the world. This company never anticipated that constructing a new bullet-train line through the mountains north of Tokyo would lead it to a new and very profitable business—in beverages. The new train line required many tunnels. In the tunnel through Mount Tanigawa, water began to cause problems, and JR East engineers drew up plans to drain it away. But inside the tunnel, construction crews had found a use for the water—they were actually drinking it. A maintenance worker, whose job was to check the safety of the tunneling equipment, thought it tasted so good that he proposed that instead of pumping it away into runoffs, JR East should bottle and market it as premium mineral water. His idea was implemented, and soon the water appeared on the market under the brand name Oshimizu. Within a very short time the water became so popular that JR East installed vending machines for it on every one of its nearly one thousand platforms in Tokyo and eastern Japan. Advertisements for the water emphasize the purity of Mt. Tanigawa's snow pack, the source of the water, and the slow process by which it percolates through the mountain's unusual geological strata, picking up healthful amounts of minerals such as calcium, magnesium, and potassium. A JR East subsidiary now offers home delivery of it in cases or twenty-liter containers, and the product line has grown to include juices as well as iced and hot teas and coffees. In 1994, sales of Oshimizu beverages were $47 million.

Spectacular creative acts like this do happen now and again in companies, but the vast majority of them are far less dramatic. Consider, for example, the American Airlines flight attendant who sent a suggestion into headquarters in Dallas, Texas, one of some forty-five thousand ideas the airline received that year from its employees. She attached a plastic lid to the suggestion form. This lid, she explained, was a cover for the metal pots that flight attendants use to serve coffee. It was meant to keep the coffee warm and to prevent it from spilling on the passengers in the event of turbulence. Standard procedure called for the catering division to provision each aircraft with ten of these lids. However, the flight attendant had noticed that at the end of each flight, at least half of the lids were being thrown away unused. She proposed that only five should be put on each flight. The airline initiated a study of her proposal. At first, the potential savings seemed negligible—each lid cost only 1.5 cents, hardly worth bothering about. It was soon realized, however, that saving five lids would mean saving 7.5 cents per flight, and with more than 2,300 flights per day on each of 365 days in the year, her idea about penny-and-a-half coffeepot lids was worth more than $62,000 in annual savings.

JR East did not anticipate its entry into the beverage business, nor did American Airlines plan to squeeze cost savings out of its in-flight coffee service. Both ideas were initiated by individuals and were entirely unanticipated by their management. Through our investigations of creativity in companies around the world—even in Japan, where Japanese and foreigners alike seem to think it is not supposed to happen—we came to realize that the majority of creative acts, whether dramatic innovations or tiny improvements, occur in this way. They are not only unplanned but completely unexpected.

Before we met, each of us had already arrived at this realization. For Sam Stern, it came during his two-year study of creativity in Japanese companies, sponsored by the Japan Management Association (JMA). The study looked in detail at projects that had received national awards from the government's Science and Technology Agency and the Japan Institute of Invention and Innovation from 1986 to 1990. An interesting fact emerged. More than half of these award-winning projects had been initiated by individuals and had not been anticipated by anyone else at their companies. Furthermore, the novelty and impact of these self-initiated projects far exceeded that of the projects initiated by management. A second phase of the JMA study compared all the award-winning projects (some two hundred of them) with a comparison sample of projects that were commercially successful but not especially creative. A similar pattern emerged: the award-winning projects were more likely to have been initiated by individuals, while those that were not especially novel were far more likely to have been planned for by management.

At about the same time, Alan Robinson was noticing a similar phenomenon in the world of continuous improvement. His studies of the best and the worst practices in the world took him to organizations in many countries. Almost all the companies he looked at made use of some kind of planned approach to continuous improvement, an approach in which *what* to improve, *by how much,* and *by whom* was decided in advance. Sometimes even a particular problem-solving method was prescribed and followed. Yet the top performers invariably placed greater emphasis on systems designed to stimulate improvements that had not been planned for. Here, too, the more novel and far-reaching improvements tended to be the unanticipated ones.

This book grew out of our common insight that companies could dramatically increase their creative performance if they recognized the true nature of their creativity and learned how to promote unanticipated creative acts. So that you can see this for yourselves, we have included many detailed accounts of how creative acts actually occurred in companies. In every case, we focused on the part of the story that is usually ignored—the unexpected origins in each instance. We often wondered why they proved to be so difficult to unearth. Perhaps a natural tendency of management is to believe that it is more in control of events than it really is, particularly when those events lead to successful improvements or innovations. Over time, corporate word-of-mouth and even official company histories obscure the unexpected origins of creative acts, substituting simplistic and misleading accounts of what really happened. Early on, we learned the danger of relying on secondhand information.

There is no shortage of advice available on ways to promote creativity in companies, but much of it seems to assume that people will suspend their critical faculties. It is hard to imagine how making chicken yells, rearranging the furniture, or expanding the cafeteria menu to include Thai food and tofu (as one recent book suggests) could have helped the JR East maintenance worker or the American Airlines flight attendant come up with their ideas. The truth is that recommendations such as these have little, if any, connection to actual creative acts. In the course of our investigations, we have been careful to connect creative acts with the actions that really contributed to them.

An entirely different perspective on managing creativity comes with recognition of the power of the unexpected. We believe that any company that follows the recommendations in this book will raise its creative performance to much higher levels.

Chapter One

THE TRUE NATURE
—*of*
CORPORATE CREATIVITY

"Microsoft's only factory asset is the human imagination," observed the New York Times Magazine writer Fred Moody. . . . After exposing an audience to the Microsoft quote, I ask a telling question: "Does anyone here know what it means to 'manage' the human imagination?" So far, not a single hand has gone up, including mine. I don't know what it means to manage the human imagination either, but I do know that imagination is the main source of value in the new economy. And I know we better figure out the answer to my question—quick.

TOM PETERS[1]

Early in the Korean War the U.S. Air Force hired Paul Torrance, holder of a newly acquired doctorate in psychology, to develop a training program that would prepare its pilots and crews to survive extreme conditions of deprivation and danger, including intense cold or heat; lack of food, water, or shelter; and being downed at sea, in the jungle, or even behind enemy lines. The immediate and urgent reason for his assignment was to prepare aircrews for the particularly brutal experience some would face as prisoners of war (POWs) in North Korea. Torrance reviewed the research literature and studied existing training programs. He also interviewed hundreds of Air Force personnel who had survived such experiences in World War II. In the end, what he found surprised him: the thing that had proved most critical for survival was something that no training program taught: *creativity.* Existing courses offered plenty of information about how to deal with a variety of hostile conditions, discussed actual cases of people who had survived and even escaped from POW camps, and often included realistic simulation exercises. But Torrance found that no matter how much training people had received, when faced with the real thing, they almost invariably had to cope with *unexpected* situations. Those who survived had combined elements of their training and life experiences to create a completely new survival technique, one they had not been taught.

In describing the importance of creativity to survival, Torrance wrote:

> *Creativity and invention are adaptive forces which have perhaps been given too little attention in connection with problems of survival and survival training. Successful survivors describe many creative and imaginative behaviors which not only solved immediate problems for them but apparently gave them renewed energy for continued adaptation.*[2]

This discovery fascinated Torrance and led him on to a distinguished research career in creativity, one that spanned more than forty years. In fact, he would later create the now widely used Torrance tests of creativity.

A Look at Corporate Creativity

Few organizations would need a formal study to convince them that creativity is important to their long-term survival. However, Torrance's study also identified the connection between creativity and the unexpected, a connection that came to light only after he looked in detail at how aircrews *actually* survived. Corporate creativity is also tied to the unexpected. But we, too, came to realize this only after our own detailed study of how creative acts are actually initiated in companies. Let us now look at three examples, each of which occurred in a different industry.

From Cheese to Clinical Medicine

Creativity can and should happen in any kind of organization, not just in high-technology companies. Consider this example from Snow Brand Milk Products, a Japanese dairy company with 8,600 employees.

In April 1980, Tomoshige Hori, a young researcher at Snow Brand, went to a symposium in Tokyo on the thermophysical properties of materials, where he happened to attend a lecture by a professor from Keio University. The subject of the lecture had nothing to do with anything Hori had worked on, was working on, or planned to work on. It was about a new way to measure the thermal conductivity of a liquid using a "hot-wire" with an electric current passing through it. Hori's job at Snow Brand was to investigate ways to make dairy products more nutritious and better tasting. He worked on such projects as improving the "bite" of yogurt or the texture of ice cream. Even though the ideas discussed in the lecture bore no obvious relation to Hori's work, or to any other work done at Snow Brand, he was intrigued and began to experiment in his lab. However, instead of using water, as described in the lecture, Hori decided to use a liquid his company had a lot of— milk. Using experimental apparatus that he built himself, he began to measure its thermal conductivity.

One midsummer afternoon, he left the lab and forgot to turn off the electric current to the thin platinum hot-wire. When he came back the milk had curdled. It normally took only twenty seconds to measure its thermal conductivity, but Hori had left the heat on for *several hours*. Glancing over the printout, he noticed that at one point a large temperature change had taken place in the hot-wire. It didn't take him long to figure out that this temperature jump had occurred at the instant when the milk curdled. He knew that the point at which milk curdled was related to cheese making, although he knew little else about this process. His curiosity aroused, he did some reading and went to talk with the people responsible for cheese production at Snow Brand. He soon found out that being able to monitor the amount of curdling in milk is crucial to making good cheese. Just as cheese manufacturers all over the world had been doing for centuries, Snow Brand relied on the subjective judgment of skilled workers who stood over the open vats of curdling milk and, using their experience, called out when it was time to "cut the curd." The timing of this decision was critical: cutting the curd too early resulted in a poor yield, but cutting it too late meant the cheese would have a poor taste. Hori realized that his discovery—that curdling could be detected by monitoring temperature changes in the platinum hot wire—could lead to a highly accurate and even automated process for making cheese. He tells what happened next:

I was convinced that I had stumbled upon something new, and reported the result to my laboratory group. The reactions from my boss and colleagues, however, were not encouraging, and it was suggested that I had better stop such anti-application-oriented or "weeds" research. I was in no position at that time to contest this decision and had to stop further work for the next one and a half years. . . .

Despite this discouraging setback, I decided that I must get the results published in a scientific journal, otherwise the idea would be put on the shelf with many others to just gather dust. I submitted a paper in English to the most authoritative journal in the field and applied for an international and national patent.[3]

Hori's paper was accepted in the *Journal of Food Science* and, when it was published, generated considerable professional interest.[4] Encouraged, Hori once again approached his management and presented them with the results of his unofficial research. He showed them several letters from prominent foreign researchers who had written to him about the *Journal of Food Science* article. The evidence of interest and the approval of such well-known experts at last proved compelling, and about three years after Hori attended the lecture that started his interest in heat transfer, the management of Snow Brand Milk at last gave his project full official support.

Even with the full support of top management, however, it took a further two years to develop the idea to the point where it could be used in actual cheese production. Two more years were needed to enlist the support of the technical personnel at Snow Brand's cheese factory in northern Japan, which had been selected to pilot the new process. Hori, who was based in Tokyo, visited the plant almost every month during this time, spending more than a week there each trip. He knew that he needed the support and expertise of the company's technical personnel if his new process was to be successfully developed. He was also well aware of the human aspects of his discovery—in particular, it would affect the prestigious jobs of the highly skilled cheese makers.

By 1988, eight years after the professor's lecture on thermal conductivity, Snow Brand Milk had installed new hot-wire probes in the curdling vats at all its mechanized cheese plants in Japan. Today, in Japan and throughout the world, hundreds of thousands of tons of cheese are produced each year using the process developed by Hori. In recognition of his creativity, Hori received a national award from the Japan Institute of Invention and Innovation in 1990.

The story does not end there. In 1992, Stoelting, a U.S. dairy equipment company, began marketing Snow Brand's system in the United States under the name Optiset. In 1997, the largest customer for Optiset was Land O'Lakes, a leading U.S. dairy company. Other U.S. cheese manufacturers have been slower to adopt the hot-wire method because of the issues it raises regarding the jobs of their skilled cheese makers, who hold important and influential positions in the industry. The hot-wire technology developed by Hori has also been used commercially to measure the viscosity of inks, paints, and chemicals and may one day even provide a way to measure the viscosity of blood without having to draw a sample.

Eliminating Your Own Job

When people discuss creativity in companies, they generally refer to spectacular innovations in *other* organizations, the ones that make good stories. Rarely do they bring up everyday examples of creativity in their *own* companies, the bulk of which are far less dramatic. Consider this example we came across at DCM-Daewoo, an Indo-Korean joint venture that produces medium-sized trucks in Surajpur, India, a town about thirty miles west of Delhi. The creative act here involved an improvement in the way windshield-washer jets were adjusted to squirt water onto the correct area of the windscreen. Previously, two workers were required to do this job: one sat inside the cab and pressed the washer button to squirt the water, and the other stood on the bumper and adjusted the jets. The worker inside the cab thought that with a simple extension-cord device attached to the windshield-wiper control arm, the worker outside the cab could activate the jets alone. With the help of the plant's continuous improvement department, he designed and built such a device and proved that it could be successfully used on the assembly line. In other words, the suggester proposed a way *to eliminate his own job*. The improvement was made, his job was eliminated, and he was reassigned to new work.

What Are Those Yellow and Black Tags?

There is also room for creativity in companies that must operate with highly standardized procedures, like the airlines, for instance. Consider this example from British Airways (BA), the largest airline in the world. In early 1993, Ian Hart, a BA baggage handler working in Terminal 4 at London's Heathrow Airport (BA's international terminal), initiated what would be an important creative act for his company. He often worked in the luggage carousel area where arriving passengers went to collect their baggage, and he found himself frequently being asked a certain question. The bags with yellow and black tags always seemed to arrive first at the carousel, and the passengers wanted to know how they could get these tags for their bags. Hart realized that the customers who were asking him this question were always the first people off each airplane, that is, BA's first-class passengers. He decided to find out more about the mysterious yellow and black tags. After some detective work, he learned that they were used for the luggage of standby passengers, including BA crew members who were deadheading, or flying as passengers to or from their work assignments. Because BA policy was to give precedence to paying customers over deadheading personnel, these employees flew on a standby basis, never knowing until the last minute if they would get a seat on a particular aircraft.

In time, Hart discovered that the current system unintentionally gave priority handling to standby passengers' luggage. Normally, passenger luggage was containerized before it was put into the cargo hold. Hart found that not only was the first-class container regularly topped off with the baggage of standby passengers, but this container was often among the *last* to be unloaded. This created a situation where first-class passengers often had to wait a long time for their luggage, whose imminent arrival they had learned to recognize by a parade of bags with black and yellow tags. Naturally, this created a poor impression of BA's first-class service. Hart proposed a change in the procedure. Rather than the first-class luggage being loaded into containers, he suggested that it be loose-loaded last into the aircraft's front hold, just before departure. On the aircraft's arrival, a BA staff member could be detailed to offload the first-class bags and get them quickly to the carousel. The idea was not a complicated one, but since it would require changing procedures worldwide and would affect many people, BA decided to test it on various routes in the summer of 1993. The trials were successful and Hart's idea became the current "First & Fast" procedure used on all of BA's inbound wide-body flights into Heathrow's Terminal 4. The average time for first-class luggage to arrive at the carousel dropped immediately from 20 to 12 minutes and by the end of 1994 had dropped to 9 minutes, 48 seconds, with some routes regularly achieving 7 minutes. Only after his idea had been implemented did someone suggest to Hart that he write it up and submit it to Brainwaves, BA's suggestion system. In 1994, it was awarded the Chairman's Customer Service Award of the Year, and Hart received £11,000 (about $18,000) as well as two round-trip Concorde tickets to the United States.

Few industries are as standardized as the airline industry, which handles large numbers of people and aircraft on a daily basis, and for which safety is paramount. But even so, Hart was able to initiate a creative act that was important to his company. First-class customers are extremely profitable to any airline and need to feel the extra attention they are paying so much for. Even in the most rigid environments, there are places and times in which creativity is not only appropriate, but desirable.

Managing for Corporate Creativity

Each of the preceding examples is an instance of corporate creativity, which we define as follows:

> *A company is creative when its employees do something new and potentially useful without being directly shown or taught.*

The tangible results of corporate creativity, so vital for long-term survival and success, are *improvements* (changes to what is already done) and *innovations* (entirely new activities for the company). As one would expect, most creative acts are improvements.

None of the improvements or innovations we have described so far were the result of a management plan. Moreover, all of them were brought about by people whom no one—including management and even the creators themselves—had previously identified as being particularly creative. Snow Brand never set out to change the way cheese was made, nor did DCM-Daewoo target its windshield-washer adjusting operation for manpower reductions. Before Ian Hart stepped forward, British Airways had no plans for high-speed handling of first-class luggage at Heathrow, and if it had, would it have asked a baggage handler to spearhead the initiative?

These examples and all the many others we looked at have led us to a critical realization about the true nature of corporate creativity. Most creative acts are not planned for and come from where they are least expected. Nobody can predict *who* will be involved in them, *what* they will be, *when* they will occur, or *how* they will happen. But this does not mean that nothing can be done. We believe that companies can dramatically increase their creative performance once they recognize the nature of their creativity and learn how to actively promote unanticipated improvements and innovations. It is here that the richest potential for promoting corporate creativity really lies. As far as creativity is concerned, the power is indeed in the unexpected.

The Six Essential Elements of Corporate Creativity

In every unexpected creative act that we have studied, six elements played a role, and we have come to believe that these elements are the key to promoting consistent corporate creativity. Although no one can predict the *specific* creative acts that will follow, the likelihood of their happening will significantly increase when these six elements are in place. "Managing" creativity is about raising probabilities, and in this respect it is similar to operating a casino. Even though casinos do not know how individual gamblers will fare at any given table, they know very well that if enough customers come and play for long enough against the house odds, the casino will make a very predictable and stable profit. In the short term, it is a matter of probability, but in the long term, profits are a matter of certainty. In much the same way, although companies cannot know where specific creative acts will come from or what they will be, they can take action to increase the frequency with which these events occur. The second half of this book will introduce these elements, explain why they are important for corporate creativity, and describe how to implement them. The six elements are:

1. Alignment
2. Self-initiated activity
3. Unofficial activity
4. Serendipity
5. Diverse stimuli
6. Within-company communication

The first element, *alignment,* is about ensuring that the interests and actions of all employees are directed toward a company's key goals, so that *any* employee will recognize and respond positively to a potentially useful idea. Companies can *function* with relatively poor alignment, but they cannot be consistently creative unless they are strongly aligned. Alignment is often overlooked; it is intangible and elusive, and as far as corporate creativity is concerned, its effects are readily visible only when a company is either extraordinarily well aligned or misaligned. Chapter Five, where we begin our discussion of alignment, tells the story of the disastrous (and, in hindsight, somewhat comical) system used in the former Soviet Union to promote "mass creativity." More than anything else, it was *misalignment* that led to the collapse of this system, begun with such high hopes in the 1920s. The system continued to strike fear into Soviet managers at all levels up until 1991, when Mikhail Gorbachev finally put it out of its misery.

The Soviet story illustrates well how destructive misalignment is to creativity. At the opposite extreme, to show how a company can align itself and how strong alignment promotes creativity, we turn in Chapter Six to the example of the IdeAAs in Action program at American Airlines. Alignment for cost savings at American Airlines is so strong that the flight attendant with the coffee-lid idea never had any doubt that her company would welcome and reward her proposal if it saved money. However, from the point of view of creativity, alignment is a double-edged sword. It can also limit a company's creativity. This, too, becomes quite apparent in the case of American Airlines.

The second element of corporate creativity is *self-initiated activity.* Even though Snow Brand Milk made cheese, it had no strategic plan to develop a new cheese-making technology. Hori chose the problem himself, initiated the development activity, and brought the new technology to his company. The JR East maintenance worker, the British Airways baggage handler, and the American Airlines flight attendant also were employees who thought their ideas might be possible, took hold of them, and made them work. One reason why self-initiated activity figures so prominently in corporate creativity is that it allows employees to pick a problem they are interested in and feel able to solve, for *whatever* reason. This means that their intrinsic motivation is much higher than would be the case if the project had been planned or picked for them by someone else. As we will describe in Chapter Seven, it is surprisingly straightforward to promote the kind of self-initiated activity that leads to creative acts.

The third element of corporate creativity is *unofficial activity,* activity that occurs in the absence of direct official support, and with the intent of doing something new and useful. Hori's unofficial activity lasted for three years, during which only he kept the idea alive. Had he let go of it at any point during those three years, it would not have been realized. When an idea is new to a company, it is often resisted and opposed. Unofficial activity gives ideas a safe haven where they have the chance to develop until they are strong enough to overcome that resistance. Furthermore, giving a project official status raises all kinds of barriers to creativity, which every planned project encounters throughout its life. Unofficially, Hori was free to experiment as he pleased, even far outside his job description, and it was during this time that he was able to make the critical connection between the thermal conductivity of milk and its curdling point, and to discover how this might be useful in cheese making. In almost every instance we examined, the essence of the creative act was arrived at during the unofficial period.

The fourth element, also evident in the dairy company example, is *serendipity.* Although this word is widely used, few people know of its unusual history and that its original meaning has been lost. When this meaning is restored, the actions that companies can take to promote serendipity become clear. A serendipitous discovery is one made by *fortunate accident* in the presence of *sagacity* (keenness of insight). If Hori had not accidentally left the heater on for an outrageous period of time while experimenting with thermal conductivity and had not recognized the significance of what he then saw, he would never have made his serendipitous discovery. Creativity often involves recombining or making connections between things that may seem unconnected. The more abstruse the connection, the greater the intellectual distance that must be traversed to make it, and the greater the role for the unexpected. Serendipity helps to bridge distances, such as the distance between the thermal conductivity of milk and its curdling point. For Hart at British Airways, serendipity occurred when a passenger asked about the significance of the yellow and black tags. We don't know how important serendipity was in triggering the DCM-Daewoo improvement. Perhaps one day one of the two workers at DCM-Daewoo showed up late, and for a while the other had to do both jobs and realized that one of them could be eliminated. Whether or not this actually happened, serendipity does play a key role in creativity and, as we shall describe in Chapter Nine, companies can do things to promote it.

The fifth element of corporate creativity is *diverse stimuli*. A stimulus may provide fresh insight into something a person has already set out to do, or it may bump that person into something different. In the case of Hori, the most significant stimulus of this type was the lecture he heard on measuring the thermal conductivity of water. However, it is impossible to predict how an individual will react to a particular stimulus, and what provokes one person may not even be noticed by another. If someone else from Snow Brand had attended the same lecture, for example, would that person have been stimulated to put together the apparatus needed to experiment with the phenomenon? In Chapter Ten, we describe what companies can do to promote diverse stimuli. While organizations should do all they can to bring diverse stimuli to their employees, they should also recognize that efforts of this kind will have limited impact. The truth is that most stimuli arise in connection with daily life or with the work itself. It is far more important for an organization to provide opportunities for its employees to tell others about the stimuli they have received and the possibilities these stimuli suggest to them. It is here that the real leverage lies.

The sixth and final element of corporate creativity is *within-company communication*. Every organization carries out planned activities and should establish the necessary lines of communication to support them. But these official channels are of limited usefulness for corporate creativity. In order for Hori to appreciate the potential of his discovery, it was crucial for him to find out more about cheese making from those who actually did it. Since no one had anticipated this possibility, he had to do this on his own. Unanticipated within-company communication is one of the things that seems to happen naturally at smaller companies, but not so naturally at larger ones. The larger the company, the *more* likely it is that the components of creative acts are already present somewhere in it, but the *less* likely it is that they will be brought together without some help. We believe that a company's creative potential increases rapidly with its size, but that without systems in place to promote unanticipated exchanges of information, this potential will never be realized. Worse, the assumption will continue to be made that creativity can only really happen in small companies. As our examples will show, this type of communication is difficult enough between employees who work at the same location. What about communication between people who work in different divisions and might never, in the normal course of events, meet each other? In Chapter Eleven, we discuss the importance of such communication and what companies can do to promote it.

At every company we studied, we met people who felt that their organization's potential for creativity was far greater than its present performance would indicate. They were right. We believe that this situation will not change until the true nature of creativity becomes generally recognized. The bulk of a company's potential creativity is virtually unreachable with the usual plan-and-control style of management, because it lies in creative acts that cannot be specifically asked for and that no amount of planning can directly cause. The key to corporate creativity lies in these unanticipated creative acts, and our six elements offer a way to realize the tremendous potential they represent.

MAIN POINTS

Most creative acts are unexpected. This is the true nature of corporate creativity and it is where a company's creative potential really lies.

Tomoshige Hori's new way to make cheese had not been planned for, or even anticipated by, Snow Brand Milk Products, a company that makes a lot of cheese.

A working definition of creativity:

A company is creative when its employees do something new and potentially useful without being directly shown or taught.

The results of creativity in companies are *improvements* (changes to what is already done) and *innovations* (entirely new activities for the company).

Even in the most rigidly proceduralized environments, there is a place and a time for creativity.

Few businesses depend more on standard operating procedures than major airlines. But British Airways certainly had room for a baggage handler's idea for "First & Fast" luggage handling, and American Airlines saved $62,000 from a flight attendant's idea about coffee lids.

The six elements of corporate creativity, which play a role in every creative act, are the key to increasing corporate creativity. They are:

1. *Alignment*
2. *Self-initiated activity*
3. *Unofficial activity*
4. *Serendipity*
5. *Diverse stimuli*
6. *Within-company communication*

Chapter Two

HOW PRECONCEPTIONS LIMIT CORPORATE CREATIVITY

The real creative ideas originate hither and yon in the individual members of the staff and no one can tell in advance what they will be or where they will crop up.

FRANK B. JEWETT
Vice President of Research and Development at AT&T, 1925–1944[1]
Organizer and First Head of Bell Labs

A particularly enduring and widely held stereotype of a creative person is that of the "lone heroic inventor," which leads companies to fall into what we call the "high-flier trap," in which substantial resources are invested in a handful of supposedly highly creative people who are granted great freedom. The stereotype has endured because it is based on partial truths as well as on a widespread misunderstanding of creativity. The creativity of the high fliers, when and if it comes about, is certainly important. However, it constitutes only a fraction of a company's creative potential.

It seems that the stereotype of the lone heroic inventor was formed, and then promulgated through both popular and academic culture, by what happened during an era sometimes referred to as the United States' Golden Age of the Independent Inventor. According to Thomas Hughes, who chronicled this period in his book, *American Genesis: A Century of Invention and Technological Enthusiasm:*

> No other nation has displayed such inventive power and produced such brilliantly original inventors as the United States during the half-century beginning around 1870.[2]

The Golden Age began at about the time when Alexander Graham Bell invented the telephone (1875) and Thomas Edison opened his Menlo Park Research Laboratory (1876), which was intended to give an acknowledged genius many assistants who could follow though on his ideas. The Golden Age had clearly ended by 1935, the first year when the number of patents issued to companies in the United States surpassed the number given to individuals, and when it was obvious that the Menlo Park model no longer worked. In companies today, with the rise of specialization and the explosion of knowledge, as well as the increasing complexity of processes, invention and creation come about very differently. The problem is that the extraordinary achievements of the great inventors have led us to overlook both the immeasurably greater number and impact of innovations made in corporate settings since the Golden Age. Like Hori's, these creative acts have received almost no attention in historical records. As a result, management tends to extract the wrong lessons from the successes of extraordinary people working during a unique period in history, a period that ended more than sixty years ago. The age of the lone heroic inventor is over. Nevertheless, many people still hold onto the image when they think about creativity. It is not hard to see why companies that fall into the highflier trap never really give themselves a chance to tap their real creative potential.

The No-Preconceptions Principle

Suppose that your company made a list of all its employees and the things each one knew about the operations of the company that no one else knew. Wouldn't you end up with a list that had something next to every name? What about a similar list of things only one or two employees knew? There would be even more entries next to every name. Surprisingly often, items from such lists become the key ingredients of creative acts. Those involved simply happen to be the one or two employees who know something relevant and whose interest is aroused, or who happen to be in the right place at the right time. In this light, it is not surprising that the vast majority of unplanned creative acts in today's companies are brought about by people that no one—including themselves—previously thought of as particularly creative. From the perspective of management, these facts may at first be disconcerting. They mean that a company can never know in advance:

- *Who* will be involved in a creative act
- *What* it will be
- *When* it will occur
- *How* it will occur

If this is the case, then any preconceptions a company holds about the *who, what, when,* or *how* will necessarily blind it to potential sources of creativity. This observation leads to the "No-Preconceptions Principle" of corporate creativity:

> *A company's creativity is limited to the same extent that it acts on preconceptions about who will be creative, what they will do, and when and how they will do it.*

The fact is that the real leverage for corporate creativity does not lie in strategies based on identifying creative people, but in promoting creativity from all employees. That is the purpose of the six elements of corporate creativity we describe in the second half of this book.

Before we discuss these six elements in detail, we ask you to accept the No-Preconceptions Principle and the associated unpredictability that is an intrinsic part of creativity. To do this, it is necessary to cast off preconceptions about corporate creativity—preconceptions that are surprisingly widespread and deeply rooted in our thinking. Until this is done, they stand solidly between a company and its creative potential.

Who Will Be Involved in a Creative Act?

A long-standing feature of "ABC World News Tonight" is its special "Person of the Week" report each Friday. Usually the segment features a prominent political, business, or social leader. But on June 14, 1991, anchor Peter Jennings told his viewers that "ABC World News Tonight" had chosen Kathy Betts, a part-time employee of the Commonwealth of Massachusetts who, incredibly, had made a discovery worth more than half a billion dollars in cash to the state, and roughly $200 million per year thereafter. For Governor William Weld, newly elected as the first Republican governor in twenty years in a state with a strong Democratic tradition, the windfall could not have come at a better time—just two weeks before state law required him to balance the budget at the end of the fiscal year on June 30. Without this new influx of money, he might well have been forced to break his important campaign promise to balance the budget without raising taxes or borrowing, while at the same time avoiding another round of unpopular cuts in state programs. Thanks to Kathy Betts, he was able to close the $460 million gap the Commonwealth had faced in its $13.5 billion budget and to end the fiscal year with a modest surplus of $29 million. For Massachusetts' 44,000 state employees, whose morale was extremely low after waves of layoffs and a ten-day furlough, it meant a respite from unremitting bad news.

Single-handedly, Kathy Betts, an engaging working mother of two small children, had changed the public perception and self-image of state workers, rescued the governor, and given the entire state a needed lift. What she did involved the entries that would have been next to her name on our imaginary list: the list of things she knew that perhaps only one or two other state workers knew. That it came as such a surprise, and made the national news, has a lot to do with the fact that she didn't fit the stereotype of a creative person. No one expected it from her— not the politicians, not the media, and not even the people in her state. To understand what she did, and why it involved something she knew that few others in her organization did, we first have to understand a little about her job and the system in which she worked.

In 1991, Kathy Betts worked three days a week in the Medicaid Department at the Massachusetts Department of Public Welfare (DPW). She liked her part-time schedule, because it allowed her to spend time with her young children. Her job was to handle Medicaid reimbursements to the Commonwealth's roughly one hundred acute care hospitals, the ones that provide short-term treatment for serious medical conditions. Medicaid, the national health insurance program mandated by the federal government for welfare recipients, requires each state to pay for basic medical coverage. The federal government reimburses the Commonwealth of Massachusetts fifty cents for each Medicaid dollar it spends.

Almost every acute care hospital has a problem with "uncompensated care," money it is owed for treatment it has provided but that patients are unable or unwilling to pay. Although hospitals can turn uninsured patients away, the law requires them to accept anyone in an emergency. The difficulty arises with how the word *emergency* is interpreted. In Massachusetts, at least, hospitals tend to err on the cautious side. Unless it is absolutely obvious to the hospital staff that the case is not an emergency, the patient will get to see a doctor, after which the hospital might as well finish the treatment. In addition to all this unplanned free care, most hospitals also have some sort of official program in which prospective patients can fill out an application for free care that the hospital might then choose to provide. Each hospital keeps records of the free care it provides and later applies to the state for financial relief. For some Massachusetts hospitals, uncompensated care costs can amount to as much as 20 percent of revenue. At Boston City Hospital, which because of its location serves as the safety net for a great number of the city's poor, the figure is more like 40 percent.

Before Kathy Betts came along, Massachusetts tried to help hospitals with their uncompensated care bills through the Department of Medical Security (DMS), an independent state agency set up specifically for this purpose. DMS was entirely separate and in fact completely across town from the DPW, where Kathy Betts worked. All hospitals in the state were required to add an uncompensated care surcharge to the cost of every service they provided (except those provided through Medicaid), including lab tests and outpatient treatment. The surcharge money, a total of some $600 million annually, was collected by the DMS, which then redistributed it to hospitals that had disproportionately high uncompensated care costs. What this scheme really amounted to was having a public agency reallocate private sector monies from the richer hospitals with low levels of uncompensated care, such as Massachusetts General Hospital, to the poorer hospitals with high levels of uncompensated care, such as Boston City Hospital. For years, this was the way the system had worked in Massachusetts.

Over a period of several months in late 1990, Kathy Betts came to recognize that if the system were changed so that the state could route these uncompensated care payments to hospitals through Medicaid rather than through its home-grown DMS surcharge system, Massachusetts might be able to get the federal government to make matching payments to the tune of fifty cents on the dollar, which the state could then keep. Her idea was this. Federal Medicaid guidelines allowed for 50 percent reimbursement for any Medicaid payments made by the state to help hospitals with disproportionately high uncompensated care burdens. To date, Massachusetts, like all the other states, used this clause mainly to get a little extra money for the one or two hospitals in the state with uncompensated care costs at distress levels, such as Boston City Hospital. Because Boston City had by far the highest uncompensated care costs in the state, always more than a standard deviation higher than the average, the Medicaid rule worked well for this purpose. Defining disproportionate uncompensated care costs to mean those "more than a standard deviation above the norm for hospitals in the state," the DPW could tap federal Medicaid money to subsidize its extra payments to Boston City. (Occasionally, application of this formula would pick up some other hospitals, but it always picked up Boston City.) Because this hospital was so important to a needy and politically powerful constituency, the DPW always found it relatively easy to get additional approval from the state legislature for the extra state funds. But this money was an extremely small amount compared to that handled by DMS, and the federal matching funds really came as an afterthought.

What Kathy Betts had come to realize was that the federal Medicaid regulations had never actually defined the word *disproportionate;* everyone had just assumed that it should mean "distressingly high." But nothing beyond a gentleman's agreement maintained this definition. In other words, whether a hospital's uncompensated care costs were disproportionate had been left largely up to the states to decide—a considerable loophole. This being the case, the Commonwealth of Massachusetts could interpret the word in a more favorable way, much more favorable, in fact. For example, the state could deem a hospital to have disproportionate uncompensated care costs if they were merely above the mean, or if they were higher than what would be considered the danger level for a private sector business, say 5 percent. With $600 million a year being paid out by the state for uncompensated care, the more that could qualify for Medicaid reimbursement of disproportionate uncompensated care costs, the more federal matching funds the

Commonwealth would receive. Betts made some discreet inquiries to friends in DMS to make sure that the money it dealt with would actually be considered uncompensated care as defined by Medicaid. Once she was satisfied on this point, she wrote a short memo to her boss, Maureen Pompeo, explaining her idea.[3] Pompeo instantly saw that the idea might work and "jumped for joy and ran with it."[4] She promptly forwarded it to her boss, the Commonwealth's director of Medicaid. But before the idea could be put into practice, many more people would have to become involved, and many things would have to fall into place.

First of all, the state's entire uncompensated care surcharge system would have to be abolished. The DPW, which handled Medicaid, would have to assume direct control. For reasons buried in the small print, the "surcharge" would have to be changed to a "tax." Kathy Betts had known all along that the federal Medicaid authorities would not match retroactive Medicaid payments, only fresh ones as they were made. Here again, however, she spotted a loophole. The state could tap federal Medicaid matching funds for the last three years of uncompensated care payments if it officially made the change to the new system in 1988, while declaring that "disproportionate uncompensated care" payments under the new system would be made every three years. This meant that the first payment, set for June 1991, would not be considered retroactive under federal guidelines, but rather would be seen as a current payment of a rather big three-year bill! It would, as it turned out, require several months of a "somewhat contentious" bureaucratic process in Washington, even involving Governor Weld himself, before Massachusetts authorities were notified (on June 2, 1991) that Kathy Betts's idea would indeed work.

Just four days later, on the morning of June 6, every acute care hospital in the Commonwealth refunded by electronic transfer to the DPW all the monies they had received under the old surcharge reallocation system since 1988. The total came to $1.04 billion! In the afternoon, the DPW wired the funds back to them as the first Medicaid "disproportionate uncompensated care" payment under the 1988 system. At the same time, a bill was faxed to Washington for the federal Medicaid money the state was now entitled to: some $520 million. The hospitals were not out a single penny, but the state now had a windfall of a half-billion dollars. The check came before the end of the month. Furthermore, since Kathy Betts's idea continued to bring an additional $150 million to $200 million to the state each year, by 1997 its value had already exceeded $1.4 billion. Not everyone was happy, however. Massachusetts had played hardball with the federal government. But as Gail Wilensky, speaking for Federal Medicaid Administration, conceded on the "ABC World News Tonight" special report:

> *I find it difficult to point the finger at the state for taking advantage of something that is outrageous, but perfectly legal.*

Whether an act that is new is also considered to be useful—and therefore creative—is very much a matter of perspective. It is true that Massachusetts's windfall was paid for by taxpayers in other states who might not be as comfortable with Kathy Betts's idea. But, back in Massachusetts, she was a heroine. A grateful Governor Weld, who, according the *New York Times,* had "received a pointed lesson in the value of state workers,"[5] introduced a special bill to the legislature. It proposed not only that a $10,000 reward be given to Kathy Betts, but also that Massachusetts set up a permanent program of rewards to try to reap cost-saving ideas from other state employees. Kathy Betts also commented to the *Boston Globe:*

> *I hope this will serve as an example that part-time workers do contribute very much to the workplace.*[6]

Kathy Betts's story illustrates well some of the reasons why in today's organizations it is impossible to predict who will be involved in creative acts. Before her remarkable discovery, no one, including herself, would have identified Kathy Betts as an especially creative person. Governor Weld got the bonanza he needed from where he least expected it—a part-time, job-sharing young working mother well down the state government hierarchy. He might have been less surprised if the $1.4 billion idea had come from a cabinet member or a senior administrator. But Kathy Betts may very well have been the *only* person in the Commonwealth of Massachusetts who could have known enough to do what she did. She also made a related point to us:

> *Sometimes in the state, things are quite fragmented. I was an experienced employee who had been with the state for twelve years. I knew all the agencies and what they did. Consequently, I could put the pieces together to get the money from the federal government. What worries me is that, as the state downsizes, it's middle managers like me who have been around a long time that are getting laid off. And when you look at who's left behind—young and inexperienced people—they simply aren't able to make the connections between the pieces that experienced employees can. And someone has to.*[7]

Often, the so-called "fat" that the "lean" corporation works so hard to shed, whether through reengineering or other forms of restructuring, is precisely this layer of employees. As far as creativity is concerned, the company is often really cutting bone and muscle. Unfortunately, it is much easier to see the *costs* of long-term employees and middle management than the *benefits* they offer, which may be indirect, delayed, or diffuse. Though these employees form the core of the organization's institutional memory and human network, they tend to become lumped indiscriminately with real waste, things that do add cost without adding value. Managing for corporate creativity is incompatible with an excessive emphasis on direct cost-cutting or poorly conceived reengineering initiatives that cut swathes through what is indirectly necessary. Cost management is necessary for survival and success, but, as Kathy Betts pointed out, too much of it hurts creativity, which is even more vital.

Oddly enough, although Kathy Betts did get a $10,000 reward, the second half of Governor Weld's proposed legislation—to put in place a system to encourage and reward cost-saving ideas—was quietly shelved after the hoopla died down. We were told that the opposition came from state employee unions, which saw such a system as a roundabout way to introduce merit pay, something they felt that Massachusetts politicians had long abused for patronage and favoritism purposes. Even worse from the point of view of creativity, in November 1995 Governor Weld issued his plan for reengineering state government. Had one of its key proposals been in force in 1991, it would have ruled out Kathy Betts's discovery. The governor wanted to limit the amount of time an employee could work for the state to ten years!

The Fundamental Attribution Error

So in the end, the Commonwealth of Massachusetts did recognize Kathy Betts's extraordinary contribution, but it failed to recognize the potential for creativity from other state employees. Why do so many organizations make the same mistake? When creative acts occur, companies work to exploit the ideas, then most often recognize and reward those involved. But they stop short of changing their systems so that they can benefit from the creative ideas of other employees as well.

Part of the reason for this reluctance to address the systemic barriers to creativity in companies lies in how people perceive events in their companies and why these perceptions are often inaccurate. "Attribution theory," developed by social psychologists, examines the way we attribute credit and blame when something happens in a company. According to this theory, our perceptions are strongly influenced by three factors: our role in the activity (participant or observer), our distance from the events in question, and whether we perceive the outcome as a success or a failure:[8]

1. A person who only observes events unfold, and is not a direct participant in them, tends to *overrate* the effect of the personal characteristics of the individuals involved and to *underrate* the effect of the system they work in.
2. In general, the more remote the observer is from the players and events, the more exaggerated this tendency becomes.
3. If a person or project is perceived as successful, everyone is likely to *overestimate* the effect of the personal characteristics of the individuals involved and to *underestimate* the effect of the system they worked in. Similarly, if a subordinate fails, his or her manager will tend to attribute the failure to the individual, rather than the system. Subconsciously or consciously, the manager knows that it is easier to deal with an individual employee than to fix the system.

In the case of creativity, these tendencies all push in the same direction: toward committing the "fundamental attribution error" of mistakenly attributing too much credit to individuals for successful acts or overly blaming them for the absence of creativity. These perceptions are important, because they affect how we think and act. A manager who believes that the success or failure of a project depends on the individual involved will focus on changing one thing—the *employee*—but if the manager recognizes the influence of the work environment, then that is what will be changed. We again and again encounter the effects of the fundamental attribution error in the companies we work with. Attribution error helps to explain the theory behind what seems to be the most common corporate strategy for creativity—one that attempts to fill positions thought to require creativity with people thought to be creative. People who believe in such a strategy will expect a book on corporate creativity to be a guide to finding and hiring creative people, or even to how to train current employees to be more creative.

Certainly, some individuals are able to be far more creative than others. Nevertheless, it does not follow that the path to increasing *corporate* creativity involves trying to hire creative people, or to replace less creative employees with others who are thought to be more creative. In fact, such an approach dooms a company to low levels of creativity, because despite the vast amount of research on individual creativity, no reliable indicators have yet emerged that would allow a company to identify those who will be creative in the future—certainly none that would have led Massachusetts to hire Kathy Betts and look to her for a billion-dollar idea. However, companies that do emphasize hiring and managing creative individuals must work with *some* criteria, despite the little that is known in this area. Unfortunately, these criteria amount to little more than inaccurate, albeit strongly held, stereotypes of creative people. In this chapter and the next, we will reveal just how inaccurate these stereotypes are. They have to be discarded, because they are very detrimental to a company's ability to develop systems that really will promote creativity.

A Bad System Will Beat a Good Person Every Time

With so little practical information available that might be used to identify "creative people," trying to fill the company with creative individuals is a losing proposition. However, even if it were possible to accurately identify creative people in advance and then pack the company with them, without a work environment conducive to creativity, the results would still be disappointing. Given the creative potential already present in most companies, the environment is the determining factor for promoting overall corporate creativity.

Consider the case of the former Soviet Union. Long before the revolution, its ideological father, Karl Marx, had identified "scientific-technological progress" as vital to the success of socialism. According to Peter Drucker:

> *Marx had the keenest appreciation of technology—he was the first and still is one of the best historians of technology.*[9]

For its entire history, the Soviet Union strongly emphasized scientific-technological progress in its efforts to catch up with the West. Prowess in science or engineering became almost a prerequisite for top-management positions in government or major enterprises. In 1980, for example, approximately 80 percent of the Soviet Politburo held engineering degrees, and by 1990 more than half the engineers in the world worked in the Soviet Union.[10] Soviet scientists and engineers were acknowledged to be among the best and most creative in the world. Without question, the country had huge creative potential. But actual scientific-technological progress fell far short of expectations. Why was this? More on this topic in Chapter Five, but in 1990, one Soviet physicist we spoke with articulated the reason very well:

> *A bad system will beat a good person every time.*

This has been recognized in the quality field for some time.[11] Curiously, the current state of thinking about corporate creativity closely parallels that of the quality movement before it shifted away from product inspection as its primary tool and toward process control. In his 1995 book, *Labor Shortages: Myth or Reality?* Malcolm Cohen predicted the five best and five worst job prospects for the next decade.[12] Interestingly, ranked just above manual labor and typist, in the fourth worst spot, was the job of production quality inspector. That production inspectors are an endangered species should not come as a surprise to anyone familiar with manufacturing. The emphasis on process improvement and on "doing it right the first time" has left a shrinking place for those whose jobs depend on catching the mistakes caused by a poor quality system. In the words of Joseph Juran, a noted authority on quality:

There is no inspector half as effective as a well-controlled process.[13]

With that in mind, let us look at the premise that a creator often needs the help of a "champion" to see an idea through to fruition. Many companies have special systems for matching a creator with a champion, usually someone from senior or upper middle management. And what is a champion? A champion is someone who breaks down barriers and fights the system on behalf of the creator. Our view of the need for a champion is somewhat different. We believe that once a champion is needed, the system has already failed. Surely, as the quality movement discovered with its inspectors, it would make more sense to change the system (or put one in place if it does not already exist) and eliminate the need for inspectors or champions. We have a dream. Perhaps one day, in the context of creativity, champions will have the same poor job prospects as their quality counterparts, the inspectors.

In the absence of an environment conducive to creativity, another preconception also flourishes, namely, that creativity often comes from social misfits with eccentric behavior, habits, and dress, who scorn management and break all the rules. Actually, as we will discuss in the next chapter, eccentricity is a poor indicator of a person's future creativity. This preconception, like the others we describe, is harmful because it encourages companies to look for creativity only from a certain type of person. It is also a self-fulfilling prophecy: in a bad system, the people who express their creativity are most often eccentric individuals with fewer inhibitions—precisely the ones who fit the profile. And so the preconception becomes even more deeply ingrained. Companies continue to expect creativity only from those employees who conform to the stereotype. They end up ignoring the majority, who constitute most of their creative potential.

The Routine and the Nonroutine

We have already discussed the imaginary list of a company's employees and the things that they alone know, or that they and only one or two other employees know. On such a list, every employee, like Kathy Betts, has something next to her or his name. But this is merely one of the reasons a company can't predict who will play a role in a creative act or what that act will be. Another reason has to do with the *routine* and the *nonroutine*.

Work is a combination of the routine and the nonroutine. The routine aspects of work should be planned and executed consistently. Assuring reliability and predictability for routine work is very important for any business; it is required, in fact, in order to deliver high-quality products and services to customers at a reasonable price. Since most work in companies today involves many people, standardization is key to efficiency, safety, and quality. But standardization does not *remove* the need for creativity—it *spreads* this need throughout the company, and even into its network of customers and suppliers. For no matter how standardized a process becomes, the unexpected can and will occur anywhere, and without warning. Since a company cannot predict when and where the unanticipated will occur, it cannot know who may become aware of it and what knowledge that person will bring to bear on it. Consider, for example, the possible actions of a production worker who encounters unusual circumstances, perhaps like those that existed immediately prior to the tragedy that released a deadly cloud of poison gas at the Union Carbide plant in Bhopal, India. Though 99 percent of his work may be routine and standardized, as it has to be in a large plant dealing with hazardous chemicals, the remaining 1 percent of his non-routine work may have a far greater impact on his company.

Japan Railways (JR) East's Oshimizu water was an entirely un-planned and unanticipated innovation. Interestingly, this company is one of the few we know of that have put into place policies specifically designed to promote ideas for new business ventures from all employees. JR East knew that it could not predict from whom such innovations would come, where they might take the company, or what interactions would need to happen before the innovations could be realized. Nor would JR East ever implement such an idea without careful evaluation—the point at which creativity should properly interact with standardization.

Today, *anyone*, including a front-line employee who executes extremely standardized procedures, might become the right person in the right place at the right time. Like Kathy Betts, he or she might be the only one in the organization who has a critical piece of information. But when something nonroutine happens, this employee also might be the only person in the organization who becomes aware of it and can react to it. Often customers are the source of these stimuli. One Boston bank clerk received just such a stimulus from one of us. Here is what happened to Sam Stern as he ended a summer's teaching at Harvard:

> *I had finished teaching my course and was about to leave to attend a conference abroad before returning to my home in Oregon. Wanting to deposit my summer paycheck into my home bank before leaving the country, I thought the easiest way was to go to a nearby branch of the bank that had issued the check, BayBank, and ask them to wire it to my home bank.*
>
> *After listening to my request, the bank clerk said, "Sorry, we can't send a wire until this check clears." When I pointed out that the check was from their bank and they could easily determine if there were sufficient funds to cover it, she said, "I don't think we can do that. Let me ask my manager." After a time she returned, reporting that it would be okay, provided I had an account with them. No, I didn't have an account with them, but I would be willing to pay a fee to have the money sent. "You can't do that. We only send wire transfers for customers with accounts at BayBank."*
>
> *I thought for a moment. "Actually, I'd like to open up an account."*
>
> *"Okay," she said, and she began following the established procedure for opening a new account: What type of checks do you want? Do you want an ATM card? Do you want a bank credit card? and so on. I told her that I didn't need any checks, didn't want an ATM card, didn't want a bank card or anything else. And so I completed the necessary forms. I opened my account with my paycheck and said, "Now I'd like to send a wire transfer."*
>
> *Again, following established procedure, she asked where I would like to send the transfer and how much money I would like to send.*

I gave her the name of my home bank in Oregon and said that I would like to send the entire balance of my newly opened account there. After completing the forms for the electronic transfer, I then told her that I wanted to close my account. "Okay," she said, pulling out the necessary forms to begin the procedure for closing an account. When at last we were done, she said, "You know something? No one has ever done that before."

Although it may appear trivial, this experience, somewhat out of the ordinary for the bank's customer service representative, was a potential opportunity for creativity. It could have alerted the bank to a possible new service for its customers, or to the need to reconsider existing policies. The customer service representative, caught at the interface between the customer and the bank's standardized procedures, was in a unique position to see this opportunity. We suspect that she took it no further, perhaps because her work environment was not conducive to her doing so.

Obviously, without the ability to change procedures easily, standardization can quickly turn into bureaucracy and produce an environment where process is more important than anything else, even common sense. But creativity can and should be expected even in the most highly standardized environments, like that of the airlines, which are perhaps more dependent on standardization than any other industry and whose entire history of increasing safety is one of systematically proceduralizing even the minutest tasks and rarest situations. And all of this is as it should be. Procedures embody the accumulated collective know-how of the organization and industry. Without detailed procedures that are strictly adhered to, air travel could neither maintain nor improve its impressive safety record. However, standardization does not rule out the possibility of creativity for airline employees, as we have already seen in the example of Ian Hart at British Airways and as we will see again in upcoming chapters.

What Will the Creative Act Be?

Just as it is impossible to know in advance who will be involved in an unplanned creative act, so a company is helpless to anticipate *what* the creative act will be, or *when* or *how* it will happen. Consider the events that led to the discovery of NutraSweet, the brand name for the low-calorie sweetener aspartame. Not only could no one have predicted these events but, in fact, they should never have happened.

NutraSweet itself, and the billion-dollar NutraSweet Company that is now part of Monsanto, would not exist but for a string of unexpected occurrences, some of which the stringent safety rules in today's chemical laboratories would explicitly prevent. Chemistry was simply done differently thirty years ago. The unlikely chain of circumstances that led to this major discovery occurred just before Christmas of 1965 in a laboratory at G. D. Searle and Co., a pharmaceutical company in Skokie, Illinois.[14]

This laboratory, led by a research scientist named Robert Mazur, was working on a new antiulcer drug. At the time, it was trying to come up with synthetic analogs of some of the body's gastric hormones that stimulate secretion of the gastric juices that cause ulcers. One of the substances about which Mazur and his colleagues were hopeful was based on a certain pentapeptide molecule—a molecule comprising five amino acids called peptides.

That morning, Mazur had asked one of his assistants, a thirty-three-year-old organic chemist named Jim Schlatter, to work on one of the building blocks for this pentapeptide molecule, a particular dipeptide (or molecule of two amino acids) called aspartyl phenylalanine methyl ester. (Much later G. D. Searle's legal department would dream up the generic name aspartame for this dipeptide, with the last two letters standing for "methyl ester"). At one point, Jim Schlatter needed to purify the compound through a process known as recrystallization. In this process, a solvent is chosen, in this case ordinary methanol, so that the substance to be purified will dissolve in it at the solvent's boiling temperature. When the resulting solution cools back down to room temperature, the impurities stay dissolved but the pure crystals of the desired compound precipitate out, because the solvent can no longer hold them in solution. Recrystallization is a very simple and routine procedure that is performed every day in chemical laboratories around the world, but on this day it would have, to say the least, very unexpected results.

Jim Schlatter took the flask containing the methanol, and the lump of dipeptide to be dissolved in it, to a steambath, in which he immersed it to heat it up, while gently swirling it around to help the process along. While he was doing this, the first accident occurred, hardly noticed by him—a phenomenon known in lab jargon as "bumping." Schlatter had put a lump of the dipeptide into the methanol, in which he wanted it to dissolve. Without his realizing it, the methanol became superheated, or heated beyond its boiling point, as occasionally happens. When Schlatter jiggled the flask, the lump of dipeptide acted as a seed for a quick burst of uncontrolled boiling. Typically, this happens extremely fast and flecks of solution fly out of the mouth of the flask, as they did in this instance. Now another important factor came into play. Schlatter did not feel this dipeptide to be even slightly hazardous—a reasonable assumption, since both of the peptide amino acids in question occur naturally, but separately, in meats, fruits, and vegetables and therefore in human beings themselves. So he was not wearing protective gloves, as he most assuredly would have in a laboratory thirty years later. Some of the liquid splattered onto his bare hands. He may have felt the drops, but they didn't really register in his consciousness. (They certainly weren't hot enough to scald him, since methanol has a much lower boiling point than water.) He didn't even think about bothering to wash his hands.[15] These are the first two reasons why all those familiar with the story believe that NutraSweet would not have been discovered (at least in this way) in a modern laboratory. So far, Schlatter had done two things that he probably would not have done thirty years later in a more tightly controlled environment: (1) he had not worn surgical protective gloves and (2) he had not immediately washed off a substance that had gotten onto his skin. But one more violation of modern procedure—the most egregious from today's perspective—was necessary before Schlatter's good observation and scientific training could take over. He would have to actually taste his chemical concoction.

After the bumping accident, which had seemed so minor that he quickly forgot about it, Schlatter moved on to other things. Later that morning, when setting up an experiment to run another reaction, he had to weigh out a chemical sample. To avoid contaminating it, since the pan of a balance might be a little dirty, it is considered good scientific practice to put something clean between the balance and the sample. Schlatter used what was then commonly used for this purpose, a special paper called glassine paper. It was extremely smooth (nothing would stick to it) and, being very thin, it used to come in stacks of a thousand or so sheets. In order to peel the top sheet off, Jim Schlatter was in the habit of licking his finger to get a better grip. According to his former boss, Robert Mazur:

> *[This was] a habit which no chemist would have nowadays. People are much more safety conscious now.*[16]

This time, when Schlatter licked his finger, he found a strange taste in his mouth—an extremely sweet taste. His first reaction was to think that it was due to the sweet roll he had eaten for breakfast. But then he remembered that he had washed his hands since then.[17] He began to wonder where the unusual taste came from. It didn't take him long to retrace his steps and identify the dipeptide as the source of the amazing taste—a taste some two hundred times sweeter than sugar.

Schlatter then told Robert Mazur of his discovery, and Mazur tasted it too, as did another chemist friend of Schlatter's. The three knew immediately that they were dealing with something very important. At that time, two other sweeteners, saccharin and cyclamate, were already in wide use in processed foods. But both were controversial: consumer groups were alleging them to be carcinogenic. In addition, many people found saccharin, a petroleum derivative, to have a bitter and metallic aftertaste. Cyclamate, which some also found to have a bitter aftertaste, was withdrawn from the market for health reasons in 1969. What really astonished the three researchers that morning was that in addition to its clean taste and the absence of an aftertaste, the new substance had a completely different chemistry from the other two sweeteners. Excitedly, Schlatter and Mazur immediately went to Byron Riegel, their department head, to tell him about the interesting new compound. Instantly realizing its significance too, Riegel exclaimed.

> *This is the best Christmas present I have ever had.*[18]

The entire sequence of events had taken place literally between breakfast and lunch.

Although Searle was a pharmaceutical company, and Schlatter had been looking for an antiulcer drug, soon Searle would be in the sweetener business. Schlatter had just discovered one of the most profitable products in the company's history. Ironically, Byron Riegel's secretary, Margaret Witt, came home that night and mentioned the discovery to her husband, who worked in a different part of Searle. John Witt, now vice president of research and development at Monsanto's NutraSweet Company, responded by saying:

So what? We're a drug company, not a food company.[19]

After Schlatter's discovery, things moved quickly for a while. Management was excited about the discovery and authorized a full-scale research study. Working full-time over the next four years, Schlatter, Mazur, and an assistant prepared between three and four hundred dipeptide compounds that were chemically similar to aspartame, comparing a number of their attributes: sweetening potency (they tasted the products themselves as they made them, also something that would be highly unusual today), preliminary safety toxicology, and estimated manufacturing costs. Ironically, after all this testing, it was the original compound—aspartame—that won out. Searle would eventually give it the brand name NutraSweet to send consumers the message that it was both natural and sweet.

But from that point it would still take more than sixteen years to bring aspartame to market. The long-term safety studies were completed in 1969, and three years later Searle petitioned the U.S. Food and Drug Administration (FDA) to approve the new sweetener. In 1981, the FDA finally approved aspartame for dry use only—that is, as a tabletop sweetener (marketed in the United States as Equal) or as the sweetener for a powdered drink such as Kool-Aid. In 1983, aspartame received full approval for use in carbonated soft drinks, by far its biggest market today. Now, NutraSweet is used in more than five thousand products from breath mints to frozen desserts and is available in more than one hundred countries. In some countries that do not produce enough sugar to meet their domestic demand, such as India, China, and several African countries, NutraSweet is blended with other sweeteners for general-purpose use. In 1985, together with G. D. Searle, its parent company, the NutraSweet Company was acquired by Monsanto. Total sales in 1996 for the NutraSweet Company were one billion dollars. In the end, like the vast majority (99.99 percent) of compounds worked on in the research divisions of pharmaceutical companies, the antiulcer drug that Mazur and Schlatter had been working on never panned out. According to Robert Mazur:

> *To find something really new, whose properties were previously unsuspected, cannot be done on purpose. That's the nature of this discovery. The company [G. D. Searle] was not a food company and had no interest in food products. It was only accidentally discovered that a chemical compound made for totally different purposes had this novel taste. And there was nothing which would have allowed you to predict that the chemical NutraSweet would have the taste it did.*[20]

Twenty-five years later, after its aspartame patents expired, the NutraSweet Company, which would never have existed if Jim Schlatter had not licked his finger, would face some severe competitive pressure. Interestingly, in the quest for new food products, one of its initiatives was to go back to its roots and try to institutionalize the serendipity that played such an important role in the company's history.[21] In late 1995, when we asked a senior executive at NutraSweet if anything had come of this initiative, the answer was, "Not really." Was this so surprising? The company was trying to predict the *what*. Perhaps it had forgotten that, before the last dose of serendipity, *it hadn't even been in the food business*. The preconceptions G. D. Searle had once held about itself were now lost. In the next chapter, we will turn to another set of preconceptions that every company must leave behind, because they too get in the way of creativity.

MAIN POINTS

A company's creativity is limited to the same extent that it acts on preconceptions about *who* will be creative, *what* they will do, and *when* and *how* they will do it.

> *Governor Weld of Massachusetts never expected a $1.4 billion idea from a part-time, job-sharing state employee, and G. D. Searle was a drug company, not a food company, until Jim Schlatter licked his finger and discovered NutraSweet.*

Every employee has something that he or she alone knows about the company, or that is known to only one or two other employees.

> *Because of her experience and detailed knowledge of the Medicaid system, Kathy Betts might well have been the only person in Massachusetts who could have come up with her $1.4 billion idea.*

For corporate creativity, the *work environment* is the dominant factor.

> *A bad system will beat a good person every time.*

Every employee's work has nonroutine aspects that may give him or her the opportunity to initiate a creative act.

Chapter Three

WHAT DO WE REALLY KNOW ABOUT CREATIVITY?

"Now let's have the 'chicken cheer,'" says the session leader. A dozen managers shed their jackets and stand up. A vice president from a Midwestern giant glances uneasily around the room, his cheeks glowing pink. The leader starts. One by one, others join in. They flap their arms and scratch at the floor with their feet. Finally, the room fills with crowing sounds a rooster would envy. Strange as it may seem, such sessions are becoming a way of business in the United States. With the intensity of itinerant evangelists, "creativity consultants" are roaming the corporate landscape preaching an appealing gospel to managers: You can learn to be creative. And business is listening. . . . Participants learn a variety of exercises intended to get their creative juices flowing. Using devices ranging from the "chicken cheer" to the flying of kites, creativity consultants try to break down rigid thinking that blocks new ideas.

EMILY T. SMITH, *Business Week,* September 1985[1]
Description of a creativity seminar

Creativity is a subject that has fascinated people for millennia. This fascination has led to considerable research and writing, most of which has focused on the personal characteristics of people who have been exceptionally creative. In this chapter, we review what is known about creativity, and whether or not a person can be taught to be more creative. The irony is that what is known is rarely applied in the business world, and what is applied doesn't really work. As we will see, what is known about how personal characteristics are related to creativity only corroborates the most important aspect of the No-Preconceptions Principle—that it cannot be known in advance who will be involved in a creative act.

The Personal Characteristics of a "Creative" Person

We first turn to a brief discussion of the following questions: How does a person's intelligence, age, or expertise influence his or her creativity?

Is a person with a propensity for taking risks really more creative? What about a less inhibited person, perhaps someone who has temporarily "chicken-cheered" his or her inhibitions away?

Intelligence and Creativity

It is commonly believed that a person's creativity increases with intelligence. Actually, the research literature shows something different. Up to a point, it does seem that the more intelligent a person is, the more creative he or she will be. But once people have enough intelligence to function in their work, this relationship no longer holds; one person is just as likely as another to be creative in that setting. If this is true (and we believe it is), then if companies already hire people who are competent to perform the work they do, their intelligence provides no further indication of their creative potential. And so we find ourselves back at the No-Preconceptions Principle.

Though intelligence and creativity (however they are defined) are now seen as separate but related attributes, not so long ago people made no distinction between the two. Historically, it was attempts to measure intelligence that eventually led psychologists to the study of creativity.[2] The earliest attempts to measure intelligence were made by Alfred Binet and his student, Theodore Simon, who developed a test for the French school system in 1905. The test was designed to identify students who were having difficulty in regular classes and might benefit from special education. The Binet and Simon test was the antecedent of all modern intelligence quotient (IQ) tests—tests that result in a single number characterizing a person's entire intellectual ability. Especially in the beginning, intelligence tests had their enthusiastic fans who believed that the tests could actually measure general intelligence, or what the British psychometrician Charles Spearman called the "g" factor. But even in the early days, intelligence tests also had critics. One of the most prominent was the psychologist Louis Thurstone of the University of Chicago, who felt that there were problems with the concept of the "g" factor. Thurstone, who also held a degree in engineering and had worked as an assistant to Thomas Edison, became a formidable adversary of the new tests. He was a founder of the Psychometric Society and the now-prestigious journal *Psychometrika,* and the developer of the popular statistical technique of factor analysis.

Thurstone hoped that factor analysis would give researchers a tool to prove that, rather than consisting of one general factor, intelligence was actually a complex mix of components.

Thurstone's ideas about intelligence were ahead of his time, and they strongly influenced another psychologist, J. P. Guilford, who would dedicate much of his career to determining the factors that made up intelligence. He would eventually identify and describe more than a hundred of them in an abstruse model he called the "Structure of Intellect." Perhaps the best-known factor in this model was *divergent thinking,* which Guilford defined as a person's ability to produce many original and different answers to a question. Divergent thinkers were more likely to be creative, he argued, than convergent thinkers, whose thought processes narrow the field toward a single "correct" answer.[3]

In 1950, when he was elected president of the American Psychological Association, Guilford used his inaugural presidential address to argue that the field of psychology should make it a priority to understand the phenomenon of creativity. His speech was a landmark in the study of creativity, and before long it had led many other psychologists to the field. In the twenty-five-year period before his address, fewer than two hundred articles on creativity had been published. By 1960, ten years later, about the same number of papers were appearing in print *each year.* In his 1950 address, Guilford also expressed his concern over the prevailing view that IQ tests also measured creative potential. As he said quite bluntly:

> *Examination of the content of intelligence tests reveals very little that is of an obvious creative nature.*
>
> *Many believe that creative talent is to be accounted for in terms of high intelligence or IQ. This conception is not only inadequate but has been largely responsible for the lack of progress in the understanding of creative people.*[4]

To this day, there is little agreement on appropriate measures for either intelligence or creativity. Because of this, studies of the relationship between the two have employed a variety of measures for each. Nevertheless, the results have been remarkably consistent. The pioneering study in this area, conducted at the University of Chicago Laboratory

Schools in 1962, showed no relation between intelligence and creativity above an IQ of about 120.[5] Similar studies of school-aged children in Minnesota conducted by Paul Torrance reached the same conclusion.[6] One of the few studies to examine the relationship between intelligence and creativity in a business context was performed by Donald MacKinnon at the University of California at Berkeley's Institute for Personality Assessment and Research. In his study, MacKinnon, too, could find no connection between intelligence and creativity above a certain level of intelligence:

> *It is clear . . . that above a certain required minimum level of intelligence which varies from field to field and in some instances may be surprisingly low, being more intelligent does not guarantee a corresponding increase in creativeness. It just is not true that the more intelligent person is necessarily the more creative one.*[7]

Our experience agrees with what has become the generally accepted view in the creativity research community: once a person has the level of intelligence necessary for the work, he or she is just as likely to be creative as anyone else in a given realm of activity. So how can anyone predict who will be involved in creative acts based on intelligence?

Does a Person's Creativity Decline with Age?

The notion that a person's creativity diminishes with age is far from new, and at first glance, research seems to confirm that it does. More than a hundred years ago, George Beard, a New York doctor who served in the Civil War, became interested in the effect of age on mental ability. After a detailed study of more than a thousand biographies of eminent people, he concluded that creativity peaks just before age forty and then begins a slow decline.[8] He likened the creative potential of each decade of a person's life to different materials: the twenties were the brazen decade; the thirties, golden; forties, silver; fifties, iron; sixties, tin; and seventies, wooden. Beard speculated that 70 percent of the world's creative output came from people younger than forty-five, and about half of that from people in their "golden decade."[9]

Eighty years after Beard's study, Harvey Lehman published the results of a long and somewhat cumbersome investigation into the relationship of creativity to age in his 1953 book, *Age and Achievement*.[10] Lehman's findings generally echoed Beard's, but he added the observation that the specific relationship varied according to the person's field. For example, he noted that creative achievement in the sciences tended to peak in the late twenties or early thirties, whereas in the humanities the age was closer to forty. Indeed, the general perception has always been that in the sciences—physics and mathematics in particular—the most creative contributions often come from relatively young people.

As for creativity in the humanities, others have recently reached conclusions similar to Lehman's—that the experience that often comes with age is more important in the humanities than in the sciences.[11] But even if the results of such studies in the arts and sciences were clear and definitive, they are not really applicable to the business world. They are certainly interesting from an academic point of view; however, since they identify only general trends, they do not offer any practical information for case-by-case prediction of a *particular* person's potential creativity in a *particular* situation. Furthermore, studies that confine themselves to extraordinarily creative acts and to people significant enough to merit biographies (as did Beard's and Lehman's studies about the arts and sciences) ignore the kinds of creative acts that happen most often in companies, like those of Tomoshige Hori or Ian Hart, the British Airways baggage handler. (Incidentally, Hart was fifty years old at the time.) The fact is that age is often an important asset in the business world, because with it comes experience. Recall Kathy Betts's analysis of her own creative act: without a dozen years of experience she could not have done what she did. Every person in an organization knows something that no one else does, and this fact alone should keep a company from looking only to its younger employees for creativity.

But there is another reason why most of the research on creativity to date does not apply to the business world. It tends to address only the creativity of individuals working in isolation. Almost none of it has taken into account the environment in which the individual works. A notable exception is George Beard himself, who unwittingly touched on the issue of the environment in 1874, when he proposed that a person's creativity is a function of enthusiasm and experience. Beard contended that experience grows continuously throughout life, while enthusiasm peaks at about thirty and then declines slowly. He imagined a period in

the lives of people when the combination of their experience and enthusiasm becomes optimal for creativity. In this sense, Beard connected
creativity with the working environment, which certainly influences enthusiasm and, to some extent, experience. There are many cases of people who became creative in later life after moving into new areas of
work where their experience was limited. Consider the people involved
in two of the creative acts described later in this book: Dick King-
Smith, the seventy-two-year-old internationally best-selling children's
author (known best for his book *Babe the Gallant Sheep Pig,* which
spawned the hit movie *Babe*) and Roland Schindler and Bud Taylor at
Kodak. Before taking up writing in his mid-fifties, King-Smith had been
a full-time dairy farmer for twenty years and then a schoolteacher. As
for the two men who pioneered Kodak's highly profitable 3-D imaging
business just before they were due to retire, Taylor was an engineer and
Schindler had been in corporate training for his entire career at the
company.

Colonel Harland Sanders, the founder of Kentucky Fried Chicken,
provides another good example of creativity in later life. Before starting
the company at age sixty-five with a social security check for $105,
Colonel Sanders was, among other things, a soldier in Cuba, a railroad
fire fighter, an insurance salesman, and a steamboat operator. Perhaps
the movement of these people into new types of work reflected or stimulated enthusiasm, which in turn sparked their creativity. In short, if
Beard were alive today, he would admit that two people of the same age
are unlikely to have the same experience and enthusiasm. With this ad-
mission, wouldn't he acknowledge what we are asserting, namely, that
a person's age is no indication of his or her creativity?

Can Too Much Expertise Limit a Person's Creativity?

Although some expertise is needed to be creative in any area—imagine
someone trying to be creative in quantum physics without knowing
something about the subject—too much expertise can also interfere with
creativity. It was Kathy Betts's detailed knowledge of Medicaid regulations and the Massachusetts state government that gave her the unique
insight necessary for her creative act. On the other hand, Tomoshige
Hori's lack of knowledge in cheese making did not keep him from bringing about an entirely new way of making cheese. When discussing how

expertise affects creativity, it is helpful to distinguish it at the very start from experience, since the two are very different. *Experience*, the sum total of the events that happen to a person, accumulates steadily over a career: the longer a person does a job, the more experience he or she has. *Expertise*, by contrast, is skill or knowledge in a particular area. Depending on the person, it may develop slowly, quickly, or not at all. As W. Edwards Deming was fond of pointing out, experience does not automatically translate into more expertise. One person might develop significant expertise from only a few years of work experience, while another might spend an entire career merely putting in time. As far as expertise is concerned, *quality* of experience, rather than *quantity*, is what is important.

The study of expertise and, in particular, expert behavior and what distinguishes it from novice behavior has long been a focus of cognitive psychology. Experts have a strong command of the facts, an understanding of the underlying principles of their fields, and an awareness of the varying opinions of other experts. But most important, from the point of view of creativity, they have developed the ability to recognize patterns that novices do not see and have "scripts" for dealing with particular problems in their field. In the world of chess, for example, top players instantly recognize patterns that are not obvious to the beginner. This crucial ability allows grand masters to beat computers that far outmatch them in raw computing power, but that apply only the brute force strategy of examining millions of possible future positions. When used in the right circumstances, the expert's patterns and scripts can be very effective. Sometimes, however, they can also limit creativity. In the corporate world, almost ninety years ago, Henry Ford recognized the dangers of the patterned behavior that often comes with expertise. He said:

> *It is not always easy to get away from tradition. That is why all our new operations are always directed by men who have no previous knowledge of the subject and therefore have not had a chance to get on really familiar terms with the impossible. We call in technical experts to aid whenever their aid seems necessary, but no operation is ever directed by a technician. Our invariable reply to "It can't be done" is, "Go do it."*[12]

Unfortunately, as Thomas Kuhn noted in *The Structure of Scientific Revolutions*, the longer a person has success with a particular paradigm, the harder it is to let it go when it no longer applies.[13]

It often happens, as in the case of Hori, that someone has no particular expertise in the area in which he or she turns out to be creative, but instead has considerable knowledge of another (perhaps related) area that proves to be important for the creative act. As Herbert Simon noted:

> *The vital point is the possession of relevant skill and knowledge, and at certain key periods in the history of science and of other domains, the relevant knowledge comes from a field other than the one to which it is applied.*[14]

The point is simple. A company cannot expect creative acts in a particular area to come only from the experts in that area. From the point of view of corporate creativity, the boundaries between areas are artificial. In companies, work requires interactions between many people, not all of whom are experts, and no one can predict who will have or come into possession of a critical ingredient needed for a creative act. JR East had a catering division with many experts on food and drink, but it was a maintenance worker who came up with the idea for Oshimizu water. This is the No-Preconceptions Principle in action; any company that looks only to its experts will be blindsided by employees like Hori or the JR worker who cross over onto the experts' turf.

The problem with expertise lies precisely in those grooved-in patterns and scripts that make people experts in the first place. Although these scripts do increase their effectiveness, at the same time they make it more difficult for them to do something fundamentally different, namely, to take apart and recombine elements of their experience in novel ways. So companies have to look for creativity both from employees who have the scripts and those who don't. Creativity can come from either.

Shedding Inhibitions and Taking Risks

The link between risk taking and creative behavior has been asserted so often that it is rarely questioned anymore. But is it really true that if employees are set free from their inhibitions, a torrent of creativity will follow? Will the consultants' "chicken-cheer" really make the managers who attended their seminars more creative? The following passage, taken from a book on creativity, articulates what has become by default the conventional wisdom on the subject:

> *Failure builds a creative character because the more failures one recovers from the better equipped one is to fail again, and thus the more risks, the more chances of success one will take. No creative idea can ever be dreamed up if its dreamer is afraid to take the risk of being called a fool. Risk-taking and creativity go hand in hand.*[15]

Actually, the assertion that failure and risk taking go hand-in-hand with creativity is not only false, but quite harmful in a corporate context. It insidiously reinforces the view that creative people are abnormal, that they thrive on risk and do things that normal people would find unthinkable. Some creative people do fit the bill, of course. Take Nikola Tesla, the inventor of alternating current, for example. He was certainly a very strange person. At meals, he would not begin eating until he had calculated the volume in cubic inches of the food on his plate; when walking, he counted his steps; and he always avoided touching other people's hair.[16] The view that creative people have to be abnormal has led many people to link creativity with mental disturbance. Max Nordau, in his best-selling 1897 book, *Degeneration*, counted Zola, Wagner, Ibsen, and Tolstoy, along with many of the Impressionists, as examples of creators who were either degenerate or diseased.[17] This notion is still alive today, though perhaps in less extreme form.

It is simplistic and misleading to associate creativity with risk taking and freedom from inhibition. It keeps companies from reaching for the potential creativity in everyone and in every situation. As Peter Drucker wrote:

> *The popular picture of innovators—half pop-psychology, half Hollywood—makes them look like a cross between Superman and the Knights of the Round Table. Alas, most of them in real life are unromantic figures, and much more likely to spend hours on a cash-flow projection than to dash off looking for "risks."*[18]

Important in this observation is the phrase "most of them." Most people involved in creative acts in companies are like Kathy Betts, Jim Schlatter, Ian Hart, and Tomoshige Hori: they are more cautious than reckless. It may well be that the especially risky creative acts have received an inordinate amount of attention in the historical record, leading to a general belief that creativity is bred by risk. Although some people are more risk-oriented than others, for corporate creativity, caution is more often in order than taking a risk.

Is There a Recipe for Creativity?

As far as creativity is concerned, the research to date seems to indicate that once employees have the basic intelligence necessary to function in their work, sometimes their age, expertise, and lack of inhibition help, and sometimes they don't. But perhaps there is a way to train people to be more creative. A recipe for creativity is indeed an attractive prospect. It could be taught to anyone who wanted it and used at will. However, as the philosopher Jacques Barzun observed:

> *If creation was a process, by this time its operation would have been reduced to formulas, recipes, which intelligence and method could apply to produce great art and great science.*[19]

Not only has no such set of rules yet been devised, but we doubt any ever will be. The variety of creativity methods that have been developed are really designed for *targeted* problem solving: they all start with a given problem in mind. But the evidence shows that, despite their popularity, they are not terribly effective at taking a company where it was not already expecting to go. (It is hard for us to imagine that people sitting in a room dreaming up ideas would have suggested that JR East start bottling the water dripping in its tunnels.) The majority of creative acts are unplanned, and each begins with awareness of an unexpected opportunity. By the time this opportunity is developed to the point where a target can be set and creativity methods brought to bear, much of the creative challenge is over. If creativity methods can help us to master anything, it is this final step. From the point of view of corporate creativity, they have low leverage precisely because they are designed to help a company end up where it is already planning to go.

One of the first models of the creative process was proposed by Graham Wallas in his 1926 book, *The Art of Thought*.[20] Based largely on the experiences and observations of the German physicist Hermann Helmholtz and the French mathematician Jules-Henry Poincaré, the Wallas model had four stages. The first, *preparation,* is concerned with the investigation of all aspects of a problem. In the second stage, *incubation,* the problem solver does not consciously think about the problem, but instead works on it unconsciously. During the third stage, *illumination,* the "happy idea," as Wallas called it, pops up. In the fourth and final stage, *verification,* the details of the idea are worked out and tested. Wallas's model, reflecting his interests, is concerned with how exceptional people think, rather than how they act. Like the other models that would follow, his also defined creativity merely as "the ability to solve a given problem."

Alex Osborn, an advertising executive in the 1930s, began what would become his life's work on creativity with a seemingly more modest goal in mind. He wanted to improve the effectiveness of business meetings, because he was frustrated by the amount of time they wasted and also by the poor decisions that often emerged from them. His frustrations led him to develop the technique of brainstorming. Described in his best-selling book, *Applied Imagination,* brainstorming is based on two principles: (1) judgment should be deferred while ideas are being generated and (2) quantity of ideas proposed breeds the quality of the outcome.[21] In his book, Osborn described how the name "brainstorming" came into being:

> *It was in 1938 when I first employed organized ideation in the company I then headed [an advertising agency]. The early participants dubbed our efforts "Brainstorm Sessions"; and quite aptly so because, in this case, "brainstorm" means using the brain to storm a problem.*[22]

Brainstorming is intended to promote fluency and flexibility in groups, each of which has been associated with creativity. *Fluency* is the ability to generate many ideas easily; *flexibility* is about coming up with many different kinds of ideas. A person who can quickly think of many uses for a paper cup is fluent, but not very flexible, if all or most of them involve using the cup as a container. Flexible thinking would produce truly different alternatives, such as using the paper cup as a cookie cutter or punching holes in its bottom to turn it into a sprinkler. In the early 1950s, when Guilford developed his Structure of the Intellect model, he too would identify fluency and flexibility as factors that contribute to divergent thinking, and hence to creativity.

Given the popular view of brainstorming as a tool for creativity, it is ironic that its real power has always been for what Osborn designed it for: better decision making and communication in meetings. Badly run meetings don't bring out what everyone really thinks or really knows. The rule of deferred judgment creates an atmosphere in which all aspects of a problem can be discussed and considered freely—ostensibly the reason for the meeting in the first place. Brainstorming does help to make meetings better. Only as an afterthought, it seems, did Osborn link brainstorming to creativity, a link that at first even he may have realized would prove to be tenuous. Good decisions often are not creative decisions, and creative decisions are not always good ones. There is no question that brainstorming brings fluency, helping a group to generate a large number of ideas. However, most research shows that brainstorming actually has minimal effect on the *creativity* of a group's solution to a problem.[23] The difficulty lies with the assumption that group fluency and flexibility will result in *creative* outcomes rather than just *good* ones. As David Perkins has observed:

Measures of ideational fluency and flexibility apparently do not relate reliably to real-world creative achievement within a discipline.[24]

The fact is that most real-world creative acts—like those of Kathy Betts and Jim Schlatter—have nothing whatsoever to do with fluency and flexibility. Jim Schlatter did not sit down and try to think of hundreds of ways to create a new sweetener. In a corporate setting, it is more the *environment* that is fluent, because it presents employees throughout the company with thousands of new possibilities every day.

Undeniably, "brainstorming" was a catchy word that captured the popular imagination of the day and became irrevocably linked with creativity. That its original purpose was to run effective meetings has been long forgotten. Eventually, even Osborn himself became convinced that brainstorming promoted creativity. Building on the groundswell of enthusiasm for his new technique, he revised his model to aim it directly at creative thinking. The new model consisted of three parts: *fact-finding, idea-finding,* and *solution-finding.* Sidney Parnes, a psychologist who worked closely with Osborn at the Creative Education Foundation (which Osborn founded in 1954), altered that model still further. The resulting Osborn-Parnes Creative Problem Solving Model has been widely used in creativity training.

Although there are many creative problem-solving methods, and the lure of the perfect recipe will no doubt lead to others, the evidence is overwhelming that none of them really works.[25] In companies, creativity does not happen magically when people are taken out of their workplace and a procedure is invoked to set up a special environment where creativity might flourish. The workplace itself is alive with the unexpected; when employees interact with it, it yields provocations no one can possibly expect. Jim Schlatter had to be working in his lab to come up with NutraSweet, and the American Airlines flight attendant had to be on duty to see the wasted penny-and-half coffee lids. Rather than fashioning artificial environments for creativity, shouldn't the company make the workplace environment always conducive to creativity?

How to Motivate for Creativity

It is almost an axiom that managers should reward behaviors they want and not reward those they don't. This seems simple and straightforward enough, but does such an approach work for creativity? Although incentives and rewards are widely used and are very effective in certain situations, the evidence is clear that for creativity they are more often counterproductive—they diminish it. Incentives and rewards provide *extrinsic motivation;* they motivate someone to work on something primarily as a means to an end—the reward. The use of rewards as positive reinforcement is central to behaviorism, a school of thought that dominated psychology for about a half-century before new research revealed its limitations.[26] The widespread consensus among psychologists today is that the more the work involves following a set algorithm, the more effective extrinsic motivation will be. But since creativity does not come from a set algorithm, extrinsic motivation often gets in the way. Creativity depends far more on *intrinsic motivation,* the desire to work on something for its own sake.

In 1971 Edward Deci, a young faculty member in the psychology department at the University of Rochester, published the results of one of the first studies on the effects of extrinsic and intrinsic motivation. His experiment with male college students showed how rewards influenced their interest in an activity. At the start, each of the subjects was told that the experiment would involve three separate sessions on three different days. In each of the three sessions, the students worked with a Parker Brothers puzzle called Soma, which was popular with college students at the time. The puzzle consisted of seven pieces, each made up of three or four one-inch cubes. The seven pieces could be put together in millions of different configurations. During each session, the participants were asked to reproduce specific configurations that were drawn for them. The twenty-four participants were divided into an experimental and a control group. In the first of the three sessions, the participants in the two groups did exactly the same thing: they tried to make as many of the configurations as they could. In the second session, however, each member of the experimental group was offered one dollar for each successfully completed configuration. Throughout the experiment, the issue of rewards was never brought up with the control group, who continued to work on the puzzle for no pay. The third session reverted to the same format as the first, with the experimental group again being asked to reproduce configurations, but without any reward.

In the middle of each of the three sessions, Deci told the students to wait for a short while until the next phase of the experiment began. During this waiting period, they were left alone in the room with a number of options to occupy their time. They could continue playing with the puzzle if they wished, or they could read a magazine (Deci placed copies of *Playboy, Time,* and the *New Yorker* on a table close by), pace around, or simply daydream. Actually, however, the waiting period was the critical stage of the experiment. For eight minutes, the students were watched to see what they did—in particular, to see if they resumed play with the puzzle and, if so, for how long. In the third session, the experimental participants, who once more were not paid for playing with the puzzle, spent significantly less time playing with it during the "break" period than did those in the control group. Moreover, they spent much less time with the puzzle than they had during their break in the first session, before the issue of money had been raised. By contrast, the control participants, who had never received any pay for working with the puzzle, steadily increased the amount of time they amused themselves with it during the breaks. It appeared, Deci wrote, that "money may work to 'buy off' one's intrinsic motivation for an activity."[27]

An often-told, though apocryphal, story illustrates how Deci's experiment might play out in real life. A grumpy old man lived next to a vacant lot that was a popular after-school gathering spot for baseball. Because the noise of the play irritated him, the old man concocted a devious plan. One day he walked over to the children and announced, "I enjoy watching you play baseball so much that from now on I would like to pay each of you a quarter every day that you play here." The children were astounded that anyone would want to pay them for something they enjoyed doing so much. Nevertheless, true to his word, the old man gave each child a quarter every day that week. But the next week the old man came out and said, "I'm sorry, I can't afford to keep paying you quarters each day. I just don't have the money. From now on I can pay only a dime." A few of the children grumbled at this, but most took it in stride, since they intended to play there anyway. In the following week, the old man reduced his payment to a nickel each, and then, a few days later, he announced the bad news, "I'm afraid I can no longer pay you anything to play." When they heard this, the children were angry and grumbled at him, "If you think we're going to play here for nothing, you're crazy." They left and never returned. The old man's ploy had succeeded. Without the children's having realized it, he had been able to rob them of the joy of playing baseball, at least in the vacant lot next to his house.

Deci's experiment was only the first of many that would build considerable evidence about the relationship of extrinsic and intrinsic motivation to creativity. Why is intrinsic motivation so critical for creativity, and extrinsic motivation so detrimental to it? The answer is that the prospect of a reward encourages people to take the quickest and surest (not necessarily the most creative) route toward gaining it. In other words, the goal becomes the reward and the reward itself captures much of their interest and energy. Teresa Amabile, who has conducted many experiments on the effects of motivation on creativity, has found that rewards reduce the creativity of children, artists, and scientists alike. To illustrate her point she uses the unlikely image of a rat in a maze searching for cheese.

> *If you [the rat] are extrinsically motivated, your primary motive is to achieve the extrinsic goal. You are working for something that is external to the maze: You have to earn the reward, or win the competition, or get the promotion, or please those who are watching you. You are so singleminded about the goal that you don't take the time to think much about the maze itself. Since you're only interested in getting out as quickly as possible, you will be likely to take only the most obvious, well-traveled route.*
>
> *By contrast, if you are intrinsically motivated, you enjoy being in the maze. You enjoy playing in it, nosing around, trying out different pathways, exploring, thinking things through before blindly plunging ahead. You're not really concentrating on anything else but how much you enjoy the problem itself, how much you like the challenge and the intrigue.*[28]

Much creativity is the result of informal poking around, experimenting, and exploiting the unexpected. In the race for the reward, not only is creativity sacrificed, but opportunities for what cognitive psychologists call *incidental learning,* the important knowledge and insight gained from such exploration, are greatly reduced.

We do not mean to suggest that those involved in creative acts should receive no rewards whatsoever. It is of course important for people to be recognized and treated fairly. Companies already provide rewards for their employees, which do influence their intrinsic motivation. However, because most companies are inclined to pay far more attention to the extrinsic part of the equation, whether consciously or not, the balance is upset from the point of view of creativity. In the words of W. Edwards Deming:

Some extrinsic motivation helps to build self-esteem. But total submission to external motivation leads to destruction of the individual. Extrinsic motivation in the extreme crushes intrinsic motivation.[29]

The success of *kaizen teian* (continuous improvement proposal) systems, used first in Japan but now around the world, is in large part attributable to their emphasis on intrinsic motivation. In fact, many of these systems—like that at the FoaMech (short for "foam and mechanisms") plant of Johnson Controls, in Georgetown, Kentucky—attain *100 percent* employee participation. FoaMech is a supplier of headrests, seat cushions, and seat adjustment mechanisms to Toyota and Ford. In 1996, literally every one of the plant's 350 employees proposed one or more ideas to the FoaMech Kaizen Program. In the business environment in which FoaMech operates, it would have been very easy—almost natural, in fact—for FoaMech to try to use rewards to motivate ideas. The automobile industry is highly competitive and cost-conscious. A supplier to an automobile companies is always under tremendous pressure to reduce costs. Not only does the supplier have to offer the lowest possible price to get business, but it often has to commit in advance to a tough schedule of price reductions (known as "givebacks" in the industry) over the life span of the product. The Johnson Controls' FoaMech plant is given monthly targets for new cost savings, which it has to meet. Since 1994, the company has been able to count on its *kaizen* program to deliver roughly half of the necessary cost savings each month. But even while it is expected to deliver an *output* measured in dollar terms, the *kaizen* department does all it can to deemphasize extrinsic rewards as far as the *inputs* are concerned. The modest rewards that are given for ideas are only loosely tied to their dollar value. The maximum reward is only $100, and *every* idea (except an entirely frivolous one) gets a reward of at least $5. The main goal is to ensure that employees propose ideas because they find it intrinsically rewarding to do so.

One example from FoaMech illustrates this well.[30] In February of 1995, Kim Darnell was team leader of a group in the plant that made the seat adjuster mechanisms—the tracks, levers, and wheels under the front seats—for the Toyota Camry. Russ Harrod was the maintenance person for her group. On her shift, Darnell was running what amounted to a small metalworking shop with some thirty people and forty-six machines. The workplace was noisy and, with so much large equipment on the production floor, it was hard for Darnell to see more than a few operators at a time. Everyone in the group, but particularly Darnell and Harrod, were frustrated by how difficult it was to communicate in this environment when problems arose. Whenever a machine began to run out of parts or give trouble, the operator's first recourse was to yell for a materials handler or maintenance person. As often as not, neither would be standing close enough to hear, so the operator would have to shut the machine down and go off to look for the person he or she needed. Similarly, if the machine actually went down, it could not be restarted until the operator could find Harrod and he arrived to fix it. Darnell was spending much of her time looking for Harrod, and Harrod never knew where he was needed until it was too late. In addition to the daily hassle this entailed, both Darnell and Harrod felt that it was unprofessional for them to have to walk around the production floor yelling for each other. They talked about the problem and decided to try to do something about it.

The idea they developed was a lighted display board that would indicate the operating status of every machine; it would hang high above the factory floor so that everyone in the group could see it easily from wherever he or she happened to be. Darnell and Harrod got their idea from machines they had seen at other plants that were equipped with alarm bells or flashing red lights to signal problems. Because bells and lights on machines would not project well in their hectic and noisy area, they set to thinking about other possibilities. In the end, they came up with a display board in which each machine was represented by four indicator lights. A yellow light indicated that the operator wanted the team leader to come to the machine, a red light called maintenance, a blue light called a materials handler, and a green light shone whenever the machine was running. Easy-to-reach buttons were provided for the operators at each machine. Once their idea was approved, it took Harrod and Darnell two and a half months to build their display board and to install all the necessary wiring.

The new board made life on the floor much simpler. The maintenance staff and the materials handlers could now quickly see where they were needed. At the time when the idea was evaluated, it was estimated that it would save some $48,000, and accordingly Darnell and Harrod were given the maximum reward of $100 to split between them. But the original cost-savings estimate fell far short of what the idea actually saved. Machine downtime was reduced from 9 percent to 2 percent, and the group's production rose by *20 percent!* As far as the reward was concerned, the fact that the idea's cost savings were underestimated at first did not matter, since the reward would have been the same anyway. Any idea worth more than $1,000 in cost savings got a reward of $100.

During her time at FoaMech, Darnell has proposed about forty ideas, of which roughly half have been implemented. She has certainly received her share of rewards from the FoaMech Kaizen Program. We asked her what she had spent them on, and her answer was revealing:

> *Actually, I haven't spent any of them. . . . I have some stashed at home, and I have some here that I have kept on my clipboard. I don't actually know how many I have. I don't really do this for the rewards, you see, I do it for the fun of it.*[31]

We believe that special care should be taken to nurture the intrinsic motivation that gives employees the desire to be creative. Not one of the people involved in the creative acts we have described so far in this book did what they did in anticipation of receiving a reward. Ian Hart did not think about submitting his idea to the British Airways suggestion system until after it had been implemented, and Kathy Betts could never have imagined that Massachusetts would enact special legislation to grant her a $10,000 reward. These two people were not racing through a maze in pursuit of the "cheese." What they did came from inside them.

We will discuss the important matter of rewards and recognition in several of the later chapters. The issues they raise are faced by every organization and have received considerable attention throughout history. More about the effects of intrinsic and extrinsic motivation on creativity are revealed in the next chapter, where we describe the collapse of the simple suggestion system and the rise of its second-generation counterpart. It would be hard to think of more damning evidence against the proposition that creativity can be promoted by extrinsic motivation, in fact, than is provided by the remarkable story in the next chapter.

MAIN POINTS

The results of research on creativity only reinforce the most important part of the No-Preconceptions Principle—it cannot be known in advance who will be involved in a creative act.

Once a person has the level of intelligence necessary to do the work, he or she is just as likely as anyone else to be creative in that realm of activity.

A person's age tells little about whether he or she will be involved in a creative act.

Risk takers are no more likely to be involved in a creative act than anyone else. In fact, most of the people involved in creative acts in companies are more cautious than reckless.

Expertise can either help or hinder creativity, or both.

Creativity methods such as brainstorming actually limit people's creativity by removing them from their workplace, which is the source of most creative acts.

Creativity depends on *intrinsic motivation,* the desire to work on something for its own sake. Extrinsic motivation damages creativity.

Chapter Four

THE DECLINE OF THE SIMPLE SUGGESTION SYSTEM
—*and the*————
RISE OF A NEW GENERATION

We attempt by rewards to stimulate the minds of our workmen directly to invention and to a continual criticism of the methods of work, tools and machines employed by them.

WILLIAM DENNY, SHIPBUILDER
Originator of the world's first corporate suggestion system
April 25, 1883[1]

The first generation of systems to promote creativity in companies was quite simple: put a suggestion box on the wall and ask employees to contribute any ideas they might have. Without question, these systems delivered valuable results and, particularly in the early days, had strong support from top management. Although the simple suggestion system was an important first step in the management of corporate creativity, the truth is that it never really worked well. Almost a century later, a new generation of systems arose—the Japanese *kaizen teian* (continuous improvement proposal) system—whose performance was better by an order of magnitude. This chapter explains the difference in performance between these two kinds of systems and tells the fascinating and little-known story of how they came into being.

The first recorded suggestion system was put into operation in 1880 at the Scottish shipbuilder William Denny and Brothers, then one of the most admired companies in Great Britain. Denny's system, designed to stimulate everything from the smallest improvements to major patentable inventions, was widely copied throughout Great Britain.

60

Interestingly, even though it is now more than a century old, the simple suggestion system is still used in many companies in the United States and Europe and even in the republics of the former Soviet Union. This outdated system persists in part because of the mistaken, but widely held, belief that creativity can be had simply by offering rewards for it.

In one sense, the goals of *kaizen teian* systems are much more modest than those of Denny's all-encompassing system. They target only part of the spectrum of corporate creativity: improvements in the immediate workplace. However, at the same time, they are far more ambitious in that they are designed to obtain ideas from literally every employee. *Kaizen teian* systems work so well because they are forced to be consistent with what really motivates people to be creative. A good *kaizen teian* system gives us a look at what becomes possible when a company begins to harness the power of the unexpected.

As we will see, the evidence is clear that *kaizen teian* systems deliver much more creativity than simple suggestion systems. Since by default the suggestion system continues to be used at many U.S. companies, while the *kaizen teian* approach is an integral part of Japanese management, the performance differences between the two actually cause disparities in national-level statistics on creativity. Ironically, if it were not for some little-known and lucky events that took place in Japan during the Occupation period after World War II, things might well have turned out very differently and Japanese companies would not have set off on such a different track from that of their Western counterparts. The story of the emergence of the second generation of systems is full of coincidences and odd turns.

An Order-of-Magnitude Difference

It is not hard to document that the second generation of systems outperforms the first—the data speak for themselves. In Japan, *kaizen teian* systems are commonplace; almost every company of any size has one. The Japan Human Relations Association publishes an annual ranking of the top 150 *kaizen teian* systems in Japan. Table 4.1 gives a small selection of these data for some of the internationally known Japanese companies on this list.[2] Companies with good *kaizen teian* systems receive a steady stream of ideas from their employees. If a working year consists of 250 days, Toshiba, for example, averages just over one proposal from each employee every five business days, or one working week.

Table 4.2 gives the results of two 1995 surveys, one performed in the United States and the other in Japan. As shown in the first row of the table, in 1995 the average Japanese employee proposed some eighteen ideas to his or her employer. Again assuming 250 working days to the year, this amounts to roughly one every three weeks. Results from systems at U.S. companies, on the other hand, were relatively disappointing: one suggestion from every six employees in the same year. Or, to look at it in a different way, the average U.S. employee proposed only one idea every six years. Furthermore, although 90 percent of ideas in Japanese companies were adopted, only 38 percent of the ideas received from employees in American companies were actually implemented. The participation rates for each country also differed dramatically: 74 percent in Japan versus 11 percent in the United States. (An employee "participated" in the suggestion system if he or she submitted an idea in that year.)

It may at first seem ironic that, despite markedly poorer results from their systems, U.S. companies paid an average reward ($458.00) more than a hundred times larger than their Japanese counterparts ($3.88). Shouldn't companies that pay more for ideas expect to get more of

TABLE 4.1.
Selected Japanese *Kaizen Teian* Systems
from the Top 150 in Japan in Fiscal 1995
(April 1, 1995 to March 31, 1996), Ranked by Total Number of Ideas.

Company	Total proposals	Proposals per person
Matsushita	2,427,015	17.9
Toshiba	2,222,042	52.6
Idemitsu Kosan	1,073,256	118.3
Toyota	764,402	13.8
Sanyo	660,427	27.5
Kubota	537,389	35.3

Source: National Annual Report on Japanese Kaizen Teian *Systems* (Tokyo: Japan Human Relations Association, November 1996) (published in Japanese).

them? Recall the discussion in Chapter Three of the effect of rewards on creativity. The smaller monetary rewards merely reflect the fact that *kaizen teian* systems are designed to stimulate and operate primarily with intrinsic rather than extrinsic motivation. As we will see in Chapter Seven, intrinsic motivation is increased when people feel they can have some impact on the work they perform. A system designed for rapid implementation of ideas—one that really works—cultivates this intrinsic motivation, in some cases to the point where money can be eliminated from the picture altogether. Extrinsic motivation reduces a person's intrinsic motivation to be creative.

You may be tempted to assume that cultural differences between the United States and Japan account for this difference in performance. However, in the United States, where the emphasis has always been on extrinsic motivation, a small but increasing number of companies are already using *kaizen teian* systems successfully. The national performance disparity, in our opinion, merely reflects the prevalent use of first-generation systems in the United States and second-generation ones in Japan. What these statistics really show, in other words, are the results of a giant unintended experiment on the effects of intrinsic and extrinsic motivation on corporate creativity.

TABLE 4.2.
Comparative Statistics at the National Level in 1995.

	United States	*Japan*
Average number of suggestions submitted per employee	0.16	18.5
Adoption rate	38.0%	89.7%
Participation rate	10.7%	74.3%
Average reward	$458.00	$3.88
Average net savings per suggestion	$5,586.00	$175.66
Net savings per employee	$334.66	$3,249.71

Source: This table is compiled from two sources: *National Annual Report on Japanese Kaizen Teian Systems* (Tokyo: Japan Human Relations Association, November 1996) (published in Japanese), and the 1995 *Annual Statistical Report on Suggestion Systems* (Arlington, Va.: Employee Involvement Association, 1995).

Note: The U.S. column reports performance based on the 1995 calendar year; the Japanese one is based on the 1995 fiscal year (April 1 to March 31, 1996). Savings for both countries are given in U.S. dollars at the exchange rate of $1 = 100 yen.

Participation Is the Key

Even though a *kaizen teian* system is similar in *form* to a suggestion system, it differs fundamentally in *substance*. The differences, in fact,
begin at the philosophical level. The majority of suggestion systems are
run to promote ideas that save money or increase revenues, and those
responsible for them are measured by their bottom-line performance.
The goal of a *kaizen teian* system is to promote employee involvement,
and its managers are held accountable for the participation rate. The
emphasis on involvement explains most of the other differences between the two systems. Any company that wishes to increase participation in its system is forced to have realistic expectations of the kinds of
creative acts that every employee is regularly capable of, to understand
what really inspires these acts and what blocks them. The result is a
system that unleashes a significant amount of unexpected corporate
creativity. The irony is that a strategy based on participation delivers far superior bottom-line performance (a net savings per employee of $3,249.71
in Table 4.2) than a strategy directly aimed at cost savings ($334.66 in sav-
ings per employee).

By rewarding participation, a *kaizen teian* system sometimes does
things that seem to make no sense from a short-term financial point
of view. For example, in such a system, an employee who makes a bad
suggestion—even one that could cause damage if implemented—is still
offered a small "participation" fee, not much different from what would
be offered if the idea resulted in cost savings. In a suggestion system,
such a proposal earns no reward at all. Here again, focusing on involvement actually leads a company to better financial decisions, for
bad ideas are usually worth much more to the company than the cost
of the participation fee. A bad idea, offered in good faith, identifies an
important learning opportunity. It pinpoints an employee who does not
understand something about his or her work, and who will remain a
potential liability until the problem is corrected.

Imagine, for example, a well-meaning hotel employee whose job is
to clean the conference rooms at the end of the day, and who notices
that the fans in the overhead projectors remain running long after the
sessions have concluded. He goes to his supervisor with a money-
saving idea: from now on, he suggests, when catering staff come across

an overhead projector with its fan still running, they should unplug it from the wall to save electricity. Were his idea to be implemented, rather than saving money, it would actually increase costs, because the fan runs for a reason: to cool the projector. Even slightly shortening the cooling cycle would accelerate the deterioration of both projectors and bulbs. But if the "bad" suggestion led to a supervisor's explaining all this, the employee would understand more about the equipment he was responsible for and would then be able to take better care of it. A "bad" idea is most often really a plea for more information. As the saying goes, "Every suggestion is an opportunity." If it's a good idea, implement it. If it's a bad one, then consider the possibility that an employee is letting you know that he or she doesn't understand some aspect of the work. Helping that person saves the company money in the long run.

How did the suggestion system come about? How did the new generation evolve into something so different from it? Why did U.S. and Japanese management practices in this regard diverge so rapidly after World War II? The story we are about to tell remains relatively unknown on both sides of the Pacific. *Kaizen teian* was a child of World War II. It was spawned in Japan because of a unique confluence of circumstances that came together for only a brief moment after the war. If these historical coincidences had not happened, *kaizen teian* might not have originated in Japan—in fact, it might never have happened at all. But it did, and by helping to unleash the tremendous power of the unexpected in Japanese companies, it profoundly changed the practice of management around the world.

Systems for Corporate Creativity: The First Generation

William Denny

In 1864, at the age of sixteen, William Denny began a five-year apprenticeship in his father's shipyard in Dumbarton, a town on the River Clyde in Scotland. For both him and his father the apprenticeship was a serious matter. Young William Denny received no special consideration. He worked in the yard for twelve hours each day and, upon returning home, studied for two more. In this way, he not only learned about shipbuilding but came to know well the workforce and the working conditions in the company. All his life, Denny had the reputation of being very kind. Once, for example, when he was still an apprentice himself, he happened to notice a carpenter's apprentice who, because he did not have proper clothing, was suffering from the blustery cold as he caulked the decks of a ship. Wanting to help, but not wishing to be ostentatious or embarrass the apprentice, Denny brought in a bundle of his own clothes the next day and hid it in the bow of the ship where he knew the apprentice would find it, which he did.

On his twenty-first birthday, Denny was made a partner in the firm, and he soon set about overhauling the shipyard's management practices, a project that would occupy him for twelve years. He knew that reform was needed. The shipyard was growing, and operating methods that had worked well when the firm was small and the owners could supervise every aspect of a ship's construction now no longer did. Denny, who wanted to retain the unique culture and reputation of his firm, realized that as the company grew larger, systems would have to do what had been done informally when the company was smaller. The systems he devised were described in a set of rules, a copy of which was distributed to every employee in the shipyard. The stated purpose of these rules was not only to make the yard more efficient and safe, but to increase the employees' interest in efficiency and safety as well. The comprehensive rules were divided into five categories. One of these categories, which Denny called "Rules for the Awards Committee to guide them in rewarding the workmen for inventions or improvements," constituted the world's first attempt to systematically promote creativity in a company.

Denny's pioneering system was started in 1880 and quickly proved to be a success. To run it, he set up a two-person awards committee consisting of a member of the engineering department and one person from outside the company, who also acted as chairman. The rules were brief and straightforward:

Any employee (exclusive of head foremen, officials of Awards Committee, and heads of departments) may claim an award from the committee on the following grounds:

a) *That he has either invented or introduced a new machine or hand tool into the works.*

b) *That he has improved any existing machine or hand tool.*

c) *That he has applied any existing machine or hand tool to a new class of work.*

d) *That he has discovered or introduced any new method of carrying on or arranging work.*

e) *That he has invented or introduced any appliance for the prevention of accidents.*

f) *That he has suggested some means by which waste of material may be avoided.*

g) *Or, generally, that he has made any change by which work is rendered either superior in quality or more economical in cost.*[3]

Cash awards from £2 to £15 were paid for each accepted idea, according to the Committee's estimate of its worth. If an idea was patentable, the rules stated that the company would give the inventor an award of £15 and pay all expenses necessary to obtain a patent in the inventor's name. Other than the stipulation that the company should have free use of the idea, the inventor was then free to pursue any other opportunities that might result from his patent. In 1884, a further incentive was added: award money would be doubled for any employee submitting five or more ideas.

By 1887, more than 600 ideas had been received, 196 of which had been accepted, and award monies of £933 had been paid out.[4] Denny's pioneering system quickly generated great interest and was to be widely copied throughout Great Britain and Europe over the ensuing decades. In 1883, in response to an inquiry from the Royal Commission on Technical Instruction about how his company stimulated the intelligence of its workforce, Denny framed his reply to encourage the Commission to adopt a broader view of the issue than merely training alone. At the Denny Shipyard, he wrote:

We attempt by rewards to stimulate the minds of our workmen directly to invention and to a continual criticism of the methods of work, tools and machines employed by them. We have not tried as

yet to induce them to attend technical classes, but a few of them do
attend such classes in the town, conducted under the control of the
Science and Art Department. . . .

Beyond such direct means of teaching, the last indirect means of
raising the technical skill and intelligence of our workmen would be
cheap and easily procured. In the interests of the whole country, there
is no property a workman should be made to feel more real and
valuable than the useful inventions of his brain. Could you obtain
this result, your committee would create the spur and stimulus to
great technical improvements, and you would develop a large amount
of genius now latent.[5]

Denny designed his system to cover the full spectrum of creative
acts, both improvements and innovations, and as far as we can tell, he
succeeded. It is only with the hindsight conferred by knowledge of how
kaizen teian systems work that it becomes easy to see two serious limitations of Denny's system. First, his system was a passive one—it waited
for proposals to react to. But more seriously, as Denny himself stated
in the above passage, his system attempted to stimulate creativity with
rewards.

Five years after Denny's death, John Patterson, the legendary founder
of National Cash Register (NCR), appeared on the scene. Patterson
was a mercurial figure who, through a chain of odd circumstances,
would almost single-handedly fire up enthusiasm for the suggestion system around the world.

John Patterson and His Hundred-Headed Brain

In 1892, John Patterson had just bought the rights to a new invention
with great potential—the cash register.[6] The cash register, Patterson
realized, would solve a big problem for store owners: their own employees stealing cash and failing to report sales. He was an enthusiastic pro-
ponent of his new product, which he pushed to quick success in the
world marketplace. In 1894, however, when a $50,000 shipment of de-
fective cash registers, several weeks' worth of production, was returned
to the company by a customer in England, Patterson was shocked to
learn that the cash registers had been sabotaged by his own employees,
who had poured acid into their mechanisms. Having previously devoted

his attention to sales and marketing, he quickly moved his desk onto the factory floor to find the cause. He discovered that his employees:

> *had no heart in their jobs; they did not care whether they turned out good or bad work. Then I looked further into conditions and I had frankly had to confess to myself that there was no particular reason why they should put heart into their work.*[7]

The conditions Patterson saw for himself were extremely unpleasant; the factory was unsafe, dark, and dingy. He acted speedily to make the necessary changes. He improved the ventilation in the production facility and made it well lit and attractive by turning it into a "daylight" factory, one whose walls and ceiling were 80 percent glass. He installed new amenities: bathrooms for use on company time, lounges, individual lockers, and an on-site laundry service to provide the employees with clean towels and aprons. He even established a medical center, staffed with newly hired doctors and nurses. And by reducing absenteeism, a new subsidized hot meals program more than paid for itself.

As Patterson also reexamined his management methods, he came to feel that it made more sense for the corporate pyramid to be supported by its base, rather than its top, in which case the company could be thought of as having a "hundred-headed brain." But one experience in particular made him realize that his vision wouldn't come about automatically. Here is how he tells the story:

> *A weigh-master who used to be with me in the coal business was working over here in the factory cleaning castings, and in a talk with him one day I asked him why he was working in that position, and why he didn't bring himself to the attention of his foreman and earn promotion through suggesting some changes. I asked him if there were no things over there which he could see should be changed, and he said, "Lots of them," but he said, "There's no use in my making any suggestions, for the foreman would only take all the credit for them, and would think I was trying to get his job." I thought to myself, "There's sense in what this workman says," and I decided then and there to try to get some plan whereby these suggestions could be brought directly to the attention of the management.*[8]

His "plan," which as far as we can determine was conceived independently of Denny's, became the first system in the United States aimed at promoting creativity in companies. The overall program was more active than William Denny's had been, since Patterson also instituted extensive programs of training and education to enhance his employees' ability to contribute.

Patterson gave the new system strong support and leadership. In the NCR system, each adopted idea received a $1 reward, and each month a number of the best ones were singled out for the "monthly roll of honor." Twice a year, a "Prize Distribution" ceremony was held, where twenty cash prizes ranging up to $30 were awarded for the best suggestions made during the previous six months. (This was a sizable amount of money at a time when Henry Ford was still a decade away from shocking the world with his then extremely generous $5-a-day wage.) The ceremonies were not small affairs; the guest list of all employees and their families sometimes came to more than six thousand people. During these ceremonies, which were presided over by Patterson himself, the top suggesters were honored with speeches, their ideas were described to the audience, and there was food, drink, and music. The factory magazine published the names and photographs of the winners.

In 1899, the size of the prizes was increased by 50 percent, and it was increased again in 1900. In 1903, when the company did not receive as many suggestions as expected, the award scheme was made even more generous. By 1904, the rate of suggestions had increased to more than seven thousand per year—with approximately thirty-seven hundred employees at the time, this amounted to roughly two per person per year—of which the company was able to use about one third.[9] Patterson had discovered that the creativity of his "hundred-headed brain" was profitable for the company as well. Because ideas were recognized and rewarded, many problems were resolved with minimal intervention by top management. Some, in fact, were resolved even before management became aware of them. But after Patterson's death in 1922, the performance of NCR's suggestion system began to decline. By the 1940s, with a workforce of about ten thousand people, the number of ideas had fallen off to only three thousand per year. Over the next four decades, the system fell into disuse. In 1987, almost one hundred years after it pioneered the suggestion system in the United States, NCR simply abolished it.

Patterson had built a progressive company that provided excellent wages and benefits for its employees. In 1929, for example, one middle-level executive at NCR earned $50,000, a huge sum for that time. But Patterson had an autocratic and temperamental personality that caused tremendous turnover in NCR's management ranks. He frequently fired managers who annoyed him. It was said that the words "It can't be done" were grounds for instant dismissal:

> *On one occasion he called in a foreman to get a report on the work in his department. The man said: "I am glad to report that we are 100 percent efficient, the men are loyal and the best we can get. Our product is as perfect as can be made."*
> *"Then you are perfectly satisfied," said Patterson.*
> *"Yes, sir, I am."*
> *"All right," retorted Patterson, "you are fired."*[10]

Undeniably, Patterson had a very unorthodox management style: "When we get to the point where all depends on one man, let's fire him."[11] Patterson once fired a new assistant comptroller after just a few hours on the job because he tried to turn the conversation over to Patterson during his welcoming dinner by remarking that his soup was getting cold. Patterson fired him for showing more interest in his food than in the company. One NCR executive once returned from a business trip with no idea that Patterson was miffed at him. He found his desk, together with the entire contents of his office, on the lawn in front of his building. They had been soaked with kerosene and set on fire. He got the message and left the grounds immediately.[12]

Ironically, this side of Patterson's character accounts for much of his influence on the course of American business. It is estimated that between 1910 and 1930, one-sixth of the nation's top executives had been trained and then fired by Patterson. This select but large group included his one-time sales manager, Tom Watson, who later became famous for his prominent role in building the IBM Corporation. John Patterson's "hundred-headed brain" (NCR's suggestion system) spread rapidly throughout American industry. The second such system in the United States was started without Patterson having to fire anyone. It was put in place at Kodak in 1898, after its president, George Eastman, was inspired by a talk Patterson gave in London.[13] As one journalist wrote in 1919, "Is Patterson an anomaly in the industrial world? No, a pioneer."[14]

In many ways, Patterson and his suggestion system were ahead of their time. Just as had happened at NCR, after some initial interest and success, suggestion systems at other companies throughout the country also eventually fell into disuse. This did not happen because workers stopped having good ideas. It was more because the predominant view of the workplace became one in which managers were expected to do the thinking and workers were expected to do what they were told. Without Patterson's enlightened view of the company as a pyramid supported more by its base than its top, suggestion systems were doomed to failure. They were nothing but a hollow promise.

The Rise of the Second Generation

In Japan, the suggestion system would turn into something very different, because of when and how it was introduced. We were first alerted to this story while reading the book *Kaizen: The Key to Japan's Competitive Success*, by Masaaki Imai, in which we came across this isolated and intriguing sentence:

> *Less well known is the fact that the suggestion system was brought to Japan . . . by TWI (Training Within Industries) and the U.S. Air Force.*[15]

Even then it was obvious to us that whatever Imai was referring to would be important to our understanding of what *kaizen teian* really was.

Although the main part of the story begins immediately after the Second World War, it is worth noting that suggestion boxes were not completely new to Japan at that time. In the eighteenth century, shoguns had used them to collect ideas from their citizens. One of the earliest uses of the suggestion box in a Japanese company was in 1905 at Kanebuchi Boseki, a textile firm whose management team got the idea during a visit to NCR in the United States.[16] Generally, however, suggestion systems in Japan prior to World War II were few and were identical to their American counterparts. Until the Second World War, U.S. firms such as NCR, Ford, and Kodak had unquestionably the best suggestion systems in the world.

But this all changed in the aftermath of the Second World War, in which Japan was truly devastated. By 1945, its industrial activity had fallen to less than one-tenth of prewar levels. During the war, some Americans had proposed that the postwar Occupation should be punitive and harsh—the same policy that Treasury Secretary Henry Morgenthau had urged for Germany. For example, George Fielding Eliot, a prominent military writer, advocated in an April 1943 issue of the *New York Herald Tribune:*

Not one brick of any Japanese factory shall be left upon another, so that there shall not be in Japan one electric motor or one steam or gasoline engine, nor a chemical laboratory, nor so much as a book which tells how these things are made.[17]

Nevertheless, cooler heads prevailed. Under the command of General Douglas MacArthur, the ensuing seven-year-long postwar Allied Occupation gave Japan a fresh start, not just politically and economically, but also in business and management. *Kaizen teian* was born in these times.

The stated purpose of the Occupation was to reengineer Japan's social and political system so that the extreme militarism that had become endemic before and during the war might be eradicated. Although the original plan had been to dismantle the country's industrial base, it quickly became clear to the Occupation authorities that if Japanese industry were not restarted quickly, widespread civil unrest, starvation, and even worker communism might be the result. Among the many initiatives undertaken at this time were two that would directly spur the creation of the second generation of systems for unexpected corporate creativity, and that would put Japan, in this regard, on quite a different path from the West. The results of these initiatives largely explain the differing national performance levels given earlier in Table 4.2.

The part of General MacArthur's command with overall responsibility for economic affairs was known as the Economic and Scientific

Section (ESS). Its primary task was to analyze what would be needed to restart the country's devastated economy and to draw up appropriate plans. Although it might seem surprising today, ESS economists pinpointed the low standards of supervision and management prevalent in Japanese industry as the major bottleneck to the desired rapid expansion. A 1949 Occupation memo made the following observation:

> *Supervision is ordinarily a "haphazard" rule-of-thumb process, and . . . in-plant training is characteristically done by putting a new man under an experienced worker to pick up his skills as well as he can. Such practices are incompatible with modern industrial methods and with the achievement of high output per worker. Neither industry nor government has developed a suitable program for the adequate training of supervisors in industrial establishments. The improvement of technology, machinery and raw materials will not assure a substantial increase in production unless the supervisors and the workmen are prepared to utilize their elements in the most effective manner.*[18]

There was never much doubt as to what this training should be. During the war, several members of the ESS had been involved with the fantastically successful TWI programs, which had been used in the United States during the war for exactly the same purpose.

TWI in the United States
The TWI Service had been one of the first emergency services set up by the Roosevelt administration after the fall of France in 1940.[19] Realizing that even if the United States did not get drawn into the coming war, it would still have to supply its friends and allies who were combatants, the government placed maximum priority on rapidly boosting industrial production and productivity, charging the TWI Service with spearheading this effort. At first, the fledgling service tried unsuccessfully to act as a national consulting and industrial problem-solving organization. But finding itself addressing the same problems repeatedly around the country, the Service soon realized that it would be completely overwhelmed if it tried to solve them all individually. An approach based on consulting would dissipate its meager resources and

would have minimal impact on the war effort. Far better would be to focus on training, since a program that was both well targeted and widely used would lead more directly to improved quality and productivity on a national scale. As did the ESS in postwar Japan, the TWI Service quickly determined that the biggest training need was at the supervisory level, for not only was industry rapidly expanding, but many experienced supervisors were leaving for the military and were being replaced by people with little or no experience. Many industries were in chaos. And so TWI set about developing appropriate programs that would have the maximum possible impact on production at the national level.

By the end of the war, TWI had developed three different programs, which became known as the "J" programs:

1. *Job Instruction Training* (JIT) taught supervisors the importance of proper training for their workforce and how to provide this training.
2. *Job Methods Training* (JMT) taught how to generate and implement ideas for continuous improvement.
3. *Job Relations Training* (JRT) taught leadership and human relations.

One of the inspired principles behind these training programs was the *multiplier effect*. In order to reach significant numbers of supervisors around the country, TWI aimed to:

> *develop a standard method, then train people who will train other people who will train groups of people to use the method.*[20]

The TWI Service was indeed able to trigger the multiplier effect it had hoped for. By the end of the war, more than 2.2 million supervisors had received TWI training. In the case of JIT, for example, the multiplier effect worked as follows. The four national directors of TWI, who developed the courses, trained ten field representatives, who in turn trained two hundred master instructors. During the course of the war, these master instructors trained twelve thousand JIT instructors, who collectively taught JIT to one million supervisors responsible for more than ten million workers, one-sixth of the nation's workforce. TWI was rightfully credited with playing a major role in the rapid expansion of American industry to the levels required to win the war.

To attain the multiplier effect, TWI had to design its programs to be effective in all possible situations in which they might be offered. Whatever the industry, the company might be large or small, new or mature, and rapidly expanding or merely continuing with business as usual. Young and inexperienced instructors might be teaching more experienced employees, perhaps even their bosses. The courses had to work even when "charismatically challenged" instructors offered them in poor physical surroundings. TWI left nothing to chance; it had to ensure that the courses developed by its core of experienced instructors would have a strong impact whoever taught them, and whenever and wherever they were taught. Just as actors have to learn their scripts, TWI instructors were required to commit the entire instructor's manual to memory, so that no matter who gave the course, it would be very close to one from a "master instructor." Very little room was left for variation.

Triggering the multiplier effect required an unusually high level of quality control to ensure that each instance of the course was a faithful copy of the original. TWI rigorously validated each new course before it was released nationally. JIT, for example, the first of the three courses, was field-tested in seventy plants over a period of six months. Once instructors received their licenses, they could be on "active" status only if they had taught a TWI course in the previous three months. Unless they followed the script in their manuals to the letter, trainers could lose their licenses. These manuals, which are in such large print that they can be read from five feet away, also showed the instructor exactly what to write on the blackboard and when to write it. Roving TWI Service inspectors checked constantly on instructors to make sure they followed the rules.

In order to track its impact, the Service monitored six hundred of its client companies throughout the war. The last survey, performed just after TWI shut down field operations in August 1945, reported the following improvements attributable directly to TWI:

- Eighty-six percent of the companies reported an increase in production of at least 25 percent.

- One hundred percent of the companies reported that training time had been reduced by more than 25 percent.
- Eighty-eight percent of the companies reported labor hours reduced by at least 25 percent.
- Fifty-five percent of the companies reported a reduction in scrap of at least 25 percent.
- One hundred percent of the companies reported that grievances had been reduced by at least 25 percent.

When looking through wartime reports, we came across an amusing letter to the TWI Service from a company president who described the results the "J" programs had brought about in his organization. However, he insisted that his letter be kept in the strictest confidence:

Under no circumstances do I want you to make public my name or that of my company. While I want you to know what this program has done for us, still I must not have it known to some of my stockholders, who would immediately ask "What have you, Mr. President, been doing all these years to overlook such a possible reduction in expenses which would have meant increased dividends to us?"[21]

Without question, the TWI programs are the most successful corporate training programs in the history of the United States.

TWI in Japan

It is easy to see why the ESS planners in General MacArthur's command, when faced with the need to train supervisors in postwar Japan, would turn to the TWI programs. If TWI's wartime success could be replicated in Japan, it would make a real difference there. With this in mind, ESS arranged for "requests for proposals" to be sent out in the United States. Two organizations bid for the contract. Even though it made the higher bid, the Occupation authorities awarded the contract to TWI Inc., a Cleveland, Ohio, company headed by Lowell Mellen, a former wartime TWI instructor in the United States. Though both bids offered to conduct TWI classes in Japan, only Mellen proposed to try to trigger the multiplier effect.[22] He went to Japan in January 1951, bringing three other instructors with him, and spent six months training a core of thirty-five "master instructors" in the three "J" courses. In the end, Mellen and his colleagues successfully laid the groundwork for an even larger multiplier effect in Japan than in the wartime United States. By 1966, it would extend to over one million, and by 1996, it is estimated, to more than ten million Japanese managers and supervisors.

When Mellen's instructors left in June 1951, the TWI programs were taken over by the Ministry of Labor, which continues to exercise formal oversight responsibilities today. The ministry has licensed a number of organizations to conduct TWI training, primary among them the quasi-governmental Japan Employment Problem Association (JEPA) and the Japan Industrial Training Association (JITA). Over the forty-five-year period from 1950 to 1995, these two associations alone produced almost 100,000 official TWI instructors. In 1995, more than 60,000 people took one or more of the regular TWI "J" courses through these two associations. Other than JEPA and JITA, three other national organizations are licensed to teach TWI, as are one-third of Japan's forty-six prefectural governments.

But official figures represent only the tip of the iceberg. Many Japanese companies send personnel to become TWI instructors, after which these people return and teach the course "off the books" internally, often modified and under a different name. Canon, for example, which has more than twelve hundred licensed TWI instructors on staff, runs its own modified TWI courses about five times per year in each of its plants. We believe that TWI's formative influence on the Japanese management style has yet to be properly appreciated by foreign observers of Japanese industry and management, or even by the Japanese themselves.

Among other things, TWI played a central role in the development of the *kaizen teian* system. The push came from TWI's JMT course, which forcefully communicated the importance of the many small improvement ideas a company might get from its employees. The developers of JMT did not recommend any particular way for a company to do this; they merely wanted to convince supervisors that subordinates could come up with many good ideas if they were given the opportunity to do so. (Perhaps JMT assumed that the main problem was to make supervisors and managers receptive to ideas from those who worked for them. Once this was done the "how-to" would follow naturally.) In the wartime United States, JMT spurred many companies to revitalize their existing suggestion systems, but in Japan, where most companies had none, the course prompted them to design a new system from scratch that would unleash their creativity. It is worth noting that although JMT was translated into Japanese in 1950, the course was not modified for almost twenty years. The timeless nature of its subject matter has meant that, even in 1997, the course remains quite close to its original version.

When JMT was released nationally in the United States in late 1942, at the height of the Second World War, here is how the U.S. TWI Service justified the new course in its December bulletin (emphasis in the original):

> *You know materials are growing scarcer. Machines are difficult to get or replace. And manpower is getting to be a critical issue.*
>
> *A big part of the answer is to develop better ways of doing the work you supervise with the manpower, machines, and materials **now available.***
>
> *Perhaps you worked out a better way to do one of the jobs you supervise today. If so, you made an important contribution to victory. But are you working out better methods every day?*
>
> *Here is a Plan that will help you develop those **better job methods now**. It will help you to produce greater quantities, of quality products, in less time.*
>
> *Look for the hundreds of small things you can improve. Don't try to plan a whole new department layout—or go after a big new installation of new equipment. There isn't time for these major items. Look for improvements on existing jobs, with your present equipment.*[23]

In other words, the JMT course is a course in continuous improvement. Not only did the participants learn and practice process improvement techniques, but to pass the course, they had to develop an actual improvement proposal themselves and submit it to their managers. Furthermore, the participants were repeatedly told that they should never stop making improvements:

Remember there will always be a better way. Keep searching for further improvements.[24]

JMT is a powerfully effective training program. But this fact alone does not explain the warm reception it received in Japan in 1951 or its subsequent enduring influence there. There were other reasons as well. First, the programs came to Japan at a unique low point in its history. Managers faced with rebuilding Japanese industry were eager for any useful advice. Moreover, as Admiral Isoroku Yamamoto had predicted might be the case, Japan was ultimately defeated because it lost the war of production with the United States. For most Japanese managers, the TWI courses were the first opportunity to learn about the American production management know-how they held in such awe—and from the very programs that had disseminated this knowledge to Americans during the war. Twenty years later, Nobuo Noda, a prominent Japanese business scholar, would write that the 1951 TWI programs offered:

a new pattern of "how to teach." Because Japan had lost much of its skilled labor force during the war, it was just what was needed and soon spread throughout the country—until TWI-instructed trainers could be seen in almost every factory.[25]

Last, and equally important from the standpoint of *kaizen teian,* during the postwar period management had lost its self-confidence in the face of serious conflict with labor, which had become rebellious to the point of instigating "production control," or factory takeovers. In the immediate aftermath of such takeovers, many of the worker-run factories actually operated more efficiently than before, a fact that, when it was made public, only added to management's embarrassment. Managers searching for a new way to operate in this uncertain environment latched onto the underlying message of the TWI programs: more democratic approaches to management are always more effective.

For these reasons, the TWI courses got a serious hearing from Japanese management, and at a particularly opportune time. According to *The Idea Book,* a Japanese book about *kaizen teian* that has been translated into English:

The forerunner of the modern Japanese-style suggestion system undoubtedly originated in the West. . . . TWI (Training Within Industries), introduced to Japanese industry in 1949 by the U.S. occupation forces, had a major effect in expanding the suggestion system to involve all workers rather than just a handful of the elite. Job modification constituted a part of TWI and as foremen and supervisors taught workers how to perform job modification, they learned how to make changes and suggestions. . . . Many Japanese companies introduced suggestion systems to follow up on the job modification movement begun by TWI.[26]

Toyota found its own version of the TWI course (called Toyota TWI, or "TTWI" for short) particularly useful in the period when it was pioneering the Toyota Production System, the world's first lean production system. Since the Toyota production system is also a system for managing continuous improvement, it is not surprising that TWI pops up when Toyota personnel think back to those times. Here is what Masao Nemoto, a former president of Toyoda Gosei and a managing director of Toyota, wrote about that period:

I endeavored to create an atmosphere which was conducive to raising our ability for improvement. An instructor's license I held in the "training within industry (TWI)" was a definite plus. While utilizing my own ideas, I never forgot to solicit ideas actively from those supervisors who worked for me.

This decade [1950-1960] coincided with the period when Toyota was thoroughly training its employees in the now well-known Toyota production system. As a TWI instructor, I worked night and day to inculcate the virtue of the Toyota system to [sic] the employees who worked under me. It was a period filled with improvement after improvement.[27]

But TWI was not the only major stimulus for the development of *kaizen teian* in Occupation-era Japan. In the passage we cited earlier in this chapter from *Kaizen: The Key to Japan's Competitive Success,* Masaaki Imai had also referred to a second influence—one, it turns out, of even greater importance and scope.

The U.S. Air Force in Japan

Unlike the ESS in General MacArthur's command, the U.S. Air Force (USAF) never planned a major intervention in Japanese management. It was more of an accident—things just turned out that way. In 1949, four years into the Occupation, the main matériel and logistics depot of the USAF in Japan was located in Tachikawa (a town in the western suburbs of Tokyo). The depot employed seven thousand Japanese civilians to assist with the tasks of supplying the USAF in the Far East with whatever it needed: food, fuel, spare parts, construction materials, ordnance, uniforms, and medicine. The civilians were also there to help repair and maintain important equipment such as aircraft and their engines, bulldozers, jeeps, and cranes. Many of them were highly skilled mechanics who had worked at Tachikawa during the war, when it had served as a base for the Imperial Army Aeronautic Forces. At war's end, when they found that the occupying Americans could still use their services, they stayed on. Because the USAF had been planning all along to use Tachikawa as a base during the postwar Occupation, it had conducted only careful pinpoint bombing of certain critical buildings, continually ensuring enough damage to keep the airfield from operating, but leaving most of it essentially intact.

It was not long before the Americans realized that their Japanese workforce had poor work habits and attitudes toward safety, were unable to operate certain equipment properly, and could not perform maintenance and repair tasks to the proper standards. In addition, there was a general lack of trust and understanding between Japanese and Americans, and both sides were frustrated by the language barrier and cultural differences. The base commander, General John P. Doyle, soon decided that he would have to provide training for his Japanese workers. The first programs offered were in basic English, warehousing, inventory, and accounting. But one obvious problem still remained: the poor management skills of the Japanese civilian managers who oversaw the Japanese workforce. All the USAF officers at Tachikawa were very concerned about the situation. Unless management skills were improved, any training given to the lower echelons of employees might well be wasted. So General Doyle gave the order to develop a new training course, one specifically aimed at inculcating in Japanese managers an understanding of the principles and techniques of modern management.

A group of five civilian USAF employees, two Americans (both fluent Japanese speakers) and three Japanese, was formed to develop the
new course and train instructors for it. Interestingly, in light of what
this group's efforts would produce, only one of the five had any prior
management experience, and this consisted of two years as a junior employee at Japan IBM prior to the war. During the five-month period
from November 1949 to March 1950, this unusual team developed a
new course it called the Management Training Program, or MTP. Even
though the rookie MTP group knew nothing about TWI (it would be
almost a year before Lowell Mellen would arrive in Japan), it wisely
chose a train-the-trainer approach too, putting the emphasis on creating
new MTP instructors rather than on having the original MTP group itself conduct many repetitions of the same course. Within a year, three
instructor training courses had been run, producing a total of 142 MTP
instructors, mostly from the USAF but, since word had begun to spread,
also from some U.S. Army bases and the Japanese government. The
early MTP courses proved successful and, because they were aimed
primarily at middle management, they tended to attract a more high-
powered group than did TWI, which targeted lower-level supervisors.
Although Japanese managers would eventually prove just as eager for
MTP as they were for TWI, MTP might have disappeared entirely if it
had not been for a rather unusual chain of circumstances. MTP's designers wrote their course for use at only a single base and put no
thought whatsoever into carrying MTP's message to a wider audience.
Although TWI was designed for national exposure, MTP was not. It
was to reach the rest of Japan almost by accident.

Recall that the initial and most important aim of the Occupation had
been to eliminate Japan's potential to make war. Since August 29, 1945,
the day General MacArthur stepped off the airplane at Atsugi Naval Air
Base, the authorities had been focused on demilitarization and (supposedly) deindustrialization. As it turned out, however, the Occupation
had two distinct phases, with the second dramatically set in motion on
the morning of June 25, 1950, when the North Korean army poured over
the border into South Korea. Occupation policy changed literally
overnight. Rather than being dismantled and neutralized, Japan was now
to be built up and strengthened as a bulwark against the worldwide
Communist threat. At Tachikawa, MTP training rapidly intensified in

order to free as many USAF personnel as possible for combat duty. Tachikawa Air Force Base was at the center of the action in the early phase of the war, when the burden of stopping the North Korean advance fell on the USAF. The base soon became stretched beyond its capacity, and matériel supply through Tachikawa threatened to become a serious bottleneck to the war effort. General Doyle knew he had to do something fast. And what he did unwittingly gave MTP the break it needed.

One of the harshest actions General MacArthur had taken early in the Occupation was to purge both the Japanese national and local governments of anyone linked to wartime aggression. Later this purge expanded to cover educators and senior executives as well, but it was particularly brutal for the military, where it applied to anyone who had held the rank of major or above. In all, more than 200,000 former industrial and military leaders were denied the possibility of employment anywhere in Japan. (From MTP's perspective, this was actually good, because as upper managers were purged, they were replaced by younger people more open to new ideas, among whom graduates of MTP would be well represented.) As the situation at the Tachikawa base became more desperate, General Doyle was driven to find a more enterprising solution. He appealed in private to MacArthur to secretly exempt Tachikawa from the purge, so that experienced Japanese former top managers could be quietly recruited to help get the base organized and operating smoothly.

MacArthur granted Doyle's request and, for the duration of the Occupation, Tachikawa became the only place in Japan where purged officers, government officials, and executives could legally work. As the word quietly went out, many of them came to offer their services. (One then-lieutenant we interviewed told us that during this time he hired as his office bookkeeper the former paymaster of the entire Imperial Japanese Navy![28]) As the Korean War progressed and things settled down at Tachikawa, most of these top managers not only took the MTP course, but worked in an environment where they could see its teachings put to use. When the Occupation came to an end in 1951 and the purge was lifted, many of these top managers drifted back into positions of leadership in Japanese government and industry. However else it might be viewed, the accidental involvement of Japanese top management in MTP was a big break for the fledgling program.

In late 1950, the Japanese Ministry of International Trade and Industry (MITI) approached the USAF for permission to take over MTP and disseminate it throughout Japanese government and industry. In MITI, the course now acquired a powerful sponsor. By July 1952, MITI had produced 256 MTP instructors, who had trained approximately 26,000 middle managers. Over the next decade, MTP usage grew rapidly in Japanese companies. In one of the few English-language references to MTP that we are aware of, F. L. Schodt, in his 1988 book, *Inside the Robot Kingdom,* spoke of this period, and of the situation at one company in particular:

> *In 1958, when Japan was swept with modern American ideas on management (and even old-fashioned companies began using English acronyms to describe them), Tomy [one of today's larger toy and robot manufacturers] adopted and adapted MTP, a "Management Training Program," developed by the U.S. Air Force.*[29]

By 1994 some eighty official MTP instructor institutes had graduated 3,430 instructors, who in turn had trained more than 1.2 million Japanese managers. The Jinji-in, or National Personnel Authority of the Japanese government, also developed a shortened version of MTP, known as Jinji-in Supervisor Training (JST). From 1952 to 1994, Jinji-in produced 47,143 instructors, who themselves trained more than 1.3 million managers. There are even modifications of the modifications to MTP. For instance, middle managers in the Tokyo Municipal Government take the Tokyo Supervisor Training (TST) course, a slightly modified version of the JST course. Another derivative course of MTP is the Management Basic Course of the Recruit Company, which, except for some differences in expression, made almost no changes to MTP. More than 100,000 managers have taken this course since its inception in 1978.

But again the official figures underestimate considerably the dissemination of MTP in Japanese industry. Just as with TWI, many companies have sent personnel to official instructor training courses who, upon their return, run MTP courses in-house, and hence off the official books. Also, many companies tailor MTP to their own situations, usually by dropping parts of the course that are not directly relevant. It is hard to discern any patterns that would permit even a gross estimate of this unofficial use. For example, since 1966, Olympus has required that all assistant managers complete the MTP course to be eligible for promotion to manager. In 1994, the company had eighteen MTP instructors on staff and had graduated 1,230 managers from the official course, including the company president. On the other hand Canon, a direct competitor of Olympus but five times its size, has chosen to use its own modified version of the course. MTP certification is required for promotion to manager and, since 1966, Canon has graduated more than five thousand managers. As of 1994, forty-two Canon employees were licensed MTP instructors. Some of the other companies that use an internally modified version of MTP include Toyota, Nissan, Sharp, Hitachi, Toshiba, Nippon Steel, Japan Air Lines, Japan Radio, and Sumitomo Electric.

What had MTP to do with the rise of *kaizen teian* in Japan? Like TWI's JMT program, one section of MTP, too, makes a powerful case for employee improvement ideas, although again *without suggesting a specific mechanism for stimulating them*. Unlike TWI, which adheres strictly to a script, MTP was conducted in a discussion format guided by the instructor. In discussing continuous improvement, the instructor first leads the students to realize that the goal is to produce more and higher-quality work in less time and with less effort by using labor, materials, and machines as efficiently as possible. The talk then turns to the students' personal experiences with improvements made in their workplaces. According to the manual, the instructor should try to elicit the following points:

1. There is no end to improvements.
2. There must first be a desire or curiosity for improvements to be conceived.
3. Even a very small improvement is worthwhile.
4. Improvements are conceived by the person who conscientiously looks out for details.
5. Supervisors must get in the habit of trying to figure out methods for improving jobs and for improving on improvements.[30]

The participants then spend considerable time discussing a most important issue: how "selling" the improvement to their boss and coworkers could go a long way toward seeing any idea through to implementation. The module ends with the following guidelines for the instructor:

> *Ask the group whether in their opinion job method improvement is more widely overlooked than any of the other phases of supervision and management in their nation.*
>
> *Finally, stress that the responsibility for method improvement rests on all levels of employees but at the same time it is up to the first-line supervisors and the higher officials to take the lead . . . in encouraging their subordinates also to work out methods improvements.*[31]

Toward a More Holistic Approach

In 1880, when William Denny took over his father's shipyard in Scotland, he knew that the growing company needed systems to do many of the things that had happened naturally when the company was much smaller. In particular, he saw the need for a system to promote unanticipated innovation and improvement. Denny's pioneering system stirred substantial interest in Great Britain and eventually spread throughout the world. Seventy years later, the *kaizen teian* system arose in postwar Japan. Both kinds of systems give an indication of the power that lies in the unexpected.

Systems for promoting creative ideas will always play a role in any organization's efforts to manage creativity. But no matter how effective they are, discrete systems alone can only unleash part of the power of the unexpected. We believe that it is time for organizations to take a holistic view of managing for creativity. The chapters that follow describe the six elements of corporate creativity and show how companies can use them to realize their full creative potential.

MAIN POINTS

Simple suggestion systems—the first efforts to promote corporate creativity—have been around for more than a hundred years. The main reason for their comparatively poor performance is that they rely on extrinsic motivation.

Kaizen teian systems—the next generation of systems to promote unexpected corporate creativity—were children of World War II. They came about through a unique confluence of circumstances that came together only for a brief moment in time after the war.

Kaizen teian systems emphasize intrinsic motivation. Most of the differences between the two generations of systems derive from this fact.

> *Those who manage first-generation systems are held accountable for their financial results, while managers of* kaizen teian *systems are evaluated on participation rates.*

Kaizen teian systems outperform suggestion systems by an order of magnitude. Since suggestion systems are prevalent in U.S. companies and almost every Japanese company of size has a *kaizen teian* system, this difference in performance shows up at the national level.

> *The average Japanese company received eighteen ideas from each employee in 1996, while the average U.S. company received less than this number from every 100 employees.*

> *The average reward a Japanese employee receives for an idea is less than 1 percent of that received by his or her counterpart in the United States.*

Chapter Five

HOW MISALIGNMENT SHUTS DOWN CREATIVITY

A visionary company creates a total environment that envelops employees, bombarding them with a set of signals so consistent and mutually reinforcing that it's virtually impossible to misunderstand the company's ideology and ambitions. . . . Far and away the biggest mistake managers make is ignoring the crucial importance of alignment (emphasis in original).

JAMES C. COLLINS AND JERRY I. PORRAS, *Built to Last*[1]

On a hit-or-miss basis, creative acts can happen in any company, but they cannot occur *consistently* over time unless a company is well aligned. In general, *to align* means "to bring into line." In a corporate setting, however, alignment has come to mean the degree to which the interests and actions of each employee support the organization's key goals. Since one cannot know in advance who will be involved in creative acts, how or when they will occur, or what they might be, the first step toward corporate creativity is to ensure that *any* employee will recognize and respond positively to a potentially useful idea. It is surprising how much a company's alignment (or misalignment) influences whether a creative act is initiated, the nature of the act itself, and the multitude of decisions (both big and small) that others will make to give or withhold support along the way. For these reasons, alignment is the first essential element of corporate creativity. Since all companies have goals, and are more likely to attain them if everyone is pulling in the same direction, the issue of alignment is as old as the existence of companies themselves.

In *Built to Last,* James Collins and Jerry Porras identified alignment as the key difference between their study's "visionary" companies (those select few that had steadily grown and prospered over a hundred-year period) and the "also-ran" comparison companies (which had not).[2] The

89

importance of alignment has also been noted in the world of quality, where the large gap between the state of the art and the state of the practice has been pointed out by many observers. Although the value of Total Quality Management (TQM) is widely known, surprisingly few companies have been successful in applying it. The authors of *Why TQM Fails and What to Do About It* also identified lack of alignment as one of the main reasons why most efforts to implement TQM fail.[3] Our own research and experience has led us to conclude that corporate creativity is more sensitive to alignment than any other aspect of business or management, and that unless a company is strongly aligned, it cannot be consistently creative.

If alignment is so important, why are well-aligned businesses so hard to find? We believe there are two main reasons. First, alignment is both *intangible* (it has to do with a company's culture and environment) and, as we will see in this and the next chapter, *hard to achieve*. Promoting and maintaining it requires consistency, sustained discipline, and significant resources and time. Too often, as management puts its day-to-day energies into improving what is measurable and easier to do, little attention is paid to alignment. Second, strong alignment is not really necessary for a low- or even medium-performing company. Companies can function with relatively poor alignment. Even in a misaligned environment, most employees will show up for work, know they are supposed to help, smile at the customers, and deliver decent products or services. Provided that it is not so severely misaligned as to be dysfunctional, the business can operate and even be profitable. Strong alignment is *necessary* only to sustain higher levels of performance and to make the company a more long-lasting concern. This is why it figures prominently in discussions of TQM (which Joseph Juran once defined as "those actions needed to get to world-class quality"[4]) and of the "visionary" companies identified in *Built to Last*.

Alignment is elusive. It is hard to discern without a holistic and total view of a company, and its effects on creativity are even harder to see unless the company is unusually well aligned or extraordinarily misaligned. While others have examined alignment from the perspective of its effects on quality, customer orientation, or overall performance, our interest here is in revealing its relationship with creativity. In order to illustrate this we have chosen two cases at opposite extremes. First, in this chapter we will describe the most horrendous instance of misalignment we have ever encountered: the former Soviet Union's "rationalization proposal" system, which was history's largest attempt to promote mass creativity in the workplace. The tragicomic nature of this system makes the effects of misalignment, normally so hard to see, very apparent. In the next chapter, we will look at American Airlines, which we believe has the best suggestion system in the world. As far as alignment is concerned, the difference is like night and day.

Lenin, Stalin, and Mass Creativity

Few foreigners realize that with the collapse of the Soviet Union in the early 1990s, the largest, and most disastrous, attempt in history to promote creativity also came to an end. Together with a graduate student and a colleague from a Russian business school, Alan Robinson studied this national effort, conducting research in some thirty Russian enterprises, interviewing present and former government officials with responsibility for it, and examining archival records, some of which were not opened for public access until 1991.[5] For almost seventy years, the USSR mandated the same system for promoting rationalization proposals (improvement ideas) in every enterprise in the country. If the system had worked, the consequences would have been far-reaching, perhaps even altering the course of history.

Within a year of the Bolshevik Revolution, the ground was prepared for the rationalization proposal system by Lenin himself. He signed the first Soviet law on inventions in order to spur the scientific-technological progress that he felt would be essential for socialist countries to catch up with the West. But Lenin was also an enthusiastic student of two American management experts: Henry Ford and Frederick Taylor, in whose ideas he saw much that could be useful to Soviet industry. Although both Taylor and Ford had pointed out the importance of employee improvement ideas, Soviet authorities would take no official action in this regard until after Lenin's death in 1924.

Somewhat ominously, the new rationalization proposal system was first proposed in an official memorandum by Feliks Dzerzinsky, a man greatly feared in the USSR who would later found (and become the first head of) the KGB. Rationalization proposals would come to be covered by the same sets of laws as patentable inventions and major scientific discoveries of abstract laws and principles. But, like so much else in the Soviet Union, the rationalization proposal program never worked properly. In fact, it did far more harm than good.

All aspects of Soviet enterprises, including their creativity, were dictated by centrally determined plans. At the national level, quotas were set for each industry and region that ultimately came down to the factory level as monthly quotas. If Soviet industry was officially aligned for anything, it was for meeting or exceeding these quotas. Or appearing to, as we will see.

One set of quotas were for rationalization proposals. Enterprise and factory directors were required to make sure not only that their employees proposed a certain number of ideas, but that these ideas had a certain "economic effect" (cost savings) and even that certain reward monies were paid out. If they did not meet their rationalization proposal quotas, managers lost their bonuses, which normally amounted to roughly half their total compensation. Worse, these quotas were sometimes inflated when they became the basis for "Socialist Competition," in which factories, towns, or even entire regions would compete with each other. Obviously, since Moscow had instituted a system of planning what could not be planned, unanticipated problems began to pop up.

The Trouble with Quotas

One problem was that of "spoof ideas." Sometimes, toward the end of the month, employees who sensed that their managers were desperate for ideas to fill their quotas would deliberately submit unworkable or silly ideas that their managers would be forced to accept and implement. At Ismeron, a state enterprise in Leningrad that manufactured measuring gauges, the general director told us of a ridiculous suggestion, timed with exquisite understanding of the pressures of his position, to replace a lathe's metal driveshaft with a wooden one. To help meet his reward quota for that month, he gratefully accepted the idea and paid the proposer the then-maximum reward of twenty thousand rubles (a lot of money at a time when a gallon of gas cost less than half a ruble). The director never implemented the idea, although by not doing so he was taking a risk. The central authorities were not stupid. Recognizing that many of the reported figures on rationalization proposals were false, they had established a scheme of surprise audits of factories by the police to make sure that accepted ideas were actually implemented. Penalties were harsh. A director's life was no joke, for while doling out money for stupid ideas, he also had his production quotas to meet, and here too, penalties for failure were equally harsh. It was a matter of balancing the danger of failing to meet the production plan with the danger of implementing a bad idea or *not* implementing it.

One spoof idea that was implemented became legendary within the Soviet Union. The suggestion came from the operator of a metal-cutting press at a large automobile plant near Moscow. His press had a standard safety mechanism on it that kept the operator's hands out of the machine as it cut the metal. The machine would cut only if the operator simultaneously held down two buttons spaced two feet apart. At a time when he knew his managers were particularly desperate for ideas to fill their quotas, this operator frivolously suggested disconnecting one of these safety buttons. The idea was gratefully accepted, rewarded, and, this time, actually implemented. (Perhaps the plant's size, prominence, and proximity to Moscow made an audit more of a threat in this case.) Unfortunately, this worker went into the history books when, within six months of his "improvement," he accidentally cut off his own hand.

Duplicate ideas were another problem. Managers would often find themselves short of proposals at the end of the month and would have to come up with many ideas quickly and submit them in their employees' names. On one occasion, we asked a group of managers at a printing machine factory how it was possible to come up with hundreds of ideas in one short meeting. The answer was unforgettable. One of them picked up a piece of paper and said, "This is one idea, *da?*" Then, folding the paper in two: "This is another idea, *da?*" Quartering the paper: "This is another idea, *da?*" He continued folding until he had created thirty-two ideas that were essentially equivalent to, but nominally different from, the first one. "You understand?" Yes, we certainly did. The managers would take one idea—perhaps for the use of a different screw on one machine—and write it up as something different and novel for every such machine in the plant. Clearly, as these front-line managers knew, it was ridiculous to set quotas for the unexpected. Nevertheless, the Soviet Union did, and the managers were caught in the middle. No one will ever know the true extent of the spoof and duplicate ideas that plagued the Soviet system. We encountered them often enough to know that the system was rife with them and that we, like the Soviets themselves, should not believe reported figures that were so obviously based on falsification at all levels. *Officially,* of course, the problem of falsification didn't exist.

As ridiculous as this aspect of the rationalization proposal system might seem, even leading companies outside the Soviet Union have fallen into the trap of setting quotas for ideas. Take, for example, 3M, one of the most admired companies in the world and one especially renowned for innovation. Since 1974, it has maintained a policy that each division should have 25 percent of its sales from products introduced within the previous five years. This policy has come to symbolize the company's culture of innovation and has received much publicity. In 1992, CEO Livio DeSimone upped the ante: now *30 percent* of sales had to come from products less than *four* years old. Until 1996, quotas for "new" products were an integral part of 3M's corporate culture, and they were enforced. Managers well knew that promotions and bonuses depended on meeting these quotas. Not surprisingly, they were generally met. (One senior executive told us that when managers needed to meet this quota, they would often do the equivalent of simply changing the color of the product from red to green. Sound familiar?)

In practice, just as quotas did in the Soviet Union, this policy created misalignment at 3M. Worse still, the policy put such pressure on research and development to turn out new products that the research labs had a natural reluctance to devote time to improving older products. Furthermore, as another 3M manager pointed out to us, it provided strong incentives for R&D to pass products on to manufacturing before their details had been fully worked out. In other words, the new-product quota often led to quality problems or other difficulties on the manufacturing side of the business. We were also astonished to be told that even in one of the company's oldest product lines, the manufacturing process was still not well enough understood to eliminate recurring problems with it. In 1996, 3M began to quietly downplay this policy.

During a visit to Honda's Saiyama plant outside of Tokyo, its operations manager told us that for the first time, his plant alone had received more than a million ideas that year. Somewhat dejectedly, he told us his problem. His system was fast becoming overloaded with ideas he did not feel were of high enough quality. How could he raise the quality of ideas without dampening the enthusiasm of employees to initiate them? Even Japanese companies with world-class *kaizen teian* programs have not been able to resist the attraction of quotas. Incredibly, some companies report an average of more than one thousand suggestions per employee per year. In individual cases, some employees are coming up with more than eight thousand per year—roughly thirty per working day! We have reviewed the *kaizen* forms of some of these unusually prolific suggesters. In almost every case, we found instances where what could easily have been described as one idea was instead reported as multiple ideas. Furthermore, many of the improvements were so minute that employees in other companies would not even bother to write them down. Sound familiar? In their quest for *kaizen* proposals, these companies have created an environment of de facto quotas, where employees (and sometimes even the whole company) are motivated by the desire to outdo each other in terms of the raw numbers. In our view, it makes no sense to manage creativity by quotas, whether implicit or explicit. It is the *substance* that counts, not the *quantity.*

In the Absence of Market Prices

In addition to all the harm that extrinsic rewards do to creativity in Western companies, in the USSR they did even more damage. Rationalization proposals received rewards based largely on the size of their "economic effect." A few enterprises with suggestion systems had existed in imperial Russia, and it is perhaps not surprising that in the intensity of the early drive for social-technological progress, Communist ideology took a back seat to what had worked before. However, a primary goal of Soviet communism was always to abolish market pricing in favor of a well-intentioned system of prices determined centrally by the Ministry of Planning (Gosplan). In a market economy, prices convey useful information. In the Soviet Union, however, prices rarely bore any relationship to the real costs of goods and services. (In the late 1980s, for example, gasoline cost less than a penny a gallon, and an airline ticket from Moscow to Leningrad could be bought for less than two dollars.) Many of the materials and supplies used by state enterprises never had any official prices set for them at all. But when numbers were needed to calculate a proposal's economic effect, Gosplan had to come up with (1) a way to determine what the prices *would have been*, had a market system been in place, and (2) an evaluation scheme based on these fictional numbers. As can be imagined, the results were comically complex—so complex, in fact, that special schools had to be set up to train "economist engineers" capable of doing all the calculations. By the time the rationalization proposal system was put out of its misery in 1992, these schools had pumped out more than *thirty thousand* graduates.

Worse, Gosplan's price schedules did not always stimulate creativity where it was needed. The director of Bolshevichka, a women's clothing factory in St. Petersburg, told us that because the price of clothing was held very low (a policy decision, since clothing was often scarce and always of low quality), the prices of textiles had to be pegged even lower. Knowing that proposals that would save large amounts of fabric would therefore be evaluated as having hardly any effect, employees rarely bothered proposing suggestions that would save fabric, however precious it might really have been to the *rodina*—the motherland.

To do their work, the economist engineers required several telephone-directory-sized books of tables and formulas. The cumbersome evaluation process took an astonishingly long time to complete. Somewhat humorously, we thought, and in a clear indication of how unworkable the system had become, one of the final decrees issued by the Central Committee just before the system's demise in 1992 required that no enterprise take more than two years to evaluate and implement an idea. Such a complex evaluation scheme—a mystery to all but the "high priests"—could often lead to ill-feeling when, for example, after a long evaluation, an idea was returned to its originator with what seemed an unjustly low economic effect assigned to it.

The removal of market-pricing information from the workplace is a mistake that companies outside the Soviet Union make too. The purpose of alignment is to influence the day-to-day decisions of employees throughout the company. But accurate and complete information is a prerequisite of good decision making. Without it, however well intentioned employees are, they are more likely to do things that are counterproductive. Many companies have policies and systems to get cost information into the hands of all employees. For example, at Hewlett-Packard's Inkjet Business Unit, every production employee knows how much it costs per minute to run the assembly line, and at Bombardier (the Canadian snowmobile and jet ski manufacturer), profits from each shift are prominently displayed. As we will see in the next chapter, American Airlines also gives employees easy access to cost information.

Throughout its history, the leadership of the Soviet Union drove hard for scientific-technological progress. Its emphasis on science and technology added a further twist, since it caused the rationalization proposal system to give strong preference to ideas containing "technical solutions." For several decades, in fact, ideas without technical content could not even be submitted. Toward the end, nontechnical ideas were starting to make a modest comeback, although most of the evaluated proposals we looked at had the words "and the proposal contains a technical solution" written approvingly by a manager in the comments column. Even in 1991, we still saw evidence of strong resistance to nontechnical ideas. At Ismeron's factory, we encountered a memorable instance of this. A simple idea had been submitted that would have saved a lot of packaging materials and labor, but it was rejected because it had no technical aspect to it. As the manager of the rationalization proposal system explained it to us, she became noticeably derogatory about it. To her, it was exactly the kind of ridiculously simple idea she would have to put up with without the law requiring technical content. Since whether a proposal was technical or not was often a matter of opinion, and the nature of the prices and rewards were so capricious, frequent disputes arose. A huge, entirely distinct (but still parallel) appeals bureaucracy was born to deal with the resulting mess.

Nevertheless, the system still perpetrated injustices that even the appeals bureaucracy was powerless to correct. We came across one such example at Mariental, a large municipal bakery in the town of Pushkin, where a worker had made a suggestion about a certain expensive spare part for the company's automated Yugoslav bread-baking equipment. Before his proposal, the part had to be purchased from the foreign manufacturer with hard currency, which was very difficult to obtain. The worker had figured out a way to make the part himself in the bakery's own machine shop. Though no one at the bakery had any doubt that the idea had saved a lot of money, according to the rules it had to be evaluated as having no economic effect whatsoever. The bakery ran into this problem when it contacted the Ministry of Trade (through which all foreign parts had to be purchased) to find out the price of the part for the purpose of determining the worker's reward. The reply came back: the price was a state secret and could not be divulged. Even though this idea had a huge economic impact, the Mariental bakery was left with no option but to treat it as a proposal with zero economic effect. While others received windfall awards for less significant and even spoof ideas, this worker received almost nothing.

How Creativity Can Threaten a Manager

There was yet another flaw to the Soviet system, which alone would have led it to disaster. In a command economy with constant shortages, no manager looked forward to receiving an idea from a subordinate that would result in significant savings in materials or equipment. For example, if a manager received a suggestion that would save hundreds of tons of steel each year, he might well end up being accused of not doing his job properly in the first place and being asked, "Why didn't you think of that before?" Even worse, at the whim of higher-ups who might need a scapegoat for not meeting their own quotas, a suggestion with huge impact could bring down on the hapless manager one of the most serious charges in the Soviet Union—*economic sabotage,* a vague charge often used by Stalin in the purges of the 1930s and 1940s. Managers would be asked, "Why have you been wasting these materials for so long?" If they were convicted of economic sabotage, they would face not only the loss of their jobs and expulsion from the Party (denying them access to important privileges such as better food, housing, and medical care), but long prison sentences and possibly even execution.

Despite the elaborate and comprehensive nature of the planning process, the resulting plans were often quite unrealistic, again for a number of reasons. First, national goals were often set in a seemingly capricious fashion by leaders who either were completely out of touch with reality or simply did not care. In *The New Russians*, for example, Hedrick Smith tells of how the outrageous cotton quotas demanded of the Republic of Uzbekistan in the Brezhnev era forced its farmers to use such vast amounts of chemical pesticides and fertilizers that the area was reduced to an environmental wasteland. In the words of an Uzbek police investigator:

> *Moscow provoked this situation, this crime—namely Brezhnev and his clique in the politburo. . . . They simply imposed on Uzbekistan a totally unrealistic cotton quota—a quota of six million tons. They simply took this number out of nowhere, frivolously. One of our records describes the [Party] plenum at which Rashidov was prom- ising to produce five and a half million tons of cotton. Brezhnev whispers his name—he says, "Sharafchik [Rashidov's most intimate nickname], please, round it up. Add half a million more." Rashidov, being a political prostitute rather than a leader immediately answers, "Yes, yes, Comrade General Secretary. We in Uzbekistan will pro- duce six million tons of cotton." That was the way it was done— "voluntarily," as we used to say.*[6]

Brezhnev's quota, according to Hedrick Smith, was impossible to ful- fill. It simply spawned "phantom crops, phony records, false book- keeping, a pyramid of lies, thievery, and bribes."[7] On paper, the quotas were always met. However, with each level falsifying the data to main- tain appearances, even top Soviet leaders couldn't trust the official fig- ures, and so they never knew the real results of their actions. Planning in such an environment could only have delivered poor results.

Economic plans dictated inputs and outputs to every Soviet enter- prise: what it would receive from its suppliers and what it was supposed to produce. The force that drove the Soviet economy—the one ingre- dient that kept it working despite all that was wrong—was *fear*. Man- agers were held to their production plans no matter what happened, even when they did not receive the very supplies the plans promised them. If something unanticipated happened, that was just too bad. In the Leninetz vacuum-cleaner factory in downtown St. Petersburg, we came across a striking example of the ingenuity such situations often called for. It was near the end of the month, and several days earlier a train carrying the factory's shipment of vacuum-cleaner hose from (Soviet) Georgia had been derailed because of the civil war there. Suddenly, the enterprise director was short of hose for fifteen thousand vacuum cleaners that were needed to meet the monthly quota in only a few days. But like so many managers we encountered in the USSR, he was a consummate problem solver. A few telephone calls gave him the break he needed. A friend who ran the city's municipal services department was able to arrange for him to "borrow" tens of kilometers of the city's water hose in return for some unspecified future favor. Factory engineers quickly set up a makeshift assembly line to cut and crimp the hose and affix nozzles and other attachments to it. In short order they had produced a plausible substitute for the waylaid Georgian hose. The vacuum cleaners may have looked a little strange to Soviet consumers, but the enterprise met its plan. How the two managers covered up the disappearance of the city's hose, we do not know. Perhaps they reported it as stolen, or lost in a fire. Maybe they simply didn't report it at all, putting the planners, for whom it remained on the books, still one step further away from reality.

The fact that managers were held strictly to their plans, whether or not the promised deliveries of supplies materialized, led to massive unofficial hoarding of raw-material inventories. In most enterprises, tight controls were placed on warehouses; often only the chief engineer and the plant director had keys to them. On one of the memorable occasions when we did succeed in getting a Soviet manager to show us his warehouse, after a lengthy unlocking procedure, he stepped aside and announced proudly (to the obvious approval of his accompanying staff), "Twenty years!" And indeed, before our eyes lay twenty years' worth of raw materials—a staggering amount of inventory for him to have been able to put aside off the books. Since the planners didn't know about it, his job and those of his subordinates (who loved working for so capable a director) would be relatively stress-free and secure for the foreseeable future. His actions and interests, and those of countless managers in similar situations around the country, were well out of alignment with the country's needs and, for that matter, with the stated goals of the country's leadership.

The Soviet cliché "We pretend to pay you, and you pretend to work" was very close to the truth. Unfortunately, the country's full-employment policy also created a particularly insidious misalignment. When we asked managers what they considered to be the biggest problem they faced, almost invariably the answer was: a lack of workers. This was surprising, for if anything, Soviet enterprises always seemed to have too many workers in them, far more than their counterparts in the West. At the vacuum-cleaner factory we just discussed, the director pointed at an assembly line which, he said, required some eighty workers, although he had only forty. When we suggested an obvious reorganization of the work that would allow it to be done easily with some thirty-five people, the manager agreed but then explained that he could not make any changes to the process without permission from Gosplan in Moscow. This meant that the only way for him to meet his production quota was to hire forty more workers. A number of experiences like this, along with some candid discussions over vodka at other enterprises made it abundantly clear that Gosplan was pursuing two conflicting goals with a deliberate strategy. On the one hand, it wanted rapid increases in productivity, but at the same time it was extremely reluctant to reallocate jobs, even within a single plant. By designing each process to maintain a desired level of inefficiency, planners could aim for a certain amount of production using exactly the number of people they wanted. And once the manufacturing process was set in stone, the Soviet system put intense pressure on everyone for maximum production.

The Stakhanovite movement that began in the early 1930s (named after the coal miner Alexei Stakhanov, who exceeded his quota by 1,300 percent) was a natural outgrowth of this misguided philosophy. Using him as a symbol of the heroic Soviet worker, the government set up a system in which all workers who exceeded their quota by 30 to 50 percent (depending on the job) would earn the title "Stakhanovite." Armed with this title, a worker had the right to special privileges including better housing, the right to shop in stores designated for high Party officials, and superior medical care. Unfortunately, the Stakhanovite movement was corrupt from the very beginning: in reality, it amounted to giving supervisors the power to dispense favors to subordinates arbitrarily. Almost anyone could far exceed his or her quota if, during the test period, he or she was granted proper tools and access to enough materials of decent quality, as Stakhanov himself was for his feat. Stories also abound of workers who damaged their production equipment (also in collusion with their supervisors) in their eagerness to attain Stakhanovite status. By 1940, more than *half* the working population of the USSR had been declared Stakhanovite, and the movement was beginning to lose steam.[8] On its face, the essence of Stakhanovism was to encourage workers to break records under *existing* conditions, but generally these very conditions had to be temporarily improved to enable this to happen. In short, there were few real Stakhanovites. By prohibiting any creative destruction unless Gosplan planned it, the government was barring the country's highly competent cadre of enterprise managers from instituting the very productivity gains that it officially sought, and that these managers could easily have delivered. The mixed signals from Gosplan with respect to unplanned ideas certainly prevented the Soviet Union from getting the creativity that Lenin and Marx envisioned would drive scientific-technological progress and lead to the triumph of communism.

The rationalization proposal system was riddled with petty rules that created misalignment. A particularly destructive one governed the situation in which an employee on piecework came up with an idea that would result in a faster production norm. Under this rule, the person was allowed to continue working at the old slower rate for six months, while his or her fellow workers were immediately switched over to the more demanding one. Naturally, employees would steer clear of proposing ideas that would incur the anger of their colleagues. Another astonishingly counterproductive rule arose from the fact that rewards were based on their economic effect over a three-year period. Since it was hard to predict this effect, rewards were paid out in installments as the effect of the idea became clear. If a newer, better idea came along during this time, the rule stated that further payments to the first suggester for the superseded idea should be immediately stopped.

Numerous employees also complained to us that their supervisors would often reject an idea, only to submit it a few months later as their own. Though not often acknowledged, the problem of supervisors stealing their subordinates' ideas (so apparent in the Soviet Union) is present in almost every company that has a suggestion system. As the 1943 wartime TWI Job Methods Training program admonished trainee supervisors, "One stolen idea will stop all others."[9] Not surprisingly, front-line employees are reluctant to tell their managers of their fears in this regard. Recall that even John Patterson was unaware of the problem at NCR until he asked a trusted employee, who had worked for him in a previous company where he had made many improvement suggestions, why he was now silent. We have seen companies go to considerable lengths to eliminate the problem of stolen ideas, including double-entry bookkeeping to ensure that a copy of every suggestion also goes to someone other than the immediate supervisor. But such measures are rarely completely successful. The real problem is that creativity is linked too directly to large rewards.

Our purpose, in this chapter and the next, is to demonstrate the key relationship between alignment and creativity, and to describe what a company can do to align itself. The Soviet rationalization proposal system was implemented in the most misaligned environment we have ever seen, and it is not surprising that it delivered so little creativity. But misalignment is not confined to the Soviet Union. As we discussed in the beginning of this chapter, well-aligned organizations are hard to find. In the next chapter, we will look at one company that is strongly aligned and show how this alignment promotes creativity. But we will also describe how alignment is a double-edged sword; at the same time that it promotes an organization's creativity, it also limits it.

MAIN POINTS

Alignment is the degree to which the interests and actions of every employee support the organization's key goals.

Corporate creativity is more sensitive to alignment than any other aspect of business or management. A company has to be strongly aligned in order to be consistently creative.

When it comes to getting a place on the company's agenda, alignment starts with two strikes against it. It is both *intangible* and *hard to achieve.* Well-aligned companies are rare.

> *This is why alignment figures prominently in discussions of Total Quality Management (which Joseph Juran defined as "those actions needed to get to world-class quality") and of "visionary" companies, those select few that have outdistanced the field over the last century.*

Any form of quotas for ideas—whether explicit or implicit— is counterproductive.

> *3M effectively abolished its creativity quotas in 1996 for precisely this reason.*

The most ambitious effort in history to promote creativity occurred in the Soviet Union. It failed largely because of extreme misalignment. But the misalignments that are so easy to see in the Soviet system can also be found in many companies in the West.

> *Although, officially, Soviet managers were supposed to encourage ideas from their subordinates, it could actually be dangerous for them to receive a very good idea—in fact, they could even be charged with economic sabotage, a crime as serious as treason.*

Chapter Six

ALIGNMENT: THE FIRST ESSENTIAL ELEMENT

I'm pleased to announce the beginning of a new program that we hope will produce big changes at American Airlines. The program I'm talking about is designed to use your creativity, your knowledge, and your ideas. As you all know, to remain competitive and profitable in this ever-changing airline business, we have simply got to find new ways to control expenses and generate revenues. . . . We want you to tell us what those better ways are. . . . We will listen, we will respond, and we will provide awards.

ROBERT CRANDALL, CEO of American Airlines
Speech to employees inaugurating the IdeAAs in Action system, 1989

If John Patterson of NCR could have seen IdeAAs in Action, American Airlines' system for corporate creativity, he would have recognized a system strikingly similar to his own. In 1996, IdeAAs in Action saved the company some $43 million. A hundred years after John Patterson pioneered NCR's system, American Airlines is the only company we are aware of that has been able to implement a suggestion system as well as Patterson did, and it could not have been so successful without its unusually high level of alignment for cost savings. As far as corporate creativity is concerned, American CEO Robert Crandall has led his company to a place very similar to where Patterson led his. We have already discussed John Patterson and his system, although not from the point of view of alignment. Let us now turn to Robert Crandall, the IdeAAs in Action system, and the exceptionally strong alignment at American Airlines.

Making the Goals Clear

Crandall joined American as its chief financial officer in 1973. As might be expected in his position, and for any executive in the soon-to-be-deregulated airline industry for that matter, his job was to keep a close eye on expenditures. But Crandall stuck out, even in the airline business, because of the relentless manner in which he cut costs. When he took over as president in 1981, employees quickly got the message that American would now be a particularly cost-conscious airline. (Throughout this discussion, it should be understood that, like most airlines, American Airlines is even more strongly aligned for safety. Whenever cost savings comes into conflict with safety, safety is the clear choice. We do not wish to imply otherwise.) Two stories about Crandall illustrate his almost fanatical attention to the budget.

Early in his tenure, as a way to serve notice to the whole organization of the new cost-consciousness with which he would expect managers to run their operations, he personally reviewed the budgets of every business unit, right down to the individual station level. For Crandall, this was also an excellent way to learn in detail about the company he had just joined. The painstaking nature of these reviews became part of the Crandall legend within the airline. And they did indeed send the desired message—a message that would strongly influence the nature of the company's creativity.

One of the smaller stations in American's system was on St. Thomas in the Virgin Islands. As a service to its customers, the station ran a small freight warehouse where it held goods upon arrival or before shipment. Some of this freight was quite valuable. For example, a major customer of American in St. Thomas was Timex, which had set up a factory there to assemble its electronic watches. The station often found itself having to store watch components in its warehouse overnight. Because these parts were expensive (and were not the only valuable things in the warehouse), it became a favorite target for burglars. In the beginning, the station had hired three full-time security guards, which did eliminate the problem. Over time, under Crandall's relentless questioning of every expense in the station's annual budget reviews, the guards were cut to two, then to one, then to a single part-timer. Finally the guards were eliminated altogether in favor of a guard dog. But still Crandall did not let up.

The subsequent sequence of budget reviews for that station have since become well known within American Airlines. It started when Crandall went over the station's expenses with its manager, George Elby. One line of Elby's budget was for "services purchased." When

Crandall inquired about this item, Elby explained that it was paid to the company that provided the guard dog. Crandall pointed out that Elby could further reduce expenses by hiring the guard dog for only three nights per week, randomized so that potential thieves could never know if the dog was inside the warehouse or not. Elby went back to St. Thomas and tried this, and it worked. The next year, at the budget review, Crandall again questioned Elby's "services purchased" item, even though it was now considerably less than before. When Elby reminded him that it paid for a guard dog on three randomly chosen nights per week, Crandall inquired whether the scheme had successfully kept the burglars away. Told that it had, Crandall gave Elby a new set of marching orders: buy a tape recorder, tape the dog barking, and then play the tape recorder on a timer, so that burglars would be fooled into thinking a real guard dog was inside the facility. Upon returning to St. Thomas, Elby did this, and it worked too![1]

A second Robert Crandall budget-cutting story has also become legendary within American Airlines. Over many years of collecting meal trays in aircraft cabins, flight attendants had come to know that most passengers did not eat the olives in their salads. Somehow this fact came to the attention of Crandall, who ordered a study to determine how much money would be saved if olives were eliminated from salads. The study showed that 72 percent of customers were not, in fact, eating their olives. Moreover, the airline paid for salads based on the number of items in them—sixty cents for up to four items and eighty cents for five to eight items. The olive was the fifth item. The olives were discontinued for a savings of roughly $500,000 per year. Soon afterward, an association of olive growers found out about this. They contacted Crandall and threatened to boycott the airline if olives were not restored to the salads. After some negotiations, American agreed to stock every flight with olives and to make them available to any passenger who requested them. This arrangement required no extra catering, since some olives were already put aboard every airplane for martinis.

It is not surprising that Robert Crandall would provide strong and visible leadership to a program like IdeAAs in Action, with its high potential for cost savings. In 1996, the program had a dedicated staff of forty-seven full-time employees to oversee the evaluation and implementation of roughly seventeen thousand ideas per year. We are aware of no other company in the world that has committed these kinds of resources to a suggestion system. Any idea that has not been closed out, one way or another, within 150 days is automatically forwarded to Crandall's desk. The threat of having a proposal "Crandalled" provides a major incentive to all the people involved in processing it to see that their own work is completed expeditiously. No one wants to be called to Crandall's office to explain why he or she has delayed an idea that could have saved the company money.

Creativity on the Front Lines

Let us now take a look at a sampling of ideas that have come into the IdeAAs in Action program from all over the company, and how these reflect the airline's strong alignment for cost savings.[2]

Flight Attendants
In January 1991, when Kathryn Kridel sent in an idea that would result in enormous cost savings for American Airlines, she was a purser on transatlantic flights. ("Purser" is the term most international airlines use for the lead flight attendant.) According to her, she might never have come up with her idea if the Gulf War had not been in progress. During this time, there was a very real fear that Iraq would try to bring the war to the West through terrorism. Because of this threat, every major international airline experienced a severe reduction in demand for transatlantic travel. Security was tight; every American Airlines crew that had to spend the night anywhere in Europe was taken to a secret location and escorted to and from the airport by armed guards. Some flight attendants were so worried about the situation that they took extended leaves of absence. Times were tense, and because the purser also acts as the flight attendant in the first-class cabin, Kridel saw the effects of this as directly as anyone. First-class passengers are usually on business, and business travel dropped off more than any other category. Very often Kridel found herself with only one or two passengers to look after. Sometimes, she had none at all.

Before every flight, American's catering division, whose system was linked to the reservations system, would calculate how many meals and drinks to load aboard, taking account of the estimated "no-shows," which on some European routes could run as high as ninety people. In first class, when the load was light, the provisioning would also be scaled down. For example, if there was only one first-class passenger and the menu offered four choices of entrée, then only one of each choice would be put on board. So far, so good. But the catering division's provisioning procedures had overlooked one item in this process. It happened to be the most expensive food item on board—the Sevruga Malossol caviar.

No matter how many first-class passengers boarded the flight, the plane was always provisioned with a 200-gram can of caviar, a comfortable amount for the full complement of thirteen passengers in the first-class cabin. Each can cost about $250. During the Gulf War, with her cabin almost always empty, Kridel couldn't help but notice that enormous amounts of caviar were going to waste. What the flight attendants and pilots themselves couldn't eat (and most quickly got tired of it) was simply thrown out upon arrival. This bothered Kridel and led her to send in an idea. It was that the airline buy its caviar in smaller cans, so that when the passenger load was light, less caviar could be put aboard.

The response from IdeAAs in Action came quickly. It was a rejection letter, thanking Kridel, but also telling her that the idea was not feasible at that time. She figured that there must be good reasons why the change could not be made and forgot all about the caviar problem. Behind the scenes, however, without her knowing it, wheels had begun to turn. In June 1993, nearly two years later, while waiting to board a flight in Miami, Kridel sat down in the crew lounge to read her E-mail. A general announcement for all pursers had been posted. It read something like this: "Effective immediately, first-class cabins will no longer be provisioned with a 200-gram can of caviar, but instead with two 100-gram cans when there are seven or more passengers, and with one can for less than seven passengers." The change affected some forty-three thousand flights per year to Latin America, Japan, and Europe. Kridel told us that she smiled to herself and thought, "Well, good. The company finally got smart." And she thought no more about it, nor about the fact that she might be owed a reward. Three months later, however, she had a nice surprise: a letter from IdeAAs in Action telling her that her idea had reduced the company's annual caviar consumption of $3 million by $567,000 that year, and that her reward was $50,000. Her coworkers dubbed her the "Caviar Queen," a name that is often used when she is pointed out to the younger flight attendants.[3]

Training

When IdeAAs in Action was started up, the very first proposal received came from a manager at the airline's training academy in Dallas, Texas. He pointed out that the academy was training crew members with brand-new fire extinguishers, purchased expressly for this purpose. He suggested that the job could be done much more cheaply with expired fire extinguishers, which could be delivered to the training academy as they were withdrawn from active service in airplanes. Although their official life was over, they would still be perfectly good for practice. His proposal was accepted and was simple to implement. Procedures were changed so that, instead of disposing of expired extinguishers, airline operations would forward them to a central collection point. From there, they would later be sent on to the training academy. Not only did this proposal completely eliminate the need to buy expensive new fire extinguishers for training, but it also made many hundreds of extinguishers available for this purpose, improving the training itself and therefore improving safety.

Maintenance

An idea that was sent in by a mechanic is particularly memorable because of what he attached to the form. On the top left side, he affixed a nut with a blue diaper pin. On the right side, a pink diaper pin held an identical nut. The mechanic explained that the blue diaper pin was holding a nut from a McDonnell Douglas DC-10, for which American was paying $1.19 apiece. The pink diaper pin was holding a nut, also from McDonnell Douglas, but for the Super-8, for which the airline was paying 79 cents. The mechanic wrote that, in his opinion, the two nuts were the same, and American should be paying 79 cents for all such nuts. The IdeAAs in Action account manager sent the idea over to the engineering department, which, working together with McDonnell Douglas, found that the two nuts were in fact the same. Because of this, McDonnell Douglas reduced the price of the nut to 79 cents, and since American used so many of these nuts each year, the estimated savings from the idea turned out to be $300,000. The mechanic received $37,500 for his idea. In general, American makes every effort to get cost and price information to its mechanics, in order to open the door to improvements such as these. Savings from the resulting ideas are tremendous, and also bring big rewards to the suggesters.

At the new maintenance center in Alliance, Texas, we were introduced to an airframe and power-plant mechanic who, with a partner, had submitted an idea in 1995 that had won the maximum reward of $50,000. The two men had collected data which showed that a particularly expensive maintenance step performed on Rolls-Royce RB211 engines during their scheduled major overhauls (roughly once every three to four years) was largely unnecessary. The standard procedure had been to remove all of the several hundred stator vanes from the turbine rotor and send them out to a subcontractor for cleaning, polishing, and rebuilding. The mechanic and his partner had shown that, at least in the engines they were working on, although it was true that every stator vane needed *cleaning*, not all of them required *polishing*, and only 20 percent of them actually needed to be rebuilt. They proposed that the engine overhaul procedure be altered so that only the vanes that actually needed it would be polished and rebuilt. The idea was referred to the engineering department for study and a decision. When it was approved, the average savings of $80 per vane meant savings of $30,000 per engine overhaul. With an average of fifty RB211 engines overhauled in the facility each year, this idea was worth more than $1.5 million and won the maximum reward. Through this and his other ideas, the mechanic told us, he had added $45,000 to his paycheck in 1995.

Pilots

In a similar way, with the thousands of flights that American operated daily, proposals that saved fuel could rapidly add up to significant amounts of money. One day in the Miami, Florida, operations center, a pilot complained to a crew dispatcher that it was ridiculous that his flight out of Miami always had to make a long detour around Homestead Air Force Base. Perhaps, the pilot pointed out, this had made sense before the base had been completely wiped out by Hurricane

Andrew, but since the base no longer existed and had in fact been officially closed, why did flights in and out of Miami continue to have to fly around the ghost base? For American Airlines, it meant that six of its flights per day out of Miami had to spend an extra eleven minutes in the air. On an annual basis, a tremendous amount of fuel was being wasted. Why not simply go *through* the old Homestead airspace, instead of *around* it?

It so happened that the crew dispatcher the pilot was talking to was an IdeAAdvocate, who had received special training and been assigned to stimulate ideas at the Miami station (more on IdeAAdvocates shortly). As she was trained to do, she challenged him to do something about his complaint. "Well, why don't you go to the Federal Aviation Administration [FAA] and talk to them?" One thing led to another, and eventually the pilot, together with the Operations Control Center and the Flight Department, approached the FAA, which accepted his proposal. The airspace over the former Homestead Air Force Base is no longer restricted, and now all airplanes (not just American's) can make a direct approach to the runways at Miami. Not only did this help the environment, but it also saved American $900,000 per year.

The SABRE System

A seemingly small idea concerning the company's SABRE automated reservations system ended up saving millions of dollars when it was implemented. Whenever American installed or upgraded a new computer terminal for this system, either inside the company or at a travel agency, the terminal had to be connected with a dedicated line to the SABRE mainframe in Tulsa, Oklahoma. Previously, technicians had installed twenty-four-pin outlets on the wall near where the terminals were to be located. This meant that SABRE users would have to buy, for about forty-five dollars, a connector cable to plug their terminals into the wall outlet. One SABRE technician proposed a new wiring procedure that eliminated the need for the customer to purchase this connector cable. Instead of installing the twenty-four-pin outlets, he proposed leaving a length of wire with a twenty-four-pin plug on it hanging out of the wall so it could be plugged directly into the back of the terminals. System-wide savings to customers were estimated to be in the millions of dollars.

Flight Dispatch

Another idea, submitted by a team of flight dispatchers, pointed out a software error in the airline's flight-planning computer program. FAA regulations require that an extra 10 percent en route reserve fuel (over and above the normal reserves) be carried for portions of the flight that are over water. Somehow, a programmer had slipped up, so that in some cases the program would also add the extra 10 percent reserve fuel for the portions of the flight that were over land. In other words, American Airlines aircraft had sometimes been carrying excess weight amounting to 10 percent of their fuel. The savings from this proposal were estimated at $900,000 annually.

Advocates for Ideas

One initiative that would prove extremely important to IdeAAs in Action arose from an early proposal to improve the program itself. More ideas would be forthcoming, the suggester argued, if the program had representatives in the field, rather than being run entirely out of headquarters in Dallas. His idea led to the IdeAAdvocates program. IdeAAdvocates are specially designated employees who agree to serve as front-line representatives of IdeAAs in Action in their home stations, where they try to increase participation and interest in the program and act as the "eyes and ears" of the center in Dallas.

Each year, every field station nominates one person to be its IdeAAdvocate. Ideally, that person is friendly, outgoing, and entrepreneurial. IdeAAdvocates are volunteers, and although they are not eligible to submit suggestions, they do earn a $100 bonus, and a further $50 in each quarter in which participation rates increase at their station. Even though the duties of the job must be carried out on the IdeAAdvocate's own time, there is no shortage of applicants for these positions, since a term as an IdeAAdvocate is generally perceived as a step toward a management position. It is also an opportunity for significant personal growth, offering a chance to learn more about the company's operations, to meet and deal with multiple levels of management, and to improve one's analytical skills. All IdeAAdvocates attend annual regional conferences, where they have

the chance to interact with other IdeAAdvocates from stations throughout the American system.

Before taking up their one-year appointments, IdeAAdvocates receive a day of training in Dallas. There they are shown how the evaluation process works and how to fill out IdeAAs in Action forms. The
group discusses the kinds of suggestions the program is looking for and
is given tips for promoting participation at their stations. While at the
training session, each IdeAAdvocate is also teamed up with an IdeAAs
in Action account manager, giving the advocate, in effect, a "buddy" at
headquarters.

After they return to their home stations, whenever Dallas initiates a
special promotion, the IdeAAdvocates are sent supporting materials to
distribute or post on bulletin boards. IdeAAdvocates are expected to
carry IdeAAs in Action forms at all times, and to take advantage of any
opportunity to encourage people to participate. A common technique
(the one used by the Miami IdeAAdvocate) is to try to turn complaints
into proposals. An IdeAAdvocate's influence can be considerable.

In 1989, one year before the IdeAAdvocate program began, IdeAAs
in Action had received a total of 16,590 suggestions. A year later, the
number had more than doubled to 36,800. The first cohort of IdeAAdvocates had quickly breathed life into IdeAAs in Action in even the re-
motest offices in American's system. In Fayetteville, North Carolina,
for example, the staff of eighteen had submitted only two IdeAAs prior
to the appointment of their first IdeAAdvocate. But within four months
after he began, they had sent in more than 350. In fact, Fayetteville's
first IdeAAdvocate proved so successful and enthusiastic that he won
a corporate Leadership Award that year. On his own, he held local con-
tests for idea submissions, and he personally washed the cars of the
winners. This story further illustrates why IdeAAdvocates are so effective: they know the people and their site, and they can do whatever
works best.

In 1996, American had 330 IdeAAdvocates. But, as one administra-
tor commented to us, the real beauty of the IdeAAdvocate program is
that after their one-year appointment is over, IdeAAdvocates never really stop being IdeAAdvocates. Once an IdeAAdvocate, always an
IdeAAdvocate. As a result, in 1996 American Airlines had about 2,000
of them working throughout its system, not just that year's 330.

To give the system even more bias for action, in 1992 it was brought under the purview of the airline's financial auditors. Not only must the IdeAAs in Action account manager personally verify that an idea has actually been implemented before approving payment of the reward, but the rules now require an audit of any idea with claimed savings of over $50,000 per year. Smaller suggestions are audited on a random basis. Since an audit verifies that what is supposed to have happened actually did happen, these controls give the system integrity and mean that the published performance data can be trusted. By subjecting IdeAAs in Action to the company's financial auditing arm, the message was sent that it would be held to the same exacting standards as any other budget account. According to John Ford, director of World Class IdeAAs in 1996, it has always been absolutely clear to those involved that "if the [audited] dollars aren't around, IdeAAs in Action won't be around."[4] So far, however, the system has been in no danger. The suggestion system has been far more than a financial sideshow for the company. In the second quarter of 1993, for example, when American ended a string of six losing quarters to report a profit of $47 million, IdeAAs in Action produced $63 million in cost savings for the year. As with everything else that American's top management holds itself and its employees directly accountable for, IdeAAs in Action has become part of the daily work flow of the company.

N659AA: A Very Special Airplane

In 1991, American ran its first company-wide campaign to give IdeAAs in Action increased visibility within the company and to get everyone involved in it. Named "IdeAAs in Flight," the campaign won significant attention from the media and even received an award from the National Association of Suggestion Systems for the best suggestion system promotional program of 1991. Created in partnership with Boeing, IdeAAs in Flight was a $50.3 million fund drive to buy American's fiftieth Boeing 757. The new plane would serve as a constant reminder of the power of creativity, because the money would be raised entirely through savings from the IdeAAs in Action program in 1991. By the end of that year, forty-nine thousand suggestions had been submitted, of which about forty-six hundred (9.3 percent) were accepted and implemented. Total cost savings were $58 million—more than enough to pay for the new airplane. But, in retrospect, the important phase of the campaign really began once this money had been raised, because IdeAAs in Flight turned into an almost year-long celebration of the IdeAAs in Action system.

It takes about two years to build a large airliner. During the seven months of final assembly of the IdeAAs in Flight Boeing 757, tail number N659AA, American was accepting delivery of one new Boeing aircraft per month. Ten employees who had submitted suggestions to IdeAAs in Flight were invited along each month on the necessary inspection and acceptance trips to Boeing's plant in Seattle, where they had the chance to watch the construction of N659AA. Boeing cooperated throughout this seven-month period, pairing each of these unusual visitors from American Airlines with a counterpart from its own organization who acted as host. Boeing even saved the scrap metal from N659AA and recycled it into special commemorative pins. These pins are still given away today by the IdeAAs in Action program as small "thank-you" items to suggesters.

Since this particular airplane was so special, it was decided that it would be the first airplane in the history of American Airlines to be given a name, which would be painted on its nose. After a company-wide "Name the Plane" contest, Linda Jo Henderson's entry of *Pride of American* was selected as the winner. In 1996, this airplane remains the only one in the American fleet with a name. Wherever it travels in the American system—and special efforts are made to ensure that it travels far and wide—American employees recognize it and remember why it is there.

The rollout and acceptance ceremony, the christening by Robert Crandall and Linda Jo Henderson, and the maiden voyage of *Pride of American* became a three-day celebration in Seattle in January 1992. Present with Crandall were eight other officers of the company, together with 194 of 1991's top suggesters, who had collectively come up with $40 million of the airplane's $50.3 million price tag. A video of highlights of the three days was produced and shown to every employee in the company. When the ceremonies concluded on January 10, all the participants climbed aboard *Pride of American* for its maiden voyage back to Tulsa, Oklahoma, and then, with some still on board, on to Dallas. *Pride of American* then went on a world tour with smaller ceremonies throughout the American system.

Creativity Through the Rearview Mirror

IdeAAs in Action is an extraordinary program that showcases the power of the potential creativity available to any company that puts systems in place to tap it. American receives frequent visits from companies that want to benchmark their own suggestion systems against it. It is hard to conceive of a company better aligned for soliciting cost-saving ideas from its employees than American Airlines. Certainly, we have encountered no present-day suggestion system that even comes close to IdeAAs in Action. As we have already noted, American's system is uncannily similar to NCR's under Patterson, from the strong leadership it receives to the rewards scheme, and even to the lavish banquets held each year (semiannually in Patterson's case) to celebrate the top suggesters and the managers who have best promoted ideas. In 1996, the 86,138 employees of the airline who were eligible to participate in the system submitted 17,109 ideas, saving the airline $43 million. The extremely strong alignment for cost savings has allowed American to create a high-performing suggestion system.

However, one does not have to delve too deeply into American's system before its limitations begin to emerge, limitations that will be as difficult for the airline to overcome as they were for Patterson. In 1996, fewer than 8 percent of the ideas submitted were actually adopted, and only 9 percent of employees participated in the system. (The statistics for Patterson's system were surprisingly similar.) Clearly, IdeAAs in Action is making use of only a fraction of the company's creative potential.

The single biggest source of proposals to IdeAAs in Action has always been the maintenance employees, whose ideas in 1996 amounted to $20.3 million, 47 percent of the system's total cost savings in that year. Some mechanics, in fact, earned as much as $100,000 for their suggestions. With the cost of the parts involved and the sheer quantities of parts moving through their hands, it is easy to see how this could happen. Are maintenance employees so much more creative than everyone else in the company? Or are they merely in a position that makes it easy for them to come up with ideas that result in huge cost savings? We think the latter. In fact, one team of suggesters, introduced to us as one of the most successful IdeAAs in Action teams at American, explicitly described to us their highly successful method for coming up with cost-saving ideas. The team member who worked in the accounting department would periodically run checks of parts expenditures, looking for particularly expensive parts that were used in quantity. When he found any that fit the pattern, he would alert the other member of the team, a lead mechanic for the large jets. This mechanic would then pull these parts off the aircraft as they came in for maintenance, examine them for patterns of wear or damage, and identify ways to reinforce them in order to prolong their usefulness. Or, if the mechanic felt that American was paying too much for a part, the team would look for cheaper alternatives. The cost savings from the resulting ideas were astounding (almost one million dollars annually), and so were the rewards the pair had received. This team's work is precisely what IdeAAs in Action is rewarding in practice. Although such activity is obviously useful for the business, it represents only a small part of the potential creativity American could be tapping.

The more a company is aligned for cost savings, the less likely it is to pursue an idea whose cost savings are not immediately apparent. Recall that when Ian Hart, the British Airways (BA) baggage handler, worked on his idea for "First & Fast," his company also had a suggestion system in place, known as Brainwaves. Luckily for Ian Hart, BA was not as strongly aligned for cost savings as American. Brainwaves, and the rewards it offered, did not even figure in his creative act. He worked on it out of interest, submitted his idea to the Brainwaves system only *after* it had been implemented, and did so *at someone else's suggestion*. Would he have done what he did had he worked in a company that was strongly aligned for cost-saving ideas? We don't think so. The chances are that he would not have moved ahead with his idea; his primary thought would have been that since it wouldn't save money, it wouldn't be what the company was looking for anyway.

Take the case of the flight attendant described in the Introduction, who saved five penny-and-a-half coffee lids per flight, for a cost savings that took everyone by surprise, including her. Presumably, the account manager for her proposal had considerable experience seeing apparently tiny ideas turn out to be large ones, but did the flight attendant? We can believe that she might have had a moment of doubt: was this going to save the kind of money that would make it worthwhile to write up? The low participation rates of suggestion systems based on cost savings merely reflect the fact that they attract only a small percentage of the ideas employees can come up with. The great number of ideas that people have but drop—because they don't think that they will generate cost savings or don't believe that the cost savings can be measured—are a substantial loss. How can one put a price on the number of first-class passengers BA retained because of Ian Hart's idea?

We have already seen how large rewards for ideas can lead to problems, which even IdeAAs in Action is not exempt from. For example, at American Airlines, the official policy is that all ideas should be worked on during the employees' own time. In reality, managers assured us, they would be stupid to follow this policy too rigorously. Most managers would wink at violations of this rule that resulted in significant savings. But from the employees' perspective, the story is quite different. Mechanics privately told us that they would never work on an idea during regular hours, because other mechanics might see what they were working on, realize that potential savings were involved, find those savings themselves, and submit the idea as their own before the originator could. Secrecy, it seemed, was paramount.

Because of the sums of money involved, one of the first things American does with a newly submitted idea is to conduct a "duplicate check," a keyword search of the IdeAAs in Action data base to see if the idea has been submitted before. If a proposal turns out to duplicate a previous one, an individualized and carefully worded rejection letter is sent to the suggester, together with a copy of the response to the original idea. If the idea is ultimately rejected, then for duplication purposes, the proposer owns the rights to it for three years. If, during this period, another employee submits a suggestion similar to the previously rejected idea or uses it explicitly and this new idea is accepted, it is treated as a team effort, and the reward is shared between the new proposer and the person holding the duplication rights.

With such large sums of money involved, American has to be careful to promote trust in the duplication rights system, and so it takes this very seriously. One story in particular illustrates this well. In the late 1960s, before American had a formal suggestion system, an employee submitted an idea to his supervisor for an improved way to handle Aircraft On Ground (AOG) parts, that is, replacement parts being rushed through the system to a grounded aircraft. (When an aircraft is grounded it costs any airline enormous sums of money.) The suggestion was to design special bags for AOG parts, with the letters "AOG" printed prominently on them to highlight their presence to airline personnel as they moved through the system. Nothing was done about the idea at the time. But when, twenty-five years later, a different person proposed the same thing to the new IdeAAs in Action program, the idea was accepted, implemented, and rewarded. When the new AOG bags were introduced into operations, the employee who had originally proposed the idea, and who still worked at American, spotted the new bags and recognized his own idea. He contacted the IdeAAs in Action center and pointed out that the company had used his idea without paying him for it. Even though his original proposal had been long forgotten, and his modern counterpart had already collected his full reward, the IdeAAs in Action program paid him an identical amount.

Duplication rights also make it extremely worthwhile for one person to beat another to the punch with an idea. Several employees at American told us of rumors that mailroom employees sometimes opened the easily recognizable letters containing suggestion forms for IdeAAs in Action and resubmitted some of them as their own. By contrast, we have never come across a single instance of employees stealing ideas in a *kaizen teian* system, where rewards are deemphasized, because no one has anything to gain from it.

You may be wondering if there is any room at American Airlines for innovation. American is known for two innovations in particular: it pioneered the frequent-flier program and the SABRE reservations system, which for the first time allowed reservations to be made without contacting the airline directly. But both of these ideas were thought of before the IdeAAs in Action system existed. This brings us to the most serious limitation of the American system. Cost savings come by doing already-existing activities better. But innovations involve the initiation of entirely new activities—activities never previously done by the company. How can a system based on cost savings promote innovation when it is aimed backward, looking to modify what the company already does? IdeAAs in Action is really one big corrective-action system, stimulating creativity, but through the "rearview mirror." The nature of the alignment at American Airlines determines the types of creativity the company will see.

The critical question concerning alignment at American is this: is it possible to imagine that anyone in the organization does *not* understand that cost savings are a major concern, or that anyone would pass up any chance for saving money? From the time we spent at American, and the conversations we had with employees at all levels there, it is clear to us that the answer is emphatically *no*. This strong alignment is what enables American's system (and NCR's in its time) to work so well. IdeAAs in Action is an exemplary suggestion system. Who can argue that it has not been a financial success, and that management should not be extremely pleased with it? However, from the point of view of creativity, it falls far short of what is possible.

Ironically, the very success of IdeAAs in Action makes it harder for American to move to a higher level of creative performance. The question that American has to face, as will other companies that presently use rewards to try to motivate creativity, is how to wean employees off these rewards and strengthen their intrinsic motivation. The greater the company's dependence on financial rewards, the deeper the hole that has been dug. British Airways got an indication of what was to come when it began talking with its unions about eliminating or reducing rewards for ideas, with the goal of moving toward a system based on intrinsic motivation. When he heard that this would involve eliminating rewards, one battle-hardened union leader is reported to have said, "Why not put up two boxes? The first could have a sign on it, 'Put your idea here if you want a reward for it,' and the second, 'Put your idea here if you don't.'"[5]

Many companies that wish to promote creativity face the tricky issue of reducing dependence on rewards. (Companies that have never before used them for creativity have a big advantage in this regard.) But it can be done. In the next chapter, we look at the *kaizen teian* system of Idemitsu Kosan, one of the largest petroleum companies in Japan. Although it began with modest rewards for ideas, the company initiated and successfully completed the transition to a rewardless system. As we will see, everyone at Idemitsu was very surprised at what happened. The rate of proposals more than doubled, and the participation rate rose to an astonishing 100 percent! Idemitsu now has one of the best *kaizen teian* systems in the world.

Understandably, employees will be skeptical of any proposals to reduce rewards for ideas. We do not believe that every company has to reduce them to zero; the kinds of ideas that Idemitsu's system gets reflect the nature both of its alignment and the absence of rewards. Whatever the mix of intrinsic and extrinsic motivation a company aims for, it is desirable in the context of a fair overall compensation system to keep the rewards as small as possible and to decouple them as much as possible from the creative act. Employees cannot be intrinsically motivated while operating under the influence of large potential rewards.

Alignment is all about making sure that the company's key goals are supported by everyone in the organization, so that every employee will make choices and decisions in accordance with these goals. For creativity, it determines the nature of the ideas that employees will step forward with, and how those who become aware of the idea will respond to it. Unless a company is strongly aligned, its creativity will remain a hit-or-miss proposition. The natural question arises: how does a company align itself?

How to Promote Alignment

There are good reasons why well-aligned companies are hard to find. The fact that it takes tremendous discipline, persistence, and hard work to align a company means that an organization has to see a real need for it. Since a company can operate and, in the short term, even be profitable without being strongly aligned, this need is far from obvious. This is why the most critical step in aligning a company is the first one—recognizing the value of alignment and that it has to be done. Because it has to do with culture, alignment is hard to pin down. And yet strong alignment, when it exists, is all-pervasive, affecting how everyone in an organization makes decisions, big and small. Once the commitment is made, it is surprisingly straightforward to get the strong alignment that is needed for creativity.

A good way to start is to seek out and identify sources of misalignment. The Soviet story is a litany of misalignments created by policies, rules, systems, and goals that were all pulling in different directions. Because these misalignments were so extreme, it is hard not to see them and the damage they caused. In most organizations, however, they will not be so easy to spot, even though they are actively working against creativity. To find them, an organization needs to scrutinize its policies and practices. Are the real interests and actions of employees in line with the company's key goals? Will employees respond positively to potentially useful ideas? Will they step forward with such ideas? Has the fear created by downsizing affected alignment and therefore creativity? Surveys and focus groups can provide insight into the perceptions and attitudes of employees. Task forces can examine policies and rules. And digging up examples of good ideas that were stymied can reveal the sources of misalignment that most directly limit the organization's creativity.

Eliminating misalignments is a start. Strong alignment requires three things:

1. *Clarity about what the key goals of the organization are.* For creativity to come from any employee, a company has to ensure that those who come into contact with a potentially useful idea will respond positively to it. An organization can make clear what it stands for in many ways. At American Airlines, every time the *Pride of American* touches down in a different city, employees are reminded that it was bought with the savings from their ideas. And every time an IdeAAdvocate challenges someone to turn a complaint into an idea, alignment spreads a little further.

2. *Commitment to initiatives that promote the key goals.* Every organization makes choices about how to spend its money and time. At American Airlines, the IdeAAs in Action program (which clearly moves the company where it wants to go) has a dedicated full-time staff of forty-seven and was launched with an impressive worldwide ceremony that cost the company more than $12.5 million. Although CEO Robert Crandall has many demands on his time, IdeAAs in Action always has a place on his schedule.

3. *Accountability for actions that affect the key goals.* Companies must hold their employees and managers accountable for decisions that affect the company's key goals. Corrective action has to be taken when these decisions are out of alignment. At American, everyone who interacts with a money-saving suggestion knows that they had better respond quickly. If they don't, the suggestion will end up on the CEO's desk. All forty-seven members of the IdeAAs in Action staff are fully aware that their program is held financially accountable: if the savings aren't there, they won't be either. This is not to say that corrective action will always require a sledgehammer; often a reminder or explanation will do the job.

MAIN POINTS

The extremely strong alignment of American Airlines for cost savings has allowed it to create a high-performing suggestion system.

In 1996, the 17,109 ideas from employees saved the company $43 million.

The nature of a company's alignment strongly influences the kinds of creative acts that will occur.

A suggestion system for corporate creativity in a company that is strongly aligned around cost savings has two major drawbacks:

1. *Cost savings is a powerful filter for ideas, and some employees are in a better position than others to come up with such ideas.*

   At American, the maintenance function was responsible for 47 percent of the total cost savings from IdeAAs in Action in 1996. Some mechanics earned more than $100,000 from the system.

2. *A system based on cost savings is aimed backward, because it is looking for savings on things the company already does. It does little to promote innovation—activity never previously done by the company.*

   American did pioneer the frequent-flier program and the SABRE system, but both of these innovations occurred outside the IdeAAs in Action system. IdeAAs in Action is really a giant (and highly effective) corrective-action system.

Strong alignment requires clarity about what the key goals of the organization are, commitment to initiatives that promote them, and accountability for actions that affect them.

Chapter Seven
SELF-INITIATED ACTIVITY

Intellectual curiosity, the desire to understand, is derived from an urge as basic as hunger or sex: the exploratory drive.

ARTHUR KOESTLER[1]

Arthur Koestler is right. People do have a natural drive to explore and create, a drive that leads them to initiate new activity. And while companies can plan for new and useful things, these take a company only in directions it has already anticipated. They will not lead a company to unanticipated places. Unexpected creative acts—the ones companies tend to ignore—will result only from *self-initiated activity*. G. D. Searle saw itself as a pharmaceutical company and had no plans to move into the food and beverage business with a revolutionary new sweetener. Massachusetts never expected to discover a different way to interpret federal Medicaid regulations that would bring it a billion-dollar windfall. Both of these unexpected creative acts were initiated by individuals. No one ever asked them to do what they did—in fact, no one even remotely anticipated what occurred. The second element of corporate creativity is *self-initiated activity*, and no unplanned creative act can happen without it. We begin by looking at one act that illustrates just how strong a person's desire to initiate something new can be. It resulted in something with implications far beyond what anyone could ever have imagined—the bar code. Not only was the bar code unplanned, but it is hard to think how the set of circumstances that brought it about could ever have been planned.

The Bar Code: Born on a Florida Beach

In 1948, Joseph Woodland and his colleague Bob Silver were both instructors at Drexel University in Philadelphia; Woodland in the mechanical engineering department, Silver in electrical engineering. One day, Silver had an appointment with the dean of engineering. When he arrived at the dean's office, the dean was still busy with his previous appointment, so Silver sat down in the outer office to wait. Since the door to the inner office was open, Silver couldn't help but overhear the conversation. The dean was talking with Sam Friedland, president of Food Fair, which remains one of the largest supermarket chains in the Philadelphia area. Friedland was trying to get the dean to initiate a research project to develop a system that could automatically capture the price of groceries at the checkout counter. Interestingly, the reason Friedland was looking for such a system had nothing to do with reducing his labor costs. He had a completely different problem in mind, one that plagued the entire supermarket industry—errors by cashiers, who would enter incorrect prices for items or simply miss them entirely. In theory, it might seem, the effects of cashier mistakes should balance out over time. However, in practice, customers were far more likely to call attention to an overcharge than to an undercharge. And supermarkets have long operated with extremely low margins. Indeed, just a few years after Friedland's conversation with the dean, a study would show that cashier errors were costing the grocery industry some 0.7 percent of sales, a huge amount of money considering the large volumes and low profit margins involved. It is really not surprising that Friedland would be looking for a way to make the checkout process error-free.

Unfortunately, Drexel University would not help him—at least not officially. Silver listened in amazement as the dean turned Friedland away, apparently because he felt such commercial projects were not part of the university's mission.[2] When he concluded his business with the dean, Silver dropped by Woodland's office and told him what had happened. After listening to Silver's account, Woodland thought for a moment. "The main problem's going to be with orientation," he said. "Whatever marks you put on an item, you'd have to be sure that the shopper or the checker or somebody would orient it properly toward the device that's going to read it." They talked for a while. Woodland suggested that shoppers could put their groceries on a belt that would carry them through a tunnel where a special device could illuminate and read phosphorescent marks on them. The presence or absence of a mark would encode the price in a binary sequence of zeros and ones. Silver was able to find three different colors of phosphorescent paint at a theatrical supply store. Woodland then persuaded a technician in Drexel's physics department to build them a crude spectrophotometer. Three months after the conversation in the dean's office, Woodland and Silver had built a prototype system and had it working. With just three colors of phosphorescent paint, their device could read prices up to only eight cents. Woodland and Silver had quickly moved from thinking about the problem to action.

At this point, events took an unexpected turn. While at Drexel, Woodland had been taking some MBA courses, one of which was in corporate finance. The course had a term paper requirement; each student had to pick a company and find out whether its stock was a good buy. Woodland picked Atlantic City Electric, only because he knew that its treasurer was in the same Rotary Club as his father. When he did his analysis of the company's stock, Woodland discovered that it was extremely undervalued and came to suspect that it would soon double in price, perhaps within six months. When, on Woodland's behalf, his father asked the company treasurer's opinion of the stock, he was told, "I'm buying all the stock I can." So Woodland borrowed all the money he could to buy Atlantic City Electric stock, and later he found out that his father and grandfather had also invested in it. As he had predicted, the stock did double in price. When he received an A+ for his term paper, he suspected that his instructor might also have come along for the ride. When Woodland sold out, he found himself with some money for the first time in his life. And when he told Bob Silver that he planned to resign his position at Drexel University and move into his grandfather's apartment in Florida for three or four weeks to think about a practical way to automate the supermarket checkout process, Bob Silver told him he was crazy.

Woodland spent his first day in Florida sitting on the beach, trying to think of some sort of code that could be put on an item's packaging. Years before, when he had been interested in getting his amateur radio operator's license, he had passed his test for Morse Code. In fact, Morse Code was the only code he knew. As he thought about his problem, he absent-mindedly pushed his fingers down into the sand. Pulling them out, he looked at them and there it was—the idea of vertical bars. In that moment on a Florida beach, the bar code was born.

However, one problem remained. How could such a code be scanned? Coincidentally, Woodland and Silver had previously worked on an idea for recording sound. At one point, they had looked into movie soundtrack technology and learned that it involved a sequence of lighter and darker patches on the film illuminated by a light beam. For an automated checkout system, Woodland figured that he could make a simple box that would sweep the item with a moving point of light in a similar fashion and detect the presence or absence of light reflected diffusely from wide or narrow phosphorescent bars.

But before the system could be patented, one more thing was needed: a device that could do the decoding automatically. Woodland returned to his parents' house in New Jersey and began drafting drawings and disclosure statements for a patent. At the same time, he got back in touch with Bob Silver. He told Silver that he had figured out a way to do what Sam Friedland had wanted. What he still needed, however, was some sort of a decoding system. If Silver could come up with something, Woodland suggested, they could file the patent as coinventors. Silver accepted the challenge. Using only three components, he designed and built a simple and somewhat clumsy system. Just one year after Silver accidentally overheard Friedland's conversation with the dean, they had done it. Consider this. If the dean had decided to go ahead with the project, would it have happened the same way? Would he have asked Woodland or Silver to work on it? Would it have happened at all?

In October 1949, Woodland and Silver filed the application for what would be the basic bar-code patent. However, they changed their coding scheme from vertical lines to a bull's-eye of concentric circles, so that it could be scanned from any direction. Three years later, in 1952, they would receive their patent, but it would be another twenty frustrating years before the bar code would be realized commercially. In the meantime, a more immediate concern arose for Woodland: finding a job. He worked for a consulting firm for several years, advising airframe manufacturers around the country about airframe hydraulics. During this time, he got married and, wanting to spend more time at home, he started to look for a company that he could stay with on a permanent basis, one that would help him exploit his bar-code patent. After considering several computer companies, he finally settled on IBM as his best prospect. In 1951 he was hired at the company's Endicott Laboratory near Binghamton in New York. Unfortunately, he had to keep his plans for the bar code on hold for a while longer. He had joined the company at the height of the Korean War. Thomas Watson, Sr., IBM's chairman, had promised President Harry Truman the full resources of the company for the war effort.[3] Woodland found himself assigned to a project that management thought he was best suited for: designing airborne electromechanical navigational units for bombers.

In January 1952, when Thomas Watson, Jr., was promoted to the presidency of IBM, Woodland took the unusual step of writing a letter to him. After congratulating Watson on his promotion, he described his idea for a supermarket scanning system, explaining why he thought it would be a good business opportunity for IBM. Somewhat to his surprise, Tom Watson wrote back promptly. His letter of February 5, 1952, reads as follows:

Dear Mr. Woodland,

Thank you for your letter of January 30. I appreciate your good wishes on my promotion.

I am very interested in your ideas with respect to supermarkets. There is a real need for some automatic means of totaling purchases at supermarkets and I have asked Mr. W. W. McDowell, our Director of Engineering, to get in touch with you to discuss in detail the thoughts you have on this subject.

Sincerely yours,

Thomas Watson, Jr.

However, once again events beyond Woodland's control were conspiring to pull him away from what he really wanted to work on. When he met with McDowell, he quickly got the feeling that IBM's director of engineering was more interested in Woodland himself than in the bar code. His intuition, as it turned out, was accurate.

Since the late 1940s, Thomas Watson, Jr., had been working on his father to move the company away from its "bread and butter" punch-card machines and into the electronic computer age. Thomas Watson,

Sr., was extremely reluctant to believe that the era of punch cards, on which he had built the company, was coming to an end. Looking back on this critical juncture in the company's history, Thomas Watson, Jr., remembered that, even in 1949,

> *I didn't think it would be prudent to run to Dad with the idea that punch cards were dying. He'd have thrown me out of his office.*[4]

But as complaints began to pour in from customers that they needed something better than punch cards, and as many of them began to switch to companies like Raytheon and RCA for their data-processing needs, the old man began to relent. Unfortunately, at the time, IBM had almost no in-house electrical engineering expertise. Sensing his opportunity one day in 1950 at a meeting in Endicott, Tom Watson, Jr., pointed out to his father the man he thought would make the ideal director of engineering to spearhead this change—W. W. McDowell, an MIT graduate. With his father's permission, he walked over to the astonished McDowell and gave him his marching orders for the next several years. He was to hire several hundred electrical engineers, perhaps even a few thousand, and move IBM into the electronic age.

When McDowell met Woodland in 1952, his real interest was to recruit one more top engineer for his group. And so it came about that Woodland found himself in a new job, this time in long-range planning. In this new position, too, he was unable to generate any enthusiasm for the bar code, although he did continue to work on it unofficially. At least one good thing came out of the reassignment, however—a change of office location that resulted in his carpooling with his neighbor, Evon Greanias, a physicist who would become an influential supporter of his at IBM. Greanias was working on optical character recognition devices and would teach Woodland much about optical engineering. In 1959, Greanias was asked to start an advanced systems technology group in a newly created division. He asked Woodland if he would join this group to lead a project on supermarket checkout technology.[5] Finally, eleven years after the conversation in the dean's office, the bar-code effort had official status.

Fairly quickly, IBM hired the Stanford Research Institute (SRI) to do a feasibility study of the idea. Even though Woodland and Silver had built their first working model ten years earlier, it was still far ahead of the technology that would allow it to be commercialized. Both integrated circuits and lasers were yet to come. Shrouded with black cloth to keep out light, their device used a five-hundred-watt incandescent light bulb that not only created serious cooling problems, but was so bright it could cause eye damage. The SRI study concluded that although the system was feasible, the benefits it offered did not come close to justifying its cost. Furthermore, the study gave no insight whatsoever into the other advantages of bar coding, such as real-time sales information and inventory control. The SRI consultants recommended shelving the project for a while and, with Woodland's reluctant agreement, it was—for ten more years. The corporate planning process had reached a decision, one that might have made sense from an official perspective but that almost kept IBM out of what would become a very lucrative market. As the initiator of the idea, however, Woodland had a different perspective—a perspective that IBM would come to need again.

Woodland had offered several times to sell his bar-code patent to IBM. However, he and his company had different views of its worth. Although the two sides did negotiate, they were never able to reach an agreement. In 1962, when Philco offered Woodland and Silver their asking price, they decided to sell. They both assumed that Philco wanted the patent for an automated mail-sorting project it was working on for the U.S. Post Office. Only at the closing did the company's attorney inform them that Philco had no intention of using the patent. The company was being sold to Ford in thirty days, and one component of the sale price was the value of Philco's patent portfolio, which the bar-code patent would beef up considerably. Ford never made use of the patent either, and later sold it to RCA. Beginning in 1966, RCA not only made the bar code an official project, but began an intensive development effort that would put it out in front of IBM for seven years.[6]

As things turned out, before IBM could get back in the running, it would have to rediscover the initiator of the bar-code idea within its own ranks and it would take something unexpected to bring this about. In 1969, the company began to feel pressure from a number of its larger customers who wanted to automate their forecasting and merchandise replenishment processes and were frustrated with the standard NCR electromechanical cash register. This prompted IBM to enter the business of point-of-sale systems and to set up a consumer transactions group of about thirty people in Raleigh, North Carolina. For the first two years, this group worked on making more intelligent cash registers by incorporating electronics into them.

In April 1971 (two years after Woodland's patent expired), this group received shocking and unexpected news. A member of the group, Alec Jablonover, attended an industry trade show in Cincinnati where RCA caused a sensation by unveiling a working checkout scanner. As people walked onto the exhibition floor, they were handed an empty can with a bull's-eye bar code stamped on each end. Some of the cans were worth a prize, but the only way to find out was to have them scanned at the RCA booth. RCA's exhibit drew the attention of all the supermarket executives, and the IBM representatives found their booth deserted. Alec Jablonover went over to investigate and was astonished by what he saw. He stayed at the booth for a long time and asked so many questions that his RCA counterparts soon identified him as an IBMer and kicked him out.

As soon as he returned to North Carolina, Jablonover reported the news to his group, which now realized that bar coding was the direction in which IBM had to move, and *fast*. Jablonover was assigned to find out what he could about bar codes. His first stop was the library, where he came across an article about the bull's-eye code in an old internal publication, and Joseph Woodland—of IBM, to his huge surprise—was featured prominently in it. Jablonover went to his manager and showed him the article. Both men realized that they had to try to locate Woodland. A good place to start was to find out if he was still with IBM. A few phone calls later, Woodland answered the phone in his office at IBM headquarters, where he was then working. Was he the person who had invented the bar code? Jablonover asked. Yes, indeed, he was. IBM management acted quickly and decisively, and by the end of the summer, Woodland had been transferred down to Raleigh. His arrival galvanized the demoralized consumer transactions group. Jablonover remembers it well:

> *His pride of ownership was very strong at all times. Actually, he sort of invigorated the whole group, because all of a sudden we felt that we really had a resource that could bring us great success.*[7]

From this point on, IBM made enormous profits from the bar code. But first, for the new technology to become widely used in the supermarket and retail industry, it had to be standardized. One of Woodland's first contributions was to head up the IBM team that would design the company's entry into the competition to choose what would become the standard Universal Product Code. There were twelve different entries, including IBM's. The RCA entry was not very different from the bull's-eye pattern that Woodland and Silver had patented in 1952. The IBM entry was based on the vertical wide-and-narrow bar design that Woodland had thought of more than twenty years before on the Florida beach, except that it incorporated several critical improvements. Although the Universal Product Code Committee rejected all the entries, the code it did adopt was patterned very closely after IBM's submission.[8] When, in 1973, this symbol officially became the standard bar code, IBM moved into the lead for good and has dominated the market for point-of-sale systems ever since. In 1992, after Woodland retired from a long and successful career at IBM, President George Bush awarded him the National Medal of Technology. The citation read:

> *for his invention and contribution to the commercialization of bar code technology, which improved productivity in every industrial sector and gave rise to the bar code industry.*

It may seem that self-initiated activity like Joseph Woodland's is the exception in corporate creativity. But as we have seen, the *majority* of creative acts in companies happen this way. Why does self-initiated activity figure so prominently in corporate creativity? Consider this. Would any company have assigned Joseph Woodland to design a supermarket scanner? He was a mechanical engineer, not an electrical engineer or a computer scientist. He was interested enough in business (recall that at Drexel he took MBA classes in his spare time) to appreciate the implications of Friedland's request. His critical insights would come from his former hobby of amateur radio and his previous dabbling in movie sound systems. In hindsight, he was perfect for the job, but who else could have sensed that but him? Woodland *self-selected* for the job. Neither Woodland nor Silver, nor even Friedland, dreamed of the wider implications that a bar-coding system would have for industry, but that is not important. The need they saw was enough for them. We have been struck by how frequently a person's point of entry into creative activity is only a minor facet of the idea's full potential, so minor, in fact, as to seem insignificant to all but the initiator. An excellent example of this can be seen in the unusual story of the development of a blockbuster product: the first practical word processor for Japanese characters.

The Point of Entry

In 1977, an electrical hardware engineer at Fujitsu named Yasunori Kanda had just begun to learn how to write computer programs.[9] Encountering all the start-up frustrations of a novice programmer, he noticed something that more experienced programmers might not have. The programs he looked at that were written by Americans were full of "remark" statements (helpful comments incorporated into the coding) that made it much easier for others to understand and use them. Japanese programmers, on the other hand, seemed to use very few remark statements in their programs. Kanda began to wonder why. He soon came to think that the problem was with the keyboards. Since all of them were designed for the English alphabet, there was no practical way to enter remark statements in Japanese. It was not a matter of asking for a different keyboard, for no such keyboard existed. If one were designed for Japanese, Kanda thought, programmers would not be so reluctant to include remark statements in their computer programs. Up to this point, however, no one had figured out an easy way to put the thousands of different Japanese characters on a simple keyboard. The straightforward solution of one key for every character would produce a keyboard the size of a large tabletop! The rudimentary Japanese typewriters then in existence amounted to little more than this.

Kanda began to think about a new type of keyboard that would permit easy entry of Japanese characters. On his own, he set off on what would prove to be an exhaustive study of the history of Western printing and character generation, ranging from the invention of the typewriter to the development of the American Standard Code for Information Interchange (ASCII) format for modern computers. At one point, we had a glimpse of the impressive breadth of his research into the history of typing and printing, when he showed us the loose-leaf binders of notes he had compiled during the project. He realized that an important point in the development of the Western typewriter had been the invention of the shift key, which at one stroke doubled the number of characters on the keyboard. Together with another Fujitsu researcher, Yoshiki Ikegami, Kanda experimented with combinations of keystrokes for the Japanese alphabetic *kana* characters that could be input as building blocks to help select one out of the thousands of possible pictogram *kanji* characters.

Realistically, mechanical typewriters were limited to one shift key, and that was enough for English. But with a computer, multifunction capability was available for any key. In roughly two years, the work of Kanda and Ikegami had led Fujitsu to develop an entirely new keyboard that would become the standard for both Japanese and Chinese characters. It may or may not have increased the number of remark statements written by Japanese programmers, but who cared? It freed communications throughout Asia by opening up a new era of widespread availability of low-cost word processing. Through Kanda's self-initiated activity, Fujitsu moved to a dominant position in word-processing equipment.

Consider this, however. If management had targeted the development of a new Japanese word processor, it probably would not have chosen a novice computer programmer like Kanda to lead the effort. If it had, could it have predicted the tiny facet of the problem—trying to make it easier for Japanese programmers to use more remark statements—that would pique his curiosity and set him off on his odyssey?

Systems with Follow-Through Go a Long Way

Fortunately, as Arthur Koestler pointed out, the desire to initiate creative acts not only already exists within most people, but is derived from an urge as deep-rooted as hunger or sex. Any actions that companies take to promote self-initiated activity only have to unleash what is already present. But action is needed, because in a corporate setting consistent and broad-based self-initiated activity does not happen by itself. In those few companies where we found high levels of it, we couldn't help but notice something that set them apart: they all had a *system* of some kind with good follow-through on employee ideas. We have come to believe that almost any system that responds efficiently to ideas will unleash considerable self-initiated activity. It may seem ironic that we should be discussing *systems* in the context of something as personal as a person's curiosity and motivation. But that is where the evidence has led us. A system sidesteps the whole issue; it doesn't care where an idea comes from or what motivated the people who initiated it.

Consider the experience of the Eastern Region of the U.S. Forest Service. In 1985, the Department of Agriculture criticized the service for its lack of creativity and bureaucratic ways. The harsh review prompted Forest Service Chief Max Peterson, who knew that these criticisms were accurate, to formulate a new "people-oriented" management philosophy, aimed at fostering creativity and innovation.[10] Pilot tests of the new management system were initiated in four national forests, one of which was the Mark Twain National Forest in Missouri. The project was so successful there that Floyd Marita, the Regional Forester for the Eastern Region, requested pilot status for his entire twenty-state jurisdiction. When this was approved, the region's pilot initiative was dubbed Project SPIRIT, with the two "I"s standing for "innovation" and "intrapreneurship."

One of the first Project SPIRIT initiatives was to breathe life into the Eastern Region's moribund suggestion system. It had been bureaucratic and unresponsive, requiring Forest Service employees, for example, to fill out a four-page form, exactly the same length as the one for rationalization proposals in the former Soviet Union. In the previous four years, the region's twenty-five hundred employees had sent in a paltry 252 ideas, a rate amounting to one idea from each person every *forty years*. Surely the Forest Service had more creative potential than this! The revamped system required only a very simple form, which employees could fill out on their computers and submit locally or E-mail directly to the regional office. From the start, it was made clear to frontline personnel that this time the Forest Service really did want their ideas and would do something about them. Line managers from headquarters traveled to every unit in the region to meet with staff in the field. One new rule spoke volumes about the new commitment to follow-through. If an idea was submitted and the suggester received no response within thirty days, then as long as the idea did not break any

laws and fell within the Forest Service's domain of activity, it was automatically approved and had to be immediately implemented. The region appointed Karl Mettke to the full-time position of "consultant on
creativity" and appointed Project SPIRIT coordinators (much like the
IdeAAdvocates at American Airlines) in each functional area and in
each of the region's sixteen national forests. No rewards were offered
for ideas, but those that were approved were awarded a silver sticker
with a picture of a skunk on it with its tail down. Rejected ideas also
got skunk stickers—with the tail *up*.[11]

Immediately, according to Karl Mettke, "came a rush of new ideas."[12]
In the first year alone, the Forest Service received six thousand ideas,
almost a hundred times more than under the old system. Over the next
three years, more than twelve thousand ideas would be sent in, of
which about 75 percent were implemented. All that had changed was
the system—the people remained the same. Their surge of self-initiated activity had been unleashed by a system that, for the first time,
took their ideas seriously.

A rush of ideas can always be anticipated when a company first im-
plements an effective system for unexpected creative acts. Indeed, it can
overwhelm a fledgling system at start-up. Several years ago, we acted as
advisers to a large apparel retailer and manufacturer. For the first time
in its more than century-long history, the company decided to put a system in place that would solicit ideas from its employees. Before the system was implemented company-wide, a small pilot test was conducted
at one factory in a department with some thirty employees. The company's CEO and its vice president of manufacturing went to meet with
the employees in the pilot area and told them that the company needed
their ideas, that any submission would be looked at promptly and seriously, and that rewards would be given for accepted ideas. The only
thing the company didn't do, despite being warned, was to prepare for
the usual surge of ideas. Top management simply could not bring itself
to believe that its regular employees, with no track record of proposing
ideas, would suddenly dream up a rash of them. Only one middle manager, part-time and unassisted, was assigned to respond to whatever suggestions came in from the pilot area. Within a few days of opening the
system for business, he was already overwhelmed. Within two weeks,

his caseload had grown to almost 130 ideas. As a quick calculation will show, the poor man never had a chance.

Account managers at IdeAAs in Action, a mature and highly automated system with staff support, estimated that each idea takes roughly four hours of work. For a new system, four hours per idea is optimistic, but taking this as a conservative estimate, this part-time middle manager had received more than *five hundred* hours of work in ten business days. And this for just a small pilot area! The situation degenerated rapidly back to what had existed before. Many employees in the pilot area never received responses to their ideas. Word quickly spread that management had been insincere, and management, realizing that start-up costs for the corporate-wide surge of ideas would tie up significant resources, lost its nerve and quietly shelved the whole project.

We believe that a stable, well-implemented system needs at least one full-time employee per five hundred employees, *if* the system is automated. At start-up, two or three times this number of dedicated staff are needed. The apparel company's senior management was quite correct: large resources are needed to start up a new system. The desire for self-initiated activity runs much deeper than many people think. In our experience, the most difficult aspect of starting up an effective system is persuading the company to dedicate adequate resources to survive the start-up. By comparison, the rest is easy.

The characteristic flood of ideas is easily explained. It consists of all the ideas that have occurred to people over time for which they previously had no practical outlet. A related phenomenon is often observed in the quality field. When an effective quality system is installed at a company for the first time, the number of defects actually goes up. It is not that quality has declined, but rather that the new system is detecting problems and defects that went unnoticed before. In the case of the Eastern Region of the U.S. Forest Service, for example, many of the early ideas had to do with eliminating the counterproductive bureaucracy that had frustrated employees for years. One of the more successful of these ideas had to do with the Forest Service's Kafkaesque purchasing procedures. We talked to Bill Millard, who served as the Project SPIRIT coordinator for the Eastern Region's procurement and property function:

As a coordinator, I went out to our field units and asked them to fire in any ideas they had that might lead to a streamlining of our procurement and property process. Out of that I had about three hundred ideas come in. One of the common ones, which came from twenty or twenty-five different people, was for the Forest Service to develop some kind of a checkwriting system to make it easier to procure over-the-counter or simplified items.[13]

Before, when rangers bought a can of floor wax for their station, the store would have to submit an invoice to the U.S. Forest Service. After the invoice had been processed though several layers of bureaucracy there, it would be forwarded to the National Finance Center and, if approved there, it would be sent on to the Treasury Department for payment. It was common for vendors to wait six months to be paid, a situation that seriously hampered Forest Service operations. Much of the Service's business is done at stores in very small towns, when, for example, the Service has to set up fire camps and buy food and other supplies for firefighters. Naturally, vendors had become reluctant to sell anything to an organization that took so long to pay them; some stores even refused to do any business with the Forest Service.

As the Project SPIRIT coordinator for procurement and property, Bill Millard led a project to improve the situation. Under the new "third-party draft" system, designated employees now have spending authority up to $2,500 and can pay on the spot with a check drawn on the account of a private company, GELCO Payment System, which won the contract for processing and reporting on expenditures. (The Forest Service could not simply use its own checks because of the nature of the spending authority granted to it by Congress.) The new plan also had to be approved by the Treasury Department and the Department of Agriculture, both of which wanted to ensure that appropriate checks and balances were in place. In the end, it is estimated that this idea saved the Forest Service some $500,000 per year. Under the old system, each purchase order had cost $142 to process—whereas each third-party draft costs only $2 or $3. Bill Millard is now on a task force charged with implementing the new system throughout the Forest Service. Other proposals received during Project SPIRIT's surge of ideas included delegating authority for many kinds of permits to the forest ranger level, eliminating duplicate forms for reporting annual leave, and using mountain bikes to patrol recreation areas rather than four-wheel-drive trucks.

Sadly, the Forest Service story did not end on a happy note. The pilot project at the Eastern Region did not last long. Worn down by what Karl Mettke called "benign neglect and passive resistance," the impetus behind the program slowly withered away.[14] By 1992, the "four magic years" (as they were described to us) were over. As the Forest Service learned, unless the system is maintained—like that at American Airlines—the stream of creative ideas will dry up.

The system at the U.S. Forest Service was impressive. So is IdeAAs in Action at American Airlines. Both have resulted in large numbers of useful ideas. However, neither of them has come close to attaining 100 percent participation. The goal of any system for corporate creativity should be to unleash self-initiated activity in *everyone*. We now turn to what we believe is one of the leading *kaizen teian* systems in the world, that of Idemitsu Kosan, the second largest petroleum company in Japan. Interestingly, the participation rate at Idemitsu reached 100 percent only after it eliminated rewards for ideas and focused on intrinsic motivation. The story of Idemitsu's rewardless system provides yet more evidence that intrinsic motivation is the key to corporate creativity. In his book, *Crazy Times Call for Crazy Organizations*, Tom Peters wrote: "The ideal employee (at every level) will execute self-initiated projects."[15] With every single employee at Idemitsu doing just this, has Idemitsu found a magical recruiting tool? Or is something else at work? Although we were impressed with every Idemitsu employee we met, we think that the company's secret lies in that "something else": an excellent system based on intrinsic motivation.

Idemitsu Kosan's Rewardless System

When twenty-six-year-old Sazo Idemitsu started a small Nippon Oil lubricating-oil dealership in 1911, he could hardly have foreseen that it would grow into the second-largest oil company in Japan. Sazo Idemitsu headed the company until 1966, before turning over leadership responsibility to his younger brother. In 1997, despite Idemitsu Kosan's rapid growth and the dramatic changes that have occurred in both Japan and the oil industry, the company has remained true to the founder's unique management principles and philosophy.

Today, with more than nine thousand gas stations throughout Japan, Idemitsu's name is well known to the Japanese. Idemitsu Kosan imports, refines, distributes, and sells petroleum and coal products through its domestic network of service stations and its six thousand liquefied petroleum gas (LPG) outlets. In 1997, Idemitsu was the largest supplier in Japan of lubricating oils, LPG, and jet fuel. In gasoline, Idemitsu's market share of 15 percent was second only to Nippon Oil's 16 percent. In addition to its petroleum operations, Idemitsu owns four coal mines in Australia, a uranium mine in Canada, and a twenty-five-megawatt geothermal energy facility in Japan and has subsidiaries around the world in engineering services, transportation, exploration, refining, stockpiling, and, most recently, marina management.

Before 1985, Idemitsu's Job Improvement Activity system offered a modest scheme of rewards. Employees who submitted ideas received gift certificates worth some $5. In 1985, Youichirou Seki, who managed the Job Improvement Activity system at the Tokuyama refinery, questioned the wisdom of this practice, for not only were rewards in conflict with the Idemitsu philosophy (that a salary is a guarantee of livelihood and not the price of piecemeal labor), but administering them had become a nightmare. Company-wide, *kaizen* proposals were coming in at a rate somewhere between 2,000 and 4,000 per week, and some employees were being awarded certificates on a daily basis. At first, Seki tried to simplify the administrative process by changing the scheme so that rewards no longer went to particular employees, but instead to their sections. Before long, however, it became obvious that the problem had not gone away. More radical surgery was needed. With the support of his boss, Seki decided to try an unusual experiment at the Tokuyama refinery. He wanted to see what would happen if rewards for ideas were eliminated entirely.

When we spoke with Seki, he told us that at the time he, like everyone else, thought that the number of improvement proposals would decline when rewards were eliminated. But he did it anyway, and, much to everyone's surprise, the opposite happened—the number actually *doubled.* In 1988, when Seki moved to the *kaizen* section at Idemitsu headquarters in Tokyo, the rewardless *kaizen* system was implemented throughout the company. Idemitsu's system would go on to become one of the best *kaizen teian* systems in Japan. In 1996, it was ranked among the top five in Japan by the Japan Human Relations Association. Moreover, the rankings were based on the total number of ideas collected at each company, giving a big advantage to companies much larger than Idemitsu. In hindsight, removing money from the creativity equation had forced Idemitsu to concentrate on what was left: intrinsic motivation and the "spiritual" reward a person gets from making an improvement to his or her work. To achieve this, Idemitsu had to ensure that each employee felt he or she was being listened to and taken seriously.

Following are two brief examples of the kinds of ideas Idemitsu receives from its *kaizen teian* system. One, suggested by a secretary at headquarters in Tokyo, was reported in the March 1995 issue of *Kaizen*, the Job Improvement Activity newsletter.

I had been sending monthly Kaizen *reports by fax to about 50 branches. I decided to send them at night when the rates were lower. The costs worked out as follows:*

Before: Regular fax time cost was 8 yen per page

8 yen × 20 pages/fax × 50 sites × 12 issues/year = 96,000 yen.

After: With a 30 percent discount at night fax costs are 5.6 yen per page

5.6 yen × 20 pages/fax × 50 sites × 12 issues/year = 67,200 yen.

The improvement was made effective in February and the total annual savings were 28,800 yen [at 90 yen to the dollar at the time, this was equivalent to $320].

A second idea was submitted in May 1996 by an employee in the public relations section of Idemitsu's headquarters in Tokyo. Idemitsu operates five refineries on the main islands of Japan. Each of Idemitsu's refineries regularly hosts visitors from outside the company, such as journalists and local student and business groups. To help these visitors understand its operations, each refinery was producing an informational brochure containing flowcharts of its processes, aerial photographs of the facility, and various statistics about its equipment and staff. Before

May 1996, each refinery designed and edited its own brochure and printed it locally. Not only did this mean higher printing costs for the company, but it was a real burden to the employees at each refinery. Idemitsu refineries, like those of many other oil and chemical companies, are highly automated and operate with a minimal staff, each of whom does many jobs. Nevertheless, someone at each refinery had to be assigned responsibility for putting out a brochure, and he or she could expect to spend considerable time on it.

The improvement idea was to introduce a common fill-in-the-blanks format for the brochure, so that each site could simply supply the necessary data and leave headquarters to handle the rest. Since all brochures are now sent to the same printing and binding companies, Idemitsu is able to negotiate a much better price. This suggestion also saved a lot of time, because instead of having a total of five employees dealing with the brochures and duplicating much of each other's work, almost everything is handled by just one person. Idemitsu estimates the annual savings from this idea at some five million yen (roughly fifty thousand dollars).

At the bottom of the *kaizen* form for this idea, the employee's supervisor had added the following comment:

> *This idea has resulted in major savings in editing time and printing costs, savings that will be lasting for the company. Well done!*

A planner from the *kaizen* department appended the following:

> *As we are very concerned to cut costs right now, this idea has great potential. It is based on a good system-wide understanding of how brochures are made in the Idemitsu Group as a whole. If it can be applied to other areas where we make brochures, it might mean big cost savings for the company.*

Idemitsu's system has broader scope than a system like IdeAAs in Action, because it seeks improvement in all aspects of the company's operations, including those that are less tangible, such as the work environment. However, the system still tends to focus on creativity through the rearview mirror. Improvements are made to what a company already does. It is also true that most of the creative acts at Idemitsu are relatively small, like that of the secretary who reduced the fax bill by $320 per year. In fact, each idea is expected to fit on a single line of a form designed for twelve proposals. But by ensuring that everyone has some experience with self-initiated activity, however small, Idemitsu has increased the probability of creative acts with large impact, because it can also expect employees to initiate activity if they should ever find themselves presented with an extraordinary opportunity.

How to Promote Self-Initiated Activity

It is surprisingly straightforward to promote the kind of self-initiated activity that leads to creative acts. The desire to be creative is already present in most people, and companies only have to unleash it. All that is needed is an effective system for responding to employee ideas. No matter what type of system it is, it must have five important characteristics:

1. *The system must reach everyone.* Since there is no way to predict who will be involved in a creative act, everyone in your organization must know about the system and have ready access to it. All the high-performing systems we are familiar with aim for full participation. Everyone at American Airlines, Idemitsu, or the Johnson Controls' FoaMech plant knows about his or her company's system and how it works.

2. *The system must be easy to use.* Few employees will participate in a system that is difficult to use. Most employees in the former Soviet Union and in the pre-1985 U.S. Forest Service were aware of their organization's systems. However, the four-page submission forms that both systems used made the process such an ordeal that it is a wonder they received any ideas at all. When the Forest Service revamped its system, it greatly simplified the submission form and made it possible to complete it on a computer or even send it in by E-mail. Idemitsu's form is so stripped down that twelve ideas fit on a single page.

3. *The system must have strong follow-through.* In the former Soviet Union, the government felt it necessary to pass a law mandating

that all ideas should receive a response within two years of submission. Clearly, Soviet enterprises were in no hurry to act on
their employees' ideas. It is hard to imagine anything more dam-
aging to creativity. Few people will send in ideas to a system that
does not give them serious attention. Effective systems have a
bias toward action. If the revamped system at the U.S. Forest
Service did not respond to an idea within thirty days, the idea
was automatically approved as long as it did not break any laws.
At American Airlines, any idea that has not been fully processed
within 150 days heads for the CEO's desk. At Idemitsu, employees are expected to initiate and implement their ideas and
only then write them up. For a system to work, employees have to
know that their ideas will receive fair and timely consideration.

4. *The system must document ideas.* High-performing systems all
require that employees write up their ideas and that records be
kept of what happens to them. The most important reason for
this documentation is *accountability.* This is what allows American Airlines to audit IdeAAs in Action just like any other budget
account. Documentation can also help others to find out about
ideas, which may lead to replication or elaboration of them elsewhere in the organization. Finally, the act of putting ideas down
on paper forces people to clarify their thinking and the presentation of their proposals. Unfortunately, too many companies
make the mistake of failing to require adequate documentation
in their systems.

5. *The system must be based on intrinsic motivation.* Each of the
systems we have described in this book has its own scheme of
rewards and recognition. In general, the less a company uses
rewards for ideas, the greater its creativity will be. Rewards
are an important feature of the IdeAAs in Action system at
American Airlines, in some cases even exceeding a person's
salary. Although employees submitted 17,000 cost-saving ideas
that saved $43 million in 1996, 91 percent of employees did not
participate in the system, and it averaged less than one idea
from every five employees. At Johnson Controls' FoaMech plant,
on the other hand, where the rewards are much more modest,

the average was three suggestions per employee in 1995, and 100 percent of the employees participated. In the same year, at Idemitsu, whose system is rewardless, employees averaged 118 ideas each, and every one of them participated too. For the best results, systems should reinforce intrinsic motivation and minimize rewards.

MAIN POINTS

Humans have a natural drive to explore and create, a drive that derives from an urge as basic as hunger or sex. It is this that leads them to want to initiate creative activity on their own.

In the first year after the U.S. Forest Service revamped its suggestion system, the rate of suggestions jumped from about sixty per year to six thousand!

Idemitsu Kosan in Japan and Johnson Controls in the United States are two companies that have 100 percent participation in their systems for ideas. Both rely on intrinsic rather than extrinsic motivation.

The majority of creative acts in companies are self-initiated, which explains why they are unanticipated by management.

When a project is self-initiated, the individual involved self-selects for the job. Frequently his or her point of entry into the activity is only a minor facet of its full potential, so minor, perhaps, as to seem insignificant to all but the initiator.

Yasanori Kanda at Fujitsu invented the first practical keyboard for Japanese characters because he wanted Japanese programmers to use more remark statements in their programs.

To promote self-initiated activity, companies only have to unleash what is already present. The key is an effective system for responding to employee ideas, which must have five characteristics. The system must:

1. *Reach everyone.*
2. *Be easy to use.*
3. *Have strong follow-through.*
4. *Document ideas.*
5. *Be based on intrinsic motivation.*

Chapter Eight

UNOFFICIAL ACTIVITY

We want what is new and wonderful, not the strange and repellent thing that you offer.

JACQUES BARZUN[1]

By definition, every unanticipated creative act begins with a period of unofficial activity, when it is worked on without direct official support. Sometimes the unofficial activity associated with a creative act lasts for minutes and sometimes, when the idea is particularly strange and re-pellent to the organization, it may last for years. Almost every creative act we examined that had significant impact on a company was associ-ated with an appreciable period of unofficial activity. Unless an organi-zation makes the space for such activity, it leaves itself little room to be consistently creative—to bring along a stream of new and useful things without being shown or taught. As the examples in this chapter will show, *unofficial activity,* the third element of corporate creativity, has benefits that are absent with official status and makes it possible for a company to go where it never expected to.

Six Hundred Fifty Dollars for a Drawer?

In 1987, American Airlines opened a new hub in Nashville, Tennessee, and set up a subsidiary airline, Nashville Eagle (now part of American Eagle), to handle all commuter flights from Nashville. Bette Swatzell was the secretary to the president of the new airline, a position which meant that she was well informed about the new company's operations and plans. In the early years, when the company was in start-up mode, everyone pitched in where they were needed to get the work done. At one point in October 1989, Swatzell was helping out in the accounts payable department. While she was there, she happened to notice some invoices for the pull-out drawers of the galley carts used to serve food and drinks on the airplanes—the so-called drawer liners. At the time when she discovered these invoices, Nashville Eagle had already bought ten brand-new Saab 340 turboprop aircraft and was planning to buy forty more. Each new aircraft came equipped with a galley cart, and Nashville Eagle bought one more as a spare. Each of the galley carts had six drawer liners. Drawer liners were hardly complicated items, Swatzell knew, but she was surprised to find that the Swiss manufacturer charged $650 for each one in the spare galley carts. Swatzell saw an opportunity to save her company some money.

Working unofficially over the next eight months, she did considerable research on her own to find a local vendor who could make the drawer liners at a more reasonable price. Her background was perfect for the job. She had lived in Nashville all her life and had many friends she could turn to for advice. Moreover, before joining Nashville Eagle, she had worked in the purchasing department at Du Pont for more than nineteen years. Swatzell asked the engineering department to contact the Swiss cart manufacturer and obtain the drawings for the drawer liners. Armed with these specifications, she contacted fifteen potential suppliers, nine of whom responded that they didn't have the equipment to do some of the fabrication steps. In the end, she obtained estimates from six different local vendors, and Nashville Eagle awarded the contract for the drawer liners to the lowest bidder, at a price of only $27.30 per drawer.

Swatzell told us that when she started working on her idea, she had been only vaguely aware of the IdeAAs in Action system, which was not yet fully in place at Nashville Eagle. It was only in early 1990, three months after she had started working on her idea and when she had already obtained two or three quotes from vendors, that a coworker alerted her to IdeAAs in Action and suggested that she should submit her idea to it. She did, and she was no doubt delighted to learn that she would be getting a reward of $28,500 for her idea, which had saved Nashville Eagle $188,000.

In Swatzell's case, Nashville Eagle was very happy with what she did. In fact, her company was so well aligned for cost savings that she never had any doubt that her idea would be welcomed. If management had become aware of her unofficial activity, they would certainly have encouraged her to continue it. In short, she had the whole organization behind her, and her idea never needed any protection. But many unexpected creative acts encounter resistance or even outright opposition at first, and for these ideas, unofficial activity often provides the protection they need.

It is hard to imagine an idea that was initially viewed as more strange and repellent than the one whose story we are about to tell. Russell Marker's unofficial activity was key to allowing him to realize his vision of finding a way to synthesize hormones such as progesterone, estrogen, and testosterone. His work had an immense impact on our world, particularly on the lives of women. By discovering a way to mass-produce these key sex hormones cheaply, Marker reduced the frequency of miscarriages, made births much safer, helped women after menopause, and paved the way for the oral contraceptive commonly known as "the pill."[2] When Marker died in 1995, one obituary pointed out (with some understatement of the figures involved) that :

> *Dr. Marker arguably has had as profound an impact on the course of human events as anyone now alive. The world's population would now be larger by literally tens of millions, especially in the poorer countries such as India, were it not for the contraceptive pill that is to this day being produced by the steroidal chemistry he developed.*[3]

The story of Russell Marker's creative act illustrates many of the benefits of unofficial activity, and why it so often gives an organization the opportunity to go where it least expects to.

Creativity Behind Enemy Lines

Russell Marker was born the son of a sharecropper in a one-room log cabin near Hagerstown, Maryland, in 1902. Surprisingly, for a person whose scientific work would change the course of history, he took no science classes in high school. Against the wishes of his father, who wanted him to become a farmer, but with his mother's support, he decided to enroll in the School of Chemistry at the University of Maryland. At the end of his sophomore year, a friend warned him that the toughest course in his junior year would be organic chemistry. Marker bought a copy of the textbook for the course and worked through it that summer. He was fascinated by the subject and did well in the course, particularly in its laboratory work. From that point on, his main interest would be in experimental organic chemistry. He would go on to earn his bachelor's and master's degrees in chemistry at Maryland, but he would astound the school by not completing his doctorate after successfully finishing his research, which was later published. The difficulty arose when his thesis adviser insisted that Marker take a basic course in physical chemistry in order to satisfy university requirements for the doctorate. Marker thought that this was ridiculous, since he had already mastered the course content on his own. Going over it again in a formal course, he argued, was a waste of his time, and he refused to do it. His adviser told him that without his doctorate, the best Marker could hope for was a career in urine analysis.

In June 1925, a doctorate-less Marker parted ways with the University of Maryland. He soon ended up at the Ethyl Gasoline Corporation.[4] His first assignment was to improve the young company's "no-knock" gasoline additive. Eventually he gained an understanding of the underlying phenomenon and was able to produce an additive that eliminated engine knock completely. Also, it was while exploring the various mixtures of compounds that prevented or aggravated knocking that he invented the now widely used octane-rating system for gasoline. Word of his unusual talent for synthesizing organic compounds spread through the chemistry community and led to many job offers. One of the visitors to his lab was Dr. Frank Whitmore, dean of physics and chemistry at Pennsylvania State College. Whitmore was so impressed with Marker that he asked him to come to Penn State, an offer that Marker would one day take up. In the meantime, Marker was contacted by Dr. Phoebus Levene, head of the chemistry department at the Rockefeller Institute, one of the most prestigious research organizations in the world. Levene told Marker that his chemists were having difficulty synthesizing certain complicated compounds he needed for his research. Would Marker be interested in joining his lab to do this work? He was, and in June 1928, he reported for work in New York.

Marker thrived at Rockefeller, enhancing his laboratory skills and his already considerable reputation for hard work (he sometimes stayed in the lab for three days straight). Over the next six years, he and Levene would publish thirty-two papers together. In 1935, he became intrigued by some articles on steroids, the solid alcohols common in both animals and plants. He found himself wanting to work on a particular subgroup of these steroids—hormones—but knew it would be difficult to get samples to experiment with, because they were scarce and prohibitively expensive. The one that most interested Marker was progesterone. When it was available at all, it cost more than one thousand dollars per gram and was necessarily used only in small dosages of one to three milligrams. Other than for research, progesterone was used primarily to increase the fertility of top racehorses. The handful of pharmaceutical companies that supplied it were based in Europe, and they obtained their progesterone by extracting it from bulls' urine in minute amounts. One thing was for certain with this process—it would never deliver enough to satisfy world demand.

Marker began to think about how the hormone might instead be synthesized, which could make it available in large quantities. He asked Dr. Levene for permission to work in this area. Levene told him that he would not allow it, for two reasons. First, he needed Marker for the other synthesis work. Second, in the adjacent laboratory at Rockefeller, a world-famous researcher, W. A. Jacobs, was already actively engaged in steroid research.

When Marker threatened to leave if he was not allowed to work on his problem, both men took their case to the president of the Institute, Dr. Simon Flexner. The meeting went badly, principally because Flexner took exception to what he considered Marker's impertinence at threatening to leave. He pounded his desk. It was an honor to work at Rockefeller, *the* place to do research. No one left unless his contract ran out or he was fired, the angry president told Marker.

Except for Marker, of course. If he couldn't work on developing synthetic hormones at Rockefeller, he would move to a place where he could. Remembering the offer from Dean Whitmore at Penn State, Marker contacted him and, much to the consternation of his wife, resigned his $4,400-a-year position at Rockefeller for a $1,800 fellowship at Penn State, funded by Parke-Davis, a pharmaceutical company. His move came right in the middle of the Depression.

Although he started off $2,600 a year poorer and without assistants or funds for equipment, Marker was free at last to search for new methods of synthesizing hormones. In his first year at Penn State, his efforts seemed to vindicate his doctoral adviser's prediction of a career in urine analysis, since he spent most of his time extracting trace amounts of hormones from animal urine. His son, Russell C. Marker, reminisced to us about that year at Penn State:

> *I can remember they would chase a little dog around the laboratory and collect his urine. They got urine from sheep and all different kinds of animals. He would come home reeking of urine and my mother would be upset because she wanted to go to the movies and here he was with all of his clothes reeking of urine.*[5]

As he came to recognize that animal urine would never yield adequate amounts of hormones, Marker began to turn his attention to plants. He knew that W. A. Jacobs at the Rockefeller Institute and others had found sapogenins (a variety of cholesterol chemically similar to steroids) in the roots of wild plants. So many people had tried and failed to find a way to alter the chemical structure of sapogenins to produce synthetic hormones that prevailing scientific opinion held that it could not be done. But Marker thought he could do it. For the next four years, he worked intensively in the laboratory, often through the night. (His son remembers this period well because of the number of times he brought his father breakfast in the laboratory.) In the end, Marker found a process, now known as "Marker degradation," to convert sarsasapogenin (a type of sapogenin) into progesterone. A variation of this process produced testosterone, which could easily be converted to estrogen. All he needed now was a plentiful source of sarsasapogenin.

Marker brought the same enthusiasm and persistence to his search for sapogenin-rich plants that he did to all of his work. At first he looked in the countryside around Penn State. Having no luck, he widened his search, mounting expeditions all over the United States with botanists he hired and retired botanists who volunteered their help. He even went north into the Canadian forests. (He funded this activity by selling

Parke-Davis the progesterone he extracted from bulls' urine.) Marker corresponded with botanists around the world, asking them to send him any plants that might contain sapogenins. Some Japanese researchers sent him a one-ounce sample of a sapogenin they had extracted, named "diosgenin." When Marker worked with this sample, he was struck by how easy it was to produce progesterone from it and he decided to narrow his search to plants that contained diosgenin. Soon his laboratory was overflowing with plants from around the world. Marker later estimated that during this time he examined more than forty thousand kilograms of plants representing more than four hundred species. He found a species of yucca called "Beth root" in North Carolina. Beth root, which contained a natural compound very close to estrogen, was the secret ingredient of Lydia Pinkham's Compound, a patent medicine widely used in the early 1900s and still in use today for menstrual pain.[6] Beth root also contained diosgenin, but only in tiny amounts.

From 1938 to 1942, the search continued for a source of raw material that would make synthetic hormones available in quantity and at a low price. If they did nothing else, Marker and his team of graduate students and botanists compiled a comprehensive list of plants containing sapogenins throughout the United States.[7] Finally, the break came. On one of his foraging trips, while spending a night at the home of a retired botanist in Texas, Marker picked up an old botany book and began thumbing through it. His eye was caught by a photograph of a strange-looking wild yam, the *cabeza de negro*. It had an enormous root, over 110 kilograms when full-grown, and it contained diosgenin. There was just one problem. It grew only deep in the jungle in the Veracruz province of Mexico.

In November 1941, Marker went to see Dean Whitmore and told him that he had to go to Mexico to find the *cabeza de negro*. At first, Whitmore did his best to discourage him. Europe was already at war (it was just weeks before Pearl Harbor) and the U.S. Embassy in Mexico City was advising all Americans to stay out of the country because of the growing pro-German sentiment there. Perhaps because he saw what the president of Rockefeller had not—that Marker would go anyway, with or without his permission—Whitmore relented and reluctantly gave his blessing (and modest financial support) to the trip. Marker departed immediately but soon returned empty-handed. He had been unable to get the necessary plant-collecting permit from the Mexican Department of Agriculture.

After waiting two months for the paperwork to go through, Marker returned to Mexico in January 1942, only to have further mishaps. The Mexican botanist hired by Marker had backed out because he was intimidated by the anti-American feelings people were showing when they realized that Marker was from the United States. A U.S. Embassy official once again urged Marker to go home. But he was not to be put off so easily. Despite speaking no Spanish, over several days he made his way across the hostile country on local buses to get to the area that the old botany book had described as the home of the *cabeza de negro*. As soon as he arrived, he went into a nearby village store and spoke with its owner. Not only did the man know of the plant, but he said that if Marker would come back in the morning, he would have two ready for him. Although both were stolen on the journey back, Marker recovered one (after bribing a policeman) and managed to get it safely back to Penn State. There he chopped a piece off the root, isolated the diosgenin in it, and converted it to progesterone.

His next step was to take the rest of the root to Detroit, where he demonstrated his new process at Parke-Davis to both its director of research and its president, Alexander Lescohier. He told the two men that with his process they could produce almost unlimited amounts of progesterone. But when he suggested that the production laboratories would be best situated close to where the *cabeza de negro* grew—in Mexico— he unwittingly struck a nerve. President Lescohier had recently been in Mexico, where he had fallen sick and had had a bad experience in a medical clinic. To say the least, he had not carried away a positive impression of Mexico. Lescohier could not bring himself to believe that a modern pharmaceutical facility could be run in such a backward country. Not only did he decline even to patent the process there, but he also refused Marker's next request: the use of a small area in a packaging plant that Parke-Davis had recently opened near Mexico City, where Marker proposed to set up the process himself. Parke-Davis was simply not interested, the president told Marker. It is rumored that his passing up the tremendous opportunity Marker had presented to him was not unrelated to his departure from the company soon afterward. Marker spent the rest of 1942 and 1943 trying to interest other major pharmaceutical companies in the commercial potential of his process but, unbelievably, he could not. If progesterone were to become widely available, he came to realize, he would probably have to bring this about himself.

In September 1943, Marker resigned his position at Penn State, withdrew half his life savings from the bank, and left for Mexico City. After trying and failing to interest several Mexican drug companies, in a moment of desperation he picked up the phone book and began thumbing through it. He noticed a company with a promising name, Laboratorios Hormona, S.A. He called and was invited to visit. There he met with the production manager, Federico Lehmann, who was astonished that, in just the time Marker had spent in Mexico that year, with no money and extremely poor equipment, he had been able to produce *three kilograms* of progesterone, worth $150,000 at the prevailing price of $50 per gram. Lehmann quickly recognized the commercial value of Marker's process and contacted the company's owner, Emerik Somlo, a Hungarian who had emigrated to Mexico in 1928. Somlo, too, immediately appreciated the importance of what Marker had brought him. Laboratorios Hormona had the laboratory capability to produce large quantities of progesterone, and before long the three men (Marker, Somlo, and Lehmann) had agreed to form a new company named Syntex, a combination of the words *synthesis* and *Mexico*. Syntex was incorporated in March 1944 and shortly thereafter it entered into large-scale commercial production of progesterone. But Marker's adventures were not over.

After one year of operations, Marker and his partners had a falling-out over the distribution of profits and the future of the company. Unable to resolve these differences, Marker left Syntex in May 1945, turning his 40 percent of the stock back to Somlo, and within two months he had started up a competitor, Botanica-Mex, which dropped the price of progesterone, first to ten dollars per gram and then to five dollars per gram. But clearly someone didn't want the new company to succeed. Many of the roots it collected were stolen, one of the Mexican women who worked for Marker was strangled and beaten, one of his night watchmen was shot, and one man who collected roots for him was killed. Because of this campaign of intimidation, Botanica-Mex stopped production in March 1946 and sold its equipment and inventory of *cabeza de negro* roots to a European drug company. In its short eight-month life, Botanica-Mex had produced more than thirty kilograms of progesterone. Syntex would go on to invent the birth-control pill and to become one of the largest pharmaceutical companies in the world. Several other major drug companies would be spun off from it, including G. D. Searle, where in 1965 Jim Schlatter would lick his finger and discover NutraSweet.[8]

Not long after the publication of his 213th and last article, in which he described a way to synthesize cortisone from certain plants, Marker withdrew from the world of chemistry completely, severing all his professional ties and even destroying his lab notes. For twenty years he seemed to have disappeared. Some thought he had been killed by Mexican natives or perhaps had gone mad. Actually, he had started a new life in Mexico, collaborating with a Mexican silversmith to reproduce eighteenth-century French and English silver artifacts. Finally, in 1969, Pedro Lehmann, Federico Lehmann's son and also a chemist, tracked Marker down and persuaded him to attend a Mexican Chemical Society banquet in his honor. In a letter to Lehmann at that time, Marker wrote the following:

> When I retired from chemistry in 1949, after 5 years of production and research in Mexico, I felt I had accomplished what I had set out to do. I had found sources for the production of steroidal hormones in quantity at low prices, developed the process for manufacture, and put them into production. I assisted in establishing many competitive companies in order to insure a fair price to the public and without patent protection from the producers.
>
> I have never returned to chemistry or consulting, and have no shares of stock in any hormone or related companies.[9]

Russell Marker's discovery was made almost entirely without official support. He gave many organizations the opportunity to make his idea official and benefit from it: the Rockefeller Institute, Parke-Davis, the major American and Mexican drug companies of the time, and even Penn State. They all chose not to take him up on the offer, and it is fortunate that their lack of support did not stop him. A company should always encourage more unofficial activity than it can possibly make official. By making room for the unofficial, an organization greatly

increases the probability of unanticipated creativity. But merely legit-
imizing unofficial activity is not enough. We have examined many unanticipated creative acts that required substantial resources or risk to
implement, and almost every one had a difficult transition from unofficial to official status, although few were as traumatic as Marker's. In
the majority of cases, in fact, the forces marshaled against the ideas
during the transition phase were so strong that they nearly didn't make
it. And while it can be difficult to decide which ideas should be made
official and when, companies can take specific action to ensure that
better decisions are made during the transition process.

In order to illustrate how this transition process occurs in companies, we now turn to an idea that, despite considerable resistance, successfully made the transition from unofficial to official status, and at
the perfect time. It resulted in one of the most successful products in
the history of Hewlett-Packard (HP): the inkjet printer. When it was
introduced in 1984, low-cost printers used dot-matrix technology, and
Japanese companies dominated this segment of the market. HP, which
was not then known for making anything low-cost (the joke was that
the initials HP stood for "high-priced"), was not even in this end of the
business. Thirteen years later, in 1997, HP dominated the low-cost
printer industry, now based on inkjet technology, with some 50 percent
of the market. In fact, with five billion dollars in sales, HP's inkjet-re-
lated business had become so large that if it were a separate company,
it would be in the Fortune 500. As successful as the inkjet printer has
been, few (even at HP) know of its modest beginnings, or that, as the
mere germ of an idea, it almost didn't survive.

When Ink Explodes

On the day before Christmas in 1978, a casual conversation over coffee occurred at HP's Palo Alto (California) research laboratory, one that
would unwittingly start the company off on a new and highly profitable
path. Two lab engineers, John Vaught and Dave Donald, and a handful
of engineers from HP's facility in Boise, Idaho, had just finished the design of the engine for HP's new laser printer, the first that would be capable of the then high resolution of 180 dots per inch. As they stood in

the hallway having a cup of coffee, the members of the group began to talk about what kind of printer they would like to have if they could have anything they wanted. The consensus was a color inkjet printer capable of high resolution, at least two hundred drops per inch. At the time of this conversation, such a printer could only be dreamed about. It was true that devices already existed that could squirt fine jets of ink droplets at paper. However, they were notoriously messy, unreliable, and expensive.

The concept of a printer that controls the flow of ink through tiny tubes is actually more than a century old. In 1867, Lord Kelvin had developed a method for electrostatically controlling the release of ink drops in one of his recording instruments.[10] In the mid-1960s, a hundred years later, interest in the inkjet idea would be rekindled when Richard Sweet of Stanford University developed an instrument for high-frequency recording that worked by rapidly turning on or off a high-speed stream of ink droplets (more than 100,000 per second) and deflecting each droplet onto its desired trajectory electrostatically, as Lord Kelvin had.[11] Although IBM did introduce a commercial printer based on Sweet's method, it was so difficult to operate and maintain that it never really caught on, except in research laboratories.

Over the 1978 Christmas vacation, John Vaught began to think about how to realize the coffee meeting's vision of a workable inkjet printer. Since he and Donald had been assigned to a project that didn't seem to be going anywhere, they began the new year experimenting on their own with inkjet printing. As their enthusiasm mounted, they found themselves spending all of their time on their new project. Their early efforts followed the same lines as everyone else's: they tried using tiny piezoelectrically activated material to squeeze a thin capillary tube containing ink and squirt it onto the paper.

Within a few weeks, the limitations of the piezoelectric approach had become apparent, and the two men knew they would have to try something different. Thinking about the way early coffee percolators worked, Vaught proposed what would prove to be the first breakthrough in the new inkjet printing technology—why not try heating the ink? Their first approach was to pass electricity through it, using the ink's electrical resistance to produce heat. They made a simple device with two electrodes. When these were energized, the ink did heat up, but no droplets came out of the end of the tube. As it turned out, ink does not have low enough resistivity to produce the necessary heat for rapid drop formation. Also, bubbles of hydrogen and oxygen were produced at the electrodes, causing them to erode quickly. Vaught and Donald tried to turn these bubbles to their advantage, igniting the explosive mixture of gases inside them by producing a small spark between the electrodes. Although this was successful, they could not see a way to generate the explosive mixture of gases rapidly enough to attain the necessary nozzle drop rate of two thousand drops per second.[12]

Both Vaught and Donald spoke to us of their fond memories of those early months in 1979. They had tremendous fun; like children at play, they were full of enthusiasm, trying first one thing and then another. They continued to search for a way to increase the drop rate and reduce electrode erosion, but with no luck. Eventually Vaught, remembering his coffee percolator, suggested eliminating the electrodes and trying to heat the ink with a resistor. This proved to be their second breakthrough. When they mounted a tiny resistor just inside the end of the tube and rapidly switched the electricity on and off, they succeeded in producing what appeared to be small explosions of ink.

Vaught and Donald had discovered an entirely new way of putting ink on paper. Rather than squeezing it out of a tube, they were shooting it out in controlled bursts. It was fast, and it wasn't messy. However, although the method worked, it would be some time before they, or anyone else at HP, really understood why. Partly because of this, the inkjet printer idea would now start to encounter resistance. Neither Vaught nor Donald would find working on the inkjet project much fun after this point; in fact, things would become miserable before they got any better.

The problem was that Vaught and Donald's experiments had put them out in front of their ability, or that of anyone around them, to explain the underlying phenomenon. Moreover, one of the reasons they were out in front was Vaught's unorthodox background for the environment he worked in. He was a self-taught engineer without a college degree, working in a culture in which academic credentials were considered very important. He was accustomed to working quite differently from those with academic training: he was an experimentalist who often began work in a new area without reading the patents or papers that would ground him in the relevant theory or practice. This being the case, Vaught was quite used to hearing from other lab researchers that his devices would not work, and this was the initial reaction to the inkjet idea. Excited by its obvious commercial potential, Vaught showed the device to anyone who would take the time to look at it. Unfortunately, neither his manager nor any of the other people who saw it shared his enthusiasm. Because its inner workings were not understood, even a number of the people who actually saw the device operating told him that his approach could not work. Vaught's reply was, "But it *is* working." The resolution to this curious impasse would have to wait until the underlying phenomenon had been explained.

This was not the only instance we came across where an experimental approach led the people involved to something that no one around them could explain. Remember Tomoshige Hori, whose experiments at Snow Brand on the thermal conductivity of milk led him to discover its previously unknown relationship to curdling. In one of our interviews with him, Hori remarked,

> It is especially important to process data first and develop the explanation or theory later.

It is inevitable that such an experimental approach sometimes leads to differences of opinion with those who use more of a "theory-first" approach. According to Thomas Hughes, in his study of the great inventors of America's Golden Age:

> Scientists unfamiliar with invention and development often denigrated this empirical approach, not realizing that to hunt-and-try was to hypothesize and experiment in the absence of theory.[13]

It would be some time before researchers at HP would learn that what was really going on inside the inkjet capillary tubes was a phenomenon known as vapor explosion. Liquid does not necessarily boil and turn into gas at its boiling point. If it is heated swiftly enough (modern inkjet printers heat each ink droplet in *two-millionths* of a second), it will remain liquid for a brief instant at temperatures higher than its boiling point, before exploding into vapor. Vapor explosion is different from boiling. It happens, for example, when water is poured into a hot frying pan full of grease, and the pan sizzles angrily and spatters little droplets of grease (not water) on whoever is holding it. As the water droplets plunge under the surface of the grease toward the bottom of the pan, they are instantaneously heated well beyond the boiling point. For a split second they remain liquid, but then they explode into vapor so violently that they send grease droplets flying out of the pan. Without Vaught and Donald's knowing it, their device was firing tiny dots of ink at the paper using vapor explosions in a similar, but controllable, way.

But back in 1979 no one had yet figured this out, and no one seemed interested in the new technology. Worse, in May of that year, just at the point when Vaught and Donald had built a working device, Vaught's manager ordered him to stop working on his inkjet idea and assigned him, against his wishes, to assist a Dr. Kanti Jain with the mechanical design of his metal vapor laser. Donald had already moved on to another project by this time, discouraged by the lack of official interest in the inkjet idea. When we spoke with Vaught, he described the several months that followed his reassignment as the worst period of his life. (His wife remembered it well, too.) The problem was not Jain, but rather that Vaught could not work on what he wanted to. He could see the tremendous potential of the new inkjet technology and wanted to make sure the idea was transferred out of the research labs to an HP division that would make use of it. But suddenly his fortunes changed. In late July, Jain announced that he was leaving for IBM, and with the champion of metal vapor lasers now working for another company, the project came to a screeching halt. As Vaught told us, if they had gotten much further with it, he might have been condemned to work on metal vapor lasers for a very long time. He was now able to return to his unofficial work on the inkjet idea, where he was soon joined by John Meyer, another researcher who was excited by the potential of the new technology, and whose assigned project also happened to have arrived at a dead end.

Little did they know that, despite the continuing resistance to the inkjet idea, events would shortly propel it to center stage. For several months Larry LaBarre, a respected old-timer at HP, had been working behind the scenes to enlist support for Vaught's idea. HP labs held regular reviews, in which some ten to fifteen projects were discussed. At one of these, the inkjet picked up a valuable supporter. Barney Oliver had been a close friend of David Packard and Bill Hewlett since their undergraduate days together at Stanford University and had almost joined HP at the very beginning. Years afterward, Hewlett and Packard were able to lure Oliver away from Bell Labs to head up HP's research and development. At the review, Vaught and Meyer made yet another pitch for resources to continue their inkjet work. Oliver, with whom LaBarre had talked earlier about the idea, listened intently, stood up at the end of the presentations, and said, "This inkjet concept is a significant piece of intellectual property, and we should treat it very carefully." Now, at last, about a year after the casual conversation over coffee, the inkjet project made the transition to official status. The two researchers obtained about $250,000, some five times more than they had asked for.[14] They got something else as well. After the review, Barney Oliver suggested to John Meyer that he get in touch with some high-temperature physicists at the California Institute of Technology. This is how HP learned for the first time that it was dealing with vapor explosion. With the additional resources and several new people assigned to the project, the group was now able to make rapid progress.

Like Russell Marker, whose vision went no further than making synthetic hormones widely available, John Vaught had always intended to hand off the inkjet technology to an HP division that could bring it to market. He knew very well that the purpose of corporate research was profit, and that no money was made by keeping an idea in the lab. Money comes only when an idea is successfully transferred to an operating division. But even so, Vaught had a personal reason for getting his ideas out of the lab:

> *Because once you transfer it, you don't have to work on it anymore. You can go and do something else. When you work in the labs, that's the idea. Either it fails and you get out of it and do something else, or you transfer it to a division that is willing to accept it, and then you can work on something else.*[15]

Although the new technology was picked up by a division, for the rest of his time at HP, John Vaught would find it difficult to get away from the inkjet printer. A few months before the Barney Oliver review,

Frank Cloutier, a section manager from the HP facility in Corvallis, Oregon, visited Palo Alto to look over the inkjet idea.[16] The project that Cloutier's group had been working on had just been abruptly terminated. Casting around for a new project, he became very excited when he saw the simple inkjet device at Palo Alto. He realized that the very people who had been freed up when his project was terminated were especially well equipped to take on the challenge of bringing an inkjet printer to market. When he returned to Corvallis and set things into motion, the inkjet was still a laboratory curiosity.

Over the next four years, the extraordinary efforts of hundreds of people in different divisions were involved in solving the problems that had to be overcome to make a commercially viable printer. A particularly momentous decision had to be made early in the project when the Corvallis team came up with the radical idea of making the entire printhead unit self-contained and disposable, eliminating at one stroke the issues of messy ink refills and printhead longevity. This idea was at first scoffed at but was eventually adopted as a central design feature. In 1996, worldwide sales of these disposable inkjet cartridges alone exceeded five billion dollars.

During the period from 1980 to 1984, John Vaught reluctantly remained on the HP laboratory team assigned to support the development of the inkjet printer. He and Dave Donald (who had returned to the project for a year) were given the job of designing and life-testing printheads. After a while, Vaught realized that as the inventor of inkjet technology, it was unlikely that he would ever again be permitted to work on another project of his own choosing at HP. As a result, just one month before the commercial introduction of HP's first inkjet printer in March 1984, Vaught resigned.

Years afterward, when inkjet technology had come to dominate the market for low-cost printers, Vaught received a number of awards for his role in its development. Each of them (the 1991 Kosar Memorial Award, the 1991 Johann Gutenberg Prize, and the 1995 Edwin H. Land Medal) was shared with Ichiro Endo, a researcher at Canon who had independently developed the same approach to inkjet printing some eighteen months earlier than Vaught. Without anyone at HP realizing it, a team of Canon researchers had been working on thermal inkjet technology (known as "Bubble Jet" at Canon) since the summer of 1977. Canon's story was somewhat different from HP's. Almost two years before Vaught began working on the inkjet at HP, Canon had assigned some forty researchers to look for ways that the company might break away from conventional xerographic approaches to printing. Endo was in a group looking into inkjet printing, and this group had started by experimenting with all the traditional inkjet technologies.

One day, a fortunate accident occurred. Someone who was refilling a bladder of ink on one of the older generation of inkjet printers left the ink syringe on a workbench, right next to a hot soldering iron. Somehow, the soldering iron fell over, and its hot tip briefly touched the neck of the ink syringe. Endo happened to see this and noticed that a small amount of ink splashed out. He was intrigued and set out to re-create the phenomenon, using a special high-speed camera to record what happened. From that point on things moved very quickly. Within three days, Endo's group had built a simple working device. Four years later, in September 1981, HP was shocked to learn that Canon was actually ahead of it in the very technology that HP thought it was pioneering. However, after a series of meetings, the two companies decided to cooperate in developing the new technology. In 1997, they share most of the $11 billion market for inkjet printers—a new technology that neither company directly planned for.

Reaping the Benefits of Unofficial Activity

The importance of unofficial activity for unanticipated creative acts also showed up in the Japan Management Association (JMA) study described in the Introduction. Recall that part of this study compared projects that had won national awards for creativity with others that had been commercially successful but not particularly creative. We have already discussed how the award-winning projects were more likely to have been self-initiated, while the not particularly creative ones were far more likely to have been initiated by management. But the two kinds of projects also differed markedly in another way: the lengths of their unofficial periods. The award-winning projects averaged thirteen months, some 60 percent longer than their not so creative counterparts.

Clearly, unofficial activity plays an important role in corporate creativity. Following are some of its more important benefits.

A Safe Haven for the Strange and Repellent

Any organization should aim for an appropriate balance between *exploiting* what it currently does and *exploring* new opportunities. Unfortunately, this balance is most often tipped against exploration, because of the opposition that new ideas tend to encounter. When an idea comes under consideration for official status, resistance to it can sharply increase. Before this point, even if it strongly challenges established thought or practice, unofficial activity is much less threatening, and so it is often much freer from resistance. While it is in the safe haven of unofficial status, an idea has the opportunity to develop from a mere embryo into something whose potential is clear.

Consider the new cheese-making process developed by Tomoshige Hori that differed so dramatically from well-established practice. When Hori first approached his manager with his yet-to-be-developed idea, the manager gave him little encouragement, pointing out that the world had been making cheese the same way for centuries. If, instead, Snow Brand had declared that it would pursue Hori's idea officially at that point, it might well have been overwhelmed by resistance from master cheesemakers and others within the company. But unofficially, over a period of several years, Hori was able to develop the idea and, through publication of his article, gain international recognition for it. Time allowed enough momentum to develop for his project to survive the critical transition to official status. Although Hori was never actively encouraged to pursue his idea, Snow Brand's tolerance for his unofficial activity gave him the space he needed to develop it until it could stand on its own.

According to one of their colleagues at HP labs, Vaught and Donald's inkjet idea was "so different that it probably would have triggered the auto-immune system of any company."[17] Certainly their manager found it strange and discouraged them from working on it. But with a year of unofficial activity, the idea grew strong enough to capture the attention of top management. It is also worth noting that in several of the creative acts we have described so far, unofficial status was needed to *protect* the ideas from top management. For example, although the dean of engineering at Drexel University saw the bar code as inappropriately commercial for his school, two instructors in his organization were able to work on it unofficially.

Getting More from Employees
Than Can Reasonably Be Asked For

There are limits to what a company can ask of its employees, but far fewer limits to what people will ask of themselves. Creativity, especially the unplanned kind, often requires extraordinary dedication and effort. What company could have asked Russell Marker to repeatedly work through the night for days at a time, or to go deep into the Mexican jungles in the middle of World War II? The intensity of Marker's dedication to his problem grew steadily during the unofficial period, to the point where it consumed all his waking hours. (Recall that a critical breakthrough came when he happened to pick up an old botany book while spending the night at a friend's house.) In short, unofficial activity is often associated with such deep commitment to a project that not only do those involved own the problem, but the problem owns them.

NutraSweet, the discovery that led G. D. Searle in an entirely new and unanticipated direction, had a very short unofficial period, a matter of only hours. But what happened during that period was crucial: first Jim Schlatter and then Robert Mazur tasted a substance that their common sense told them was most probably harmless. Although it was unlikely that they were in any real danger, their company could never have asked them to do this, because it would have been conducting unauthorized experiments on humans. Unofficially, however, Schlatter and Mazur were able to bend the rules intelligently.

Ability to Cross Official Boundaries

Corporate creativity often involves combining ideas, knowledge, and skills in ways that are new and unanticipated to the organization. Boundaries that can seriously hamper official activity sometimes hardly matter for unofficial activity. Not surprisingly, in the majority of creative acts we have looked at, the key boundary crossings occurred during the unofficial period, in which:

- Russell Marker, a chemist, thinking that the plant kingdom held the key to his problem, taught himself botany and went on plant-foraging expeditions all over North America.
- Tomoshige Hori went to a lecture on a topic that had nothing to with his work and was so taken by the idea of thermal conductivity that he began tinkering with it in the lab, using milk.
- John Vaught and David Donald moved from mechanical design and electronics into chemistry and even into vapor explosions, an abstruse area of physics.
- A JR East maintenance worker in the Mt. Tanigawa tunnel tasted the water there and began to think far outside his official job description.
- Bette Swatzell, a secretary, discovering that Nashville Eagle was paying $650 for drawer liners for its galley carts, began soliciting bids from outside vendors, normally a job for the purchasing department.

With official status, too, come targets of some kind, and these alone can reinforce existing boundaries or create entirely new ones. Consider what might have happened had HP targeted the development of an inkjet printer too early, before the critical insight of heating the ink. At that time, inkjet printing meant squeezing drops of ink out of tubes. If HP had put together a team of specialists representing all the myriad aspects of this technology, would this team have been able to leave behind all that they knew in favor of something they knew nothing about—exploding the ink? Official status only makes it more difficult to cross the boundaries that stand in the way of creativity. Unofficially, most boundaries exist only in the minds of those who see them.

Improved Decision Making About New Opportunities

We will long remember the researcher from a prominent U.S. company who approached us during a break in one of our seminars. He told us that during his twenty-year career he had worked on a variety of official projects, not one of which had succeeded. Unfortunately, he is not the only person with a story like this. Companies constantly face decisions about which new projects to fund but have to make these decisions without possessing all the information they would like. A high failure rate is only to be expected. Early on in our work, we noticed an interesting pattern: companies that have little unofficial activity in relation to official activity are particularly prone to making such bad decisions. Companies that maintain higher levels of unofficial activity tend to make better decisions.

The reason for this, we believe, is that more extensive unofficial activity provides these companies with better information. Since unofficial activity is much less resource-intensive than official activity, work on far more ideas can be supported unofficially than officially. Each idea in the pool is given an opportunity to develop to a point where its potential usefulness becomes clearer, and better decisions are the result. Had the researcher attending our seminar worked at a company that maintained a larger base of unofficial projects, his story might well have been different. Far from being useless redundancy, a larger pool will help a company avoid wasting substantial resources on projects that lead nowhere.

At HP, the decision to make the inkjet printer into a commercial venture was timely and successful. That HP could make a good decision like this is no accident. Like many companies, HP wants to have far more unofficial activity at its central research laboratory than will ever be made official. John Vaught and David Donald's idea was only one of many being considered for funding in the Barney Oliver lab review. When it made the decision, however, management was not speculating on vague promises but could visualize the printer's potential more accurately because of the two researchers' unofficial work.

Some companies, recognizing the importance of unofficial activity, have established policies that encourage certain employees to devote a specified percentage of their time to unofficial projects. HP's policy is 10 percent, but companies such as Toshiba and 3M go even higher, to 15 percent. However, as Lewis Lehr, a former chairman and CEO of 3M, once pointed out,

> *Only a small percentage actually make use of this 15-percent option at a given time.*[18]

If such policies are intended to do anything more than legitimize unofficial activity, we find them silly, because interpreted literally they bear no relationship to the way corporate creativity really occurs. First of all, they often violate the No-Preconceptions Principle, since they are usually confined to a select group of people (most often in R&D)—those thought to be the ones who will come up with ideas. Many of the creative acts described in this book—such as those of Kathy Betts (worth more than $1.4 billion) and the JR East maintenance worker (worth more than $150 million)—required unofficial activity from a person who normally would be outside such a predetermined group. Second, no one can ever predict *when* a particular individual will need time for unofficial activity, and how much he or she will need. The bar code took thirty years; NutraSweet required only two to three hours. Besides, most people are involved in a major creative act only once, if at all, in their careers.

Furthermore, much of the benefit of unofficial activity comes from the *individual* having to make room for it. Hori once commented to us that several young researchers at his company had remarked to him that they could be more creative if they had more time. Hori's response had been that it would be a mistake for Snow Brand simply to give them more free time. *Make* the time for your unofficial activity yourselves, he told them; being *given* it won't help you to be more creative. We believe that Hori is right. Encouraging unofficial activity at the corporate level is not enough. What really matters is that when individual employees see the need for it, they do it.

How to Promote Unofficial Activity

Unless an organization makes a space for unofficial activity, relatively few creative acts will occur. Only the most stubborn individuals will pursue projects without official support. It is important, therefore, for a company to legitimize unofficial activity, so that official activity does not squeeze it out. Most policies that specify the percentage of time employees should spend on unofficial activity are in fact intended for just this purpose. We asked a senior executive at 3M how his company had arrived at the figure of 15 percent. His response was that if 3M had picked a percentage that was too small (say 5 percent), it would have sent the message that unofficial activity was not worth paying attention to. On the other hand, too high a figure (25 percent, for example) would have turned unofficial activity into something that had to be managed. Any company that makes such a "percentage-of-time" policy for unofficial activity should be careful to emphasize its symbolic nature.

Percentage-of-time policies are not the only way a company can make it clear that unofficial activity is encouraged. In addition to its 10 percent rule, Hewlett-Packard has a long-standing policy that lab supplies may be freely used for unofficial activity, and it strives to give researchers access to labs and any equipment they need. Johnson Controls' FoaMech plant gives its Employee Involvement Teams the freedom and support they need to pursue and implement ideas they initiate, like the lighted display board described in Chapter Three. American Airlines encourages its employees to work on improvement ideas outside of working hours, but often winks at such unofficial work when it is done on company time. However a company gets the message out, the important thing is that every employee knows that the company wants him or her to work unofficially when an opportunity arises to do something new and potentially useful.

Much can be done to increase general awareness of the importance of unofficial activity to improvement and innovation. When internal publications describe the creative acts of employees, they should stress the role that unofficial activity played in them. It is unfortunate that this role is so often overlooked, because the essential connections for most creative acts are made during this period. Recall that in the JMA study, projects that had won awards for creativity had unofficial periods some 60 percent longer than their not so creative counterparts. Most creativity in companies would not happen without unofficial activity. Unless a company gets this message out, it is unlikely that individual employees will make the time for unofficial activity, or that their managers will either.

It is also important to ensure that unofficial activity is not hidden. Employees should be aware of the unofficial activity of their colleagues, and managers should know about the unofficial activity of those who work for them. Not only will this further legitimize unofficial activity as people see it going on all around them, but others who learn about a budding creative act might be in a position to help it along. In this respect, Barney Oliver, the head of HP's Research Laboratories, played a key role in the development of the inkjet idea when he steered Vaught and Meyer to the physicists at the California Institute of Technology, where they discovered that they were dealing with a phenomenon they had never heard of before—vapor explosion. But there is a danger involved when management becomes aware of unofficial activity. In their enthusiasm, managers may be tempted to pull a good idea out of unofficial status before it is sufficiently developed. If Russell Marker had contacted the president of Parke-Davis at the time of his first small success with Beth root in North Carolina, and if the president had immediately approved lavish funding for Marker to build a progesterone plant in North Carolina and buy up all the Beth root crops, would the birth-control pill ever have come about?

Ideally, a company should have far more unofficial activity going on than could possibly be supported officially. Determining which activity to make official is critical to any company's future, because bad decisions miss opportunities and waste resources. Ideas that need extensive resources to develop, involve significant risk, or that people cannot implement by themselves should be independently reviewed by different people at different times and in different ways. Recall that HP almost lost the inkjet printer idea because Vaught and Donald's manager did not support it. Fortunately, others looked at the idea and it was able to gain official status. Things did not turn out so well for Parke-Davis. Russell Marker's idea for a process to produce synthetic hormones really had only one chance at the company. Because of a single bad experience as a tourist in Mexico, the president himself rejected it out of hand, leaving no room for others in his company to give it serious consideration. One person alone is unlikely to see all the possibilities in an idea. Multiple reviews are a must. The additional costs of these reviews pale in comparison with the money that is wasted on projects doomed to fail before they start.

Main Points

Unofficial activity, work done without direct official support, is what makes it possible for a company to go where it never expected to.

Neither HP or Canon, the two companies that share most of the $11 billion world market for inkjet printers, ever planned this revolutionary new product—it came to them through unofficial activity.

Every unexpected creative act begins with a period of unofficial activity, which might be a matter of minutes or years.

Unofficial status brings some important benefits that are often lost with official status:

It provides a safe haven for the strange and repellent, in which ideas have the opportunity to develop into something with clear potential.

It allows a company to get more from its employees than it could reasonably ask for. There are limits to what a company can ask of its employees, but there are few limits to what people will ask of themselves.

Unofficial activity does not recognize official boundaries. Official boundaries often prevent the unanticipated combining of ideas, knowledge, and skill that is so important to creativity. To an unofficial project, these boundaries don't exist.

Unofficial activity brings improved decision making about new opportunities. Because unofficial activity is much less resource-intensive than official activity, far more ideas can be supported unofficially than officially. The result is that companies that maintain higher levels of unofficial activity tend to make better decisions about which projects to fund.

Chapter Nine

SERELANDIPITY

*No discovery of a thing you **are** looking for, comes under this description.*
HORACE WALPOLE[1]

Although the word *serendipity* is widely used, few people know where it came from or what it actually means. The word was introduced into the English language in 1754 by Horace Walpole. Since then, it has certainly entered the language, but an important aspect of its meaning has been lost. Today, an unforeseen event that turns out to be fortunate (such as when two people bump into each other on the street) is often wrongly described as "serendipitous." As it is now used, the word means something quite different from what Walpole intended. It is only when the full and original meaning of serendipity is restored that the actions that companies can take to promote it become clear. *Serendipity,* the fourth element of corporate creativity, is present in every creative act whether it is apparent or not. Before we discuss the true meaning of the word and its fascinating history, let us first look at an actual example of it.

Finally, Something to Put a Universal Solvent In

When Teflon was invented at Du Pont in 1938, the joke within the company was that "if Du Pont ever invented the Universal Solvent, now it had something to put it in."[2] Teflon is indeed a strange substance—it doesn't burn, melt, or dissolve in any known solvent, and it remains unaffected by acids or other corrosive elements. Because its extraordinarily high resistance makes it one of the best electrical insulators known, Teflon has become a staple of the cable and telecommunications industry, and a highly profitable product for Du Pont.

Teflon was discovered at Du Pont's Jackson Laboratory in Wilmington, Delaware, in the course of research into new refrigerants.[3] Roy Plunkett was one of the researchers involved in this work. At one point, he was trying to figure out how to synthesize a certain Freon compound. For his experiments in this area, he thought he would need roughly a hundred pounds of an intermediate product, tetrafluoroethylene gas, which he and his assistant Jack Rebok set about making. As they produced the gas, they bottled it in cylinders, which they then stored in dry ice. Each cylinder held exactly one kilogram of tetrafluoroethylene, and Plunkett planned to draw on his supply as needed. On the morning of April 6, 1938, in preparation for an experiment, Rebok fetched one of the partially used cylinders and hooked it up to the lab apparatus. But when he opened the valve on the cylinder, nothing came out. Rebok was surprised that it appeared to be empty and asked Plunkett to come over and take a look. The two men were certain that they had not used anywhere near a kilogram of tetrafluoroethylene from this cylinder and at first suspected that the problem lay with the cylinder's valve: perhaps it was stuck or blocked. After playing with it for a while, they finally opened the valve fully and pushed a piece of wire through it into the cylinder. Still, no gas came out. Plunkett was intrigued. By the weight of the cylinder, Plunkett could tell it was not empty. Nevertheless, whatever was inside the cylinder was clearly not tetrafluoroethylene gas. Plunkett took the valve off the cylinder, and when he turned the cylinder upside down, some waxy white powder fell out. He then inserted a piece of wire into the neck of the cylinder and scraped it around inside. Even more powder came out. But Plunkett still did not have enough material to account for the cylinder's weight. Curious, he sent the tank down to the machine shop with a work order for it to be sawed open.[4]

Once it was opened, Plunkett and Rebok found the same white powder packed tightly into the bottom and sides of the cylinder. Plunkett realized immediately what had happened—the tetrafluoroethylene had polymerized spontaneously into a solid. When a gas polymerizes, its molecules bond together, usually irreversibly, in extremely long chains. Until that moment, it had been thought that tetrafluoroethylene could not polymerize. However, Plunkett had demonstrated that not only does the gas polymerize, but it does so *spontaneously.* The reason turned out to be two factors that no one had previously considered: the high pressure in the tank and the catalyzing help provided by the metal walls inside the cylinder. In fact, the extremely high pressures necessary to manufacture polytetrafluoroethylene, which in 1944 would be given the trademark name of "Teflon," would forever make it a hazardous operation. Not only was Teflon difficult to make—until quite recently only one company other than Du Pont had the facilities to do it—but it was so intractable a substance that it was even more difficult to find any uses for it.

Applications for Teflon took considerable time to develop. In 1945, a figure who would prove pivotal in the history of Teflon arrived at Du Pont: Wilbert L. Gore. For the next ten years or so, he worked on a Du Pont task force assigned to conceive useful products from Teflon. But when another group within the company found a way to make a thermoplastic version of Teflon (allowing it to be molded in machines), "Du Pont felt that was good enough, and our group was dissolved," as Gore put it.[5] But he continued to believe that Teflon had real potential and in his spare time worked on it in the basement of his house. In the fall of 1957, almost twenty years after Plunkett's discovery, Gore's son Bob, a junior chemical engineering major at the University of Delaware, came downstairs to find his father very frustrated. Knowing Teflon's unique properties as an electrical insulator, Bill Gore had been attempting to find a way to coat wire with it, but nothing seemed to work. Dejectedly, Gore showed some of his failed efforts to his son. As he was doing so, Bob Gore happened to notice a roll of 3M sealant tape made of Teflon. He asked his father if, instead of coating wire with Teflon, the wire couldn't be sandwiched between two pieces of tape instead. Soon afterward, Bob wished his father good night and went upstairs to bed.

At four o'clock in the morning, an excited Bill Gore shook his son awake. The idea had worked! The following night, using the sandwich method, father and son were able to make good ribbon cable. Over the next four months, Bill Gore tried to talk Du Pont into entering the wire business, but the company's policy remained firm. Although it was ready to manufacture Teflon, its business was to supply raw materials, not end-use items, since it never wanted to be in competition with any of its customers. When Gore requested permission to set up his own wire company, proposing to obtain his supply of Teflon from Du Pont, the company gladly gave it to him. On January 1, 1958, after mortgaging their house and taking four thousand dollars out of savings, Bill and his wife Vieve formed their new company, W. L. Gore and Associates. At first, they produced Teflon-insulated ribbon cable in the basement of the Gore home in Newark, Delaware. But over the next two decades, the company grew rapidly and branched out into other applications of Teflon, most notably when it introduced GoreTex in 1973. Today, Gore-Tex fabric, which is waterproofed with a thin membrane of Teflon, is widely used for sports and outdoor clothing. By 1986, when Bill Gore died, his company had annual sales of more than $300 million and had plants in the United States, Japan, India, and Europe. And all this was built on Roy Plunkett's serendipitous discovery back in 1938.

What Does Serendipity Really Mean?

Walpole's "serendipity" has a long history. For him, it all began with a childhood fairy tale. In 1557, the Venetian publisher Michele Tramezzino printed *Peregrinaggio di tre giovani figliuoli del re di Serendippo: Tradotto dalla lingua persiana in lingua italiana da M. Christoforo Armeno* (Peregrinations of the Three Young Sons of the King of Serendip: Translated from the Persian Language into the Italian Language by Christoforo Armeno).[6] Nearly two centuries later, Horace Walpole read the tale as a child in its English version: *The Travels and Adventures of the Three Princes of Serendip.* Years afterward, when he was searching for a word to describe the way he often arrived at useful insights, he would remember this story. A friend of his had already come up with a name for Walpole's special process of discovery—he called it "sortes Walpolianae" (Walpolian accidents).

Walpole was a prolific letter writer, whose lifetime correspondence amounted to more than nine thousand letters. His wide range of interests, and his learning, worldliness, and keen powers of observation destined his correspondence to become an important part of England's literary and historical record. It was at the beginning of a long letter to a friend, dated January 28, 1754, that Walpole invented the word *serendipity* to describe the way in which he had discovered something interesting about the coat of arms of the Medicis:

This discovery indeed is almost of that kind which I call serendipity, *a very expressive word, which as I have nothing better to tell you, I shall endeavour to explain to you: you will understand it better by the derivation than by the definition. I once read a silly fairy tale,* called The Three Princes of Serendip: *as their highnesses travelled, they were always making discoveries, by accidents and sagacity, of things they were not in quest of: for instance, one of them discovered that a mule blind of the right eye had travelled the same road lately, because the grass was eaten only on the left side, where it was worse than on the right—now do you understand* serendipity?[7]

Serendip, the setting of the fairy tale, is the ancient name for the island of Sri Lanka (formerly also known as Ceylon), derived from the Sanskrit word *Sinhaladvipa* (island of the Sinhalese people). In the story, the king of Serendip, deciding to test his three sons and give them some experience of the world, contrived a way to be angry with them, so that he could banish them from his kingdom. Their subsequent adventures are the subject of the story. Ironically, by failing to give in his letter the full context of the example he used from the story, Walpole initially misled his friend as to the meaning of the new word, since he deemphasized the "accidents" that prompted their discoveries and gave only an example of "sagacity." In a double irony, in the 240 years since the invention of the word, popular usage has reversed this mistake. According to the *Oxford English Dictionary*, *serendipity* is now used to mean

the faculty of making happy and unexpected discoveries by accident.

This modern definition puts the emphasis almost totally on accidents and leaves out sagacity, the other aspect of serendipity as Walpole defined it. Sagacity is derived from the Latin noun *sagicitas* ("keenness of perception") and means, also according to the *Oxford English Dictionary*:

gifted with acuteness of mental discernment; having special aptitude for the discovery of truth; penetrating and judicious in the estimation of character and motives, and the devising of means for the accomplishment of ends.

Part of the appeal of the fairy tale is the exaggerated sagacity of the three princes, and in the episode Walpole referred to in his letter, they put on a memorable display of it. The crucial scene happens early in the story, when the brothers meet a camel driver who has lost his camel. The princes had seen signs on their journey that the camel had passed along their way and decided to have some fun by seeing if they could fool the driver into thinking they had actually seen his camel. "Was it blind in one eye?" asked the oldest. "Wasn't it also missing a tooth?" the middle brother inquired. The third brother then observed that the camel had been lame. Hearing them describe his camel so accurately, the camel driver could not but believe that the brothers had actually seen it and, on their advice, he backtracked more than twenty miles along the road the brothers had taken. Having no luck, he returned the next day to find the three brothers eating a meal not far from where he had left them. He accused the brothers of lying to him. "You can well judge from our information about your camel if we made fun of you or not," said the first brother, who added that the camel had been carrying a load of honey on one side and a load of butter on the other.[8] The second prince interjected that the camel had been carrying a woman. And she had been pregnant, the third brother chipped in. This time the brothers had gone too far. Unfortunately for them, they had unwittingly succeeded in convincing the camel driver that they had actually stolen his camel. The camel driver went to a judge, who sent the three brothers to jail.

Their arrest and conviction was reported to the emperor, who had a campaign under way to reduce robbery and banditry on his country's highways. Intrigued by the fact that the brothers steadfastly maintained their innocence, the emperor summoned them in order to hear their story for himself. He, too, found their explanation hard to believe and sent them back to prison. But soon afterward, the camel driver found his lost camel and was honorable enough to request an audience with the emperor in order to admit his mistake. The brothers were immediately released and brought into the emperor's presence. If they hadn't seen the camel, the emperor asked, how had they known so much about it? The following passage from the *Peregrinaggio,* in which the princes explain their first three observations, is what Walpole would remember so clearly decades after he had read it as a child. The first brother said:

"I guessed that the lost animal must have had only one eye, because along the way he had covered I had noticed that on one side the grass had been eaten in spite of the fact that it was very bad, while it was not so on the other side of the road where the grass was very good. So I thought that the camel must have been blind in the eye facing the side of the road where the grass was good, and had not eaten it because he could not see it, while he had eaten the bad grass he had seen on the other side."

The second brother said: "I guessed, Sire, that the camel was lacking a tooth, because I had noticed on the way many cuds of chewed grass of such a size that they could have come out only from the empty space of a missing tooth."

"And I, Sire," added the third, "guessed that the lost camel must have been lame because I had clearly noticed the tracks of only three camel feet, while at the same time I noticed the trace of a dragged foot."

The words of the three young brothers inspired infinite admiration on the part of the emperor, so that he felt the greatest esteem for their intelligence and decided that he would favor and honor them as they deserved.[9]

While it is true that the three princes do have fortunate accidents—such as their encounter with the camel driver and their subsequent joke-turned-sour that drew them to the attention of the emperor—the *Peregrinaggio* emphasizes their sagacity far more. Certainly, Walpole, in referring to his own characteristic of making discoveries in this way, was less likely to see it as meaning "accident-prone" than "sagacious." Accidents happen to everyone. If, in his letter's first example, Walpole misled his friend by not explicitly mentioning an accident, his second example was more balanced:

*One of the most remarkable instances of this **accidental sagacity** (for you must observe that **no** discovery of a thing you **are** looking for, comes under this description) was of my Lord Shaftsbury, who happening to dine at Lord Chancellor Clarendon's, found out the marriage of the Duke of York and Mrs. Hyde, by the respect with which her mother treated her at table.*[10]

For corporate creativity, Walpole's rich meaning of *serendipity* is much more helpful than its dumbed-down version. The word *serendipitous* does not apply to a person or an event—it is an adjective that qualifies the nature of a discovery. Serendipity always combines something from the people involved and something from the situation in which they work. The problem has been that people who observe creative acts attribute either too much to the accident or too much to sagacity. In reality, the two are interdependent—an accident can only be "fortunate" if the people involved are able to see something of value in it. The three princes in the fairy tale appeared to be sagacious about absolutely everything. In real life, however, a person is sagacious in particular domains in which he or she can turn an accident into a fortunate one. A person's domain of sagacity is the result of his or her specialized knowledge, life and work experiences, personal characteristics, and interests. It was because Jim Schlatter was able to bring his sagacity to bear on the unexpected events that happened to him that they became fortunate accidents. Very fortunate, in fact, since the result was NutraSweet.

It might seem that a company cannot do much to promote serendipity. Actually, as we will see, this is far from the case. Even the accidents themselves are not magical occurrences. They reflect a spectrum of underlying probabilities of events that will happen, but cannot be individually predicted, when people interact with phenomena they do not fully understand. In hindsight, it is often clear that the "lucky" accident almost had to happen eventually.

Let us look more closely at the unexpected event at the heart of the Teflon story—the cylinder appearing to be empty so much earlier than expected. In fact, until several decades after Plunkett's discovery, suppliers of tetrafluoroethylene gas had trouble ensuring that it actually got to their customers in gaseous form, without spontaneously polymerizing in the cylinders before it arrived. It was not until the advent of special inhibitors to *prevent* polymerization that the problem was finally solved.[11] Tetrafluoroethylene gas is notoriously unstable under pressure. It *wants* to polymerize and has done so many times both before and since Roy Plunkett first noticed it. Because Plunkett had produced more than forty-five cylinders of it, the chances were that polymerization, an irreversible process, had actually occurred in many of them. Plunkett, of course, added the other ingredient of serendipity—sagacity.

Today, if a chemist found a prematurely empty cylinder of tetrafluoroethylene, spontaneous polymerization is probably the first thing he or she would think of. But to Plunkett, who in 1938 *knew* that tetrafluoroethylene wouldn't polymerize, it was a complete surprise. It is often assumed that a discovery such as Teflon is simply a matter of chance. But the perception that an event has occurred by chance merely reflects a person's state of knowledge at the time, and the unpredictability of that particular event to him or her. When accidents are chalked up to chance, there is no option but to conclude that nothing can be done to increase the frequency of serendipitous discoveries.

But the truth is that accidents do have definite causes, and although we cannot predict them individually, we know that they will happen and so can do some planning for them. Consider, for example, a police department in a major city. Many people drive automobiles in their jurisdiction, so the police expect accidents to occur with a certain regularity, although the department cannot predict when, where, and how each of them will happen. The accidents are caused by the underlying phenomena that always come into play when many people drive cars in a traffic system. Each individual car accident always has specific causes. In the workplace, unforeseen events (fortunate ones, we hope) can be expected to arise in a similar manner as people interact with each other and their work.

Some of the fortunate accidents that are provoked in this way, like the polymerization of the tetrafluoroethylene in its cylinder (try to stop it!), occur frequently, whereas others occur with only moderate or low frequency. Sometimes accidents even occur in a continuous "drizzle" of minor events, each so tiny that even the most motivated and interested observer fails to notice it. Perhaps this happened to Roy Plunkett—maybe slight polymerization had been occurring for a long time in the cylinders he was working with. Let us now look at another example of serendipity, in which the person involved was "drizzled" with accidents for years, but saw nothing until a "cloudburst" came along.

A Dead Chicken Started It All

In October 1992, the *Genetic Engineering News* announced that Jason Shih, a professor of poultry science at North Carolina State University, had made a discovery with a potentially major impact on the environment. Each year, the United States alone generates more than a million tons of poultry feathers. With no significant practical use for them, most go straight into landfills. Before Shih's discovery of a method to break down keratin—the protein that makes up feathers—the poultry industry had taken for granted that feathers were nothing but waste. But Shih had now opened the door to using them as a cheap and plentiful source of protein for animal feed.

Biochemical researchers had dreamed for years of finding a "keratinase," an enzyme that would hydrolyze keratin, that is, break it down into its constituent amino acids. The industry had been trying to hydrolyze feathers for a long time using acid or steam, but the process was crude and had a serious drawback: it destroyed many of the keratin's amino acids, and animals were capable of digesting only 70 percent of what remained. Curiously, by the time of his discovery, Shih had been holding on to the idea that a keratinase might exist for more than *eighteen years*. In 1974, as a postdoctoral fellow at Cornell University, he had asked his professor, Milton Scott: "Why can't feathers be converted to amino acids?" Professor Scott had laughed. His response was the opinion of most scientists of the day: "Finding a way to do that would require a massive undertaking, like shooting a man to the moon."[12]

Like shooting a man to the moon. That phrase would stick with Shih for many years. Without it he might never have made his important discovery. Eleven years later found Shih on the faculty of the poultry science department at North Carolina State University, working on ways to convert manure into usable products such as methane, animal feed supplements, and fertilizers—none of which had anything to do with keratinase. In the old days, when farms were family-operated and smaller, farmers had regarded manure as a blessing, because it could be spread on their land as fertilizer. But with the advent of large-scale commercial farming, manure became a major problem. Even the smallest poultry or hog farm puts out more manure than can be spread locally without completely submerging all plant life. The thousands of hogs or tens of thousands of hens on larger farms generate tons of manure daily. In countries other than the United States, which have even less land to spread manure on, the disposal problem has become acute.[13] In fact, the problem of disposing of high volumes of animal waste is probably the single most important challenge faced by the animal products industry worldwide.

In 1984, Jason Shih was developing a new type of "digestion" process for animal manure. Most commercial digesters at that time, including sewage treatment plants for human waste, operated with aerobic bacteria, that is, bacteria that need oxygen to do their work. Although they are quite fast, aerobic digesters also eat up tremendous amounts of energy, making them prohibitively expensive for farmers. Shih's group was working on an *anaerobic* digester, one in which the bacteria degrade the manure in the absence of oxygen, using much less energy. Anaerobic digesters were not new; they had been widely used in China since the turn of the century. But their bioreaction rates were so slow as to preclude their use for high-volume waste streams. However, in the lab at least, Shih had managed to increase substantially the efficiency of an anaerobic digester by raising its reaction temperature from the normal thirty-five degrees centigrade to fifty degrees centigrade, and by substituting special "thermophilic" bacteria that thrived in higher-than-normal temperatures. The resulting process promised to efficiently break down manure into methane (valuable because it could be burned for energy) and carbon dioxide, with solid by-products useful as animal feed and liquid by-products useful as nutrients for aquaculture.

A pilot thermophilic anaerobic digester was set up at North Carolina State University's research farm to see how it could handle the manure from four thousand laying hens. Since these farms are designed to use gravity wherever possible to move both the eggs and manure, the chickens are kept in elevated cages. Their eggs roll down a clever system of chutes, which deliver them gently to a conveyor system. Their excreta fall directly through the bottom of the wire cages onto hard flooring, where a system of scrapers pushes the droppings into a channel. There, an auger (a slow-turning large screw running the length of the channel) moves it into the digester. It was this system that would precipitate Shih's serendipitous discovery.

For some time, Shih and his group had noticed a drizzle of minor but interesting events: the few feathers that also fell through the mesh of the cages and got mixed in with the excreta always seemed to disappear in the digester. Although Shih had long been aware of this, somehow he didn't think about it any further until one day a chicken escaped from its cage and happened to get caught and crushed in the scraper and auger system. Despite the efforts of farm workers to get to it in time, the dead chicken was pushed into the digester. Then came not a drizzle, but a cloudburst—the dead chicken completely disappeared, feathers and all! Shih now realized that something inside the digester had to be breaking down the feathers and set out to find it.

From that point on, it was only a matter of time before Shih was able to isolate the bacterium responsible: *bacillus licheniformis*, strain PWD-1 (PWD stands for "poultry waste digester"). How do the bacteria break down keratin? By producing an enzyme—precisely the keratinase that Shih's professor had suggested could never be found. The point had been made in so memorable a way, in fact, that it left Shih curious and motivated for eighteen years. Though Shih never specifically worked on the problem before the dead-chicken incident, his sagacity derived from his intense interest in it.

Serendipity Can Help You Find What You Seek

Serendipity led Roy Plunkett and Jason Shih off in an unexpected direction, but it can also help those who already have a specific problem in mind. Sagacity intensifies as a person comes to be more absorbed by a problem. The process of studying a problem from every angle, of getting stymied and blocked by it, of thinking about it all the time, can sharpen a person's sensitivities to the point that, *for that problem domain alone*, he or she finds significance in events that others do not even notice. Also, the longer someone investigates a phenomenon, the more likely it is that his or her interaction with it will produce a fortunate accident. In such cases, rather than sparking completely new activity, serendipity points the way to a different solution to the problem. An oft-cited example is that of Charles Goodyear, who after almost two decades of frustration in his search for a useful form of rubber, discovered the answer to his problem—vulcanization—when he accidentally dropped a mixture of rubber and sulfur on a hot stove. At that instant, he was probably the only person in the world who could have appreciated the significance of the unsightly mess he was looking at. Given the extraordinary lengths he had gone to in his research, he was also probably the only person in the world to whom such a perverse accident could have happened in the first place.[14] A second example where serendipity redefined the approach to an existing problem occurred at Du Pont. Although it is much less widely known, it led to an important improvement to a product we all use every day.

It is commonly thought that the first commercial product made of nylon was hosiery. Not so. Nylon was first used for toothbrush bristles. In 1936, the toothbrush (having changed little since its invention in China in the late fifteenth century) was essentially the same as it is today, except for one thing.[15] The bristles came from hogs raised specially for this purpose in China and Siberia. When, in May 1934, Wallace Carothers discovered nylon, the first practical synthetic fiber, Du Pont immediately targeted synthetic bristles as a potential application. But as it turned out, Carothers would play hardly any role in this endeavor, or in any other work at Du Pont for that matter. For two years after his historic discovery he suffered from severe depression, to the extent that he had to seek psychiatric help. Eventually, in the summer of 1936, he committed suicide. Meanwhile, in early 1936, Du Pont had hired Alan Smith, a recent Ph.D. from the University of Illinois, to work with Carothers on X-ray diffraction techniques for polymers. But when Smith turned up for work, Carothers was in Europe on a rest trip. While waiting for his return, Smith was given the temporary assignment of figuring out how to produce large-diameter filaments of nylon. Someone else had already worked on the problem before him and had devised a highly impractical approach that involved trying to extrude the nylon onto a slow-moving belt. Apart from being too slow, the process required super-high polymers, whose molecules had extra long chains, twice as long as those Du Pont was planning to use in ordinary fibers. Such material would be not only expensive to make, but extremely viscous and so hard to handle.

For the first several months, Smith tried to work along the same lines as his predecessor and became quite frustrated. But one night, while working late in the laboratory, he needed to empty a sample of nylon from an autoclave. He looked around for a trash can but could not see one. Finally, he noticed a bucket in the corner and went over to empty his autoclave there. The bucket happened to have some water in it. As Smith poured the contents of the autoclave into it, he noticed that the liquid polymer, upon hitting the water, immediately congealed into a stringy mess. Smith reached into the bucket to pull some of it out. He was able to stretch it in his hands, a natural thing for him to try, because he knew that nylon had to be drawn in order to develop its strength, just as steel is forged by hammering it. By throwing his material away in an unusual place and being alert enough to see the result, Smith had stumbled across the quenching process for nylon, a process that immediately made it possible for Du Pont to manufacture nylon filaments of any desired diameter, and at a respectable speed. In quenching, the fiber is spun out of its solution in a spinerette, then extruded into a water bath, after which it can be readily drawn. According to Smith, even the pilot process was profitable. Serendipity had solved a key problem for Du Pont.[16]

Redundancy and Randomness:
The Raw Material of Creation

Long before corporations became interested in how to manage creativity—in fact, long before corporations existed at all—Mother Nature managed creativity through the process of biological evolution. An understanding of evolution won't necessarily help companies with planned and targeted creative acts, but it does help them manage the unplanned. In fact, it is hard to think of anything that is *more* unplanned than evolution. Humans might wish evolution to be the story of millions of years of steady and predictable progress toward Homo sapiens, but prevailing scientific opinion does not support this view. Ironically, if evolution had actually been a targeted and linear process, life would probably not have evolved much beyond single cell amoeba. Why is this? According to the evolutionary biologist Stephen Jay Gould:

> *If each step in an [evolutionary] sequence were adaptive and leading to optimal form and optimal fit of morphology to an immediate environment, then there would be no flexibility left for future change for adaptation for that environmental alteration which will wipe out a lineage that is too specialized, too well fit, too committed to a*

previous environment. Organisms must remain imperfect, full of unused potential for change.[17]

An often-cited example of such unused potential for change is the heron's wing. The heron uses its wings not only to fly, but also to shade a patch of water from the sun in order to better see the fish it is trying to catch. The question is: how did the heron's wing evolve? A wing is useless, it seems, until it is fully developed. Diminutive wings are too small to fly with or to serve as much of a sunshade. How did evolution take birds from *no* wings to *full* wings, with every stage of development conferring even more advantage than the last? Darwin himself suggested an answer. Since a fraction of a wing is useless for flying, it must have originally sprouted for some other purpose. The prevalent theory is that the feathers help to retain warmth. Moreover, the need for warmth was greatest for the small dinosaurs that would evolve into birds, because they had the largest surface-area-to-volume ratio and so were most prone to heat loss. Over millions of years, as feathers covered wings and enlarged through stages of evolutionary advantage, new and unanticipated uses emerged. Once the wing reached a certain size, herons could fly and shade the waters to catch more fish. But in the beginning, the feathers certainly had unused potential for change. And they still do—but who knows what it is?

Evolution has proved to be creative, and the engine of its creativity is randomness and redundancy. Corporate creativity is no different. If companies were to have no redundancy whatsoever, they would be optimized for their present environment and would limit themselves to doing only what could be planned. For species that are subject to natural selection, also, zero redundancy is not a recipe for survival. As Roger Kimmel, who was involved in the development of 3-D imaging at Kodak (which we will discuss in Chapter Eleven), remarked:

Sometimes a company can have so much focus that it can miss the opportunity that is right next to it.[18]

At some point, every company must be able to move away from what it already does. There is value in being able to look and move in directions other than straight ahead. When a company strategically uses random-ness and redundancy, it opens itself to serendipity.

How to Promote Serendipity

Serendipity occurs when fortunate accidents happen to sagacious peo-ple. There are three approaches a company can take to promote it:

1. Increase the frequency of accidents that could turn out to be fortunate.
2. Increase awareness of the accidents that do occur.
3. Increase the company's domain of sagacity to turn more accidents into fortunate ones.

One way to increase the frequency of accidents is to promote a bias for action, toward tinkering, toward empirical research work. Jason Shih might never have made his discovery had he worked only with pencil and paper at his desk—it took an accident that could only have oc-curred in an actual running process. Roy Plunkett, intrigued, did not hesitate to have the empty cylinder of tetrafluoroethylene sawed in half. For a person to act is to expose him- or herself to a drizzle of potentially fortunate accidents.

The second approach to promote serendipity is to increase aware-ness of the accidents that do occur. Serendipitous events happen in companies more often than people realize. Perhaps there is a tendency to downplay their importance because people feel uncomfortable de-pending on accidents that come from a source they feel powerless to control—the environment. How do the employees at NutraSweet feel about the fact that their company, and their jobs, wouldn't exist but for a lucky accident (Jim Schlatter's licking his finger)? It is important for everyone to know that when accidents happen, they are driven by un-derlying phenomena that it is worth understanding further. A general principle is "Don't overlook exceptions." When Ichiro Endo of Canon saw the hot soldering iron touch the syringe and ink spurt out, he quickly set up a high-speed camera to learn what had happened. An ex-ception, however small, may be the fortunate accident that sparks a serendipitous discovery.

But a company can do more to promote serendipity than just pro-voking and catching accidents. It can also take action to raise the chances that these accidents will turn out to be fortunate, that is, that they will meet with sagacity. To do this, an organization must enlarge the domain in which it is sagacious and deliberately create unused po-tential for change, that is, redundant capacity in human potential for change. Some companies believe in training people only for what they need to know to do their current job. This amounts to optimizing for an *existing* or *predetermined* situation. An organization should encourage its employees to take classes that are not directly related to their work, to go to conferences where they are not making a presentation, to take study leaves or sabbaticals with the purpose of learning something dif-ferent. One can never know when new knowledge will become useful. Until it does, like the heron's wing for flight, it represents an unused capacity for change. An additional idea to increase a company's sagac-ity comes from the list discussed in Chapter Two, the list of all em-ployees and the things that each knows about the company's operations that no one else does. Although there will always be something next to each name, the shorter the list the better, because then a given acci-dent will fall into the areas of sagacity of more people. How does a com-pany shorten the list? Frequent job rotation, even across functions, is one route; visits to customers and suppliers by people who don't often deal with them is another. Without some redundancy, there is little room for serendipity.

MAIN POINTS

As originally defined by Horace Walpole in 1754, serendipity combines a fortunate accident with sagacity.

An alert Roy Plunkett discovered Teflon while trying to figure out why a cylinder of tetrafluoroethylene gas appeared to be empty earlier than expected.

Fortunate accidents are rarely "one-shot" events. They arise when people interact with each other and their work. They are often a continuous drizzle of tiny, almost imperceptible events that may escape the attention of all but the most alert and motivated observers. Occasionally, a cloudburst comes along and makes these events easier to see.

For years, feathers had been disappearing into the manure digester at North Carolina State University's experimental farm, and no one really thought much about it. But when a dead chicken fell in—and disappeared entirely—it led the way to a new enzyme that could solve a major waste disposal problem in the poultry industry.

Fortunate accidents (the first half of the serendipity equation) can be promoted through strategies that provoke and exploit accidents.

A bias for action will cause more potentially fortunate accidents to occur, and spreading the word not to overlook exceptions will make employees more aware of them when they do happen.

Sagacity (the second half of the equation) can be promoted by expanding the company's human potential beyond its immediate needs.

If companies have no redundancy or randomness at all, they are optimized for their present environment and so are limited to only what they can anticipate and plan.

Chapter Ten
DIVERSE STIMULI

The genius, according to [Henry] James, has an enormous capacity for perceiving similarities among disparate things; his mind jumps across the grooves cut by common experience. His is also a sensitive mind; every stimulus starts multiple trains of thought, wildly free associations. "In such minds," says James, "subjects bud and sprout and grow."

JACQUES BARZUN[1]

One reason why no one can predict who will be involved in a creative act, what it will be, or when or how it will happen is that it is impossible to know in advance what sort of stimulus will lead a particular person to initiate one. Recall that it was a casual conversation over coffee that set off the chain of events leading to Hewlett-Packard's inkjet printer, and that it was first-class passengers repeatedly asking about the yellow and black tags that led to British Airways' "First & Fast" luggage service. The fifth element of corporate creativity is *diverse stimuli,* the sparks for creative ideas. A stimulus can either give a person fresh insight into something he or she has already set off to do or push that person in a completely new direction. While companies can do things to identify diverse stimuli and provide them to their employees, the impact of such efforts on creativity will be limited, for two reasons. First, the majority of stimuli arise in connection with the work itself. Second, what serves as a powerful stimulus for one person may not even be *noticed* by someone else. This unpredictability means that efforts to *give* people stimuli will necessarily have a low success rate. The real leverage lies in helping employees *get* the stimuli, and in creating opportunities for them to bring these stimuli back into the organization where they can be put to use.

Before we discuss the actions that organizations can take to give diverse stimuli to their employees, and why most of these stimuli arise in connection with work, we will first take a closer look at just how diverse and specific to the individual such stimuli can be. Consider, for example, what led George Miller, the Australian director and producer of the *Mad Max* and *Road Warrior* movies (starring Mel Gibson), to undertake a new project—the film *Babe*, a box-office smash hit about a pig who wanted to be a sheepdog.

If Pigs Could Talk

A British Airways long-haul flight from Sydney, Australia, to London in 1986 found George Miller listening to a children's audio channel through his headset. The program happened to include a series of book reviews given by a woman whom Miller described as a very school-marmish lady whose manner and too-perfect English brought to mind the quintessential British nanny. One of the books she reviewed for her young audience was *The Sheep Pig*, by the British children's author Dick King-Smith. She told her listeners that the book had won a prize and then began to tell its story. It was about a young orphan pig called Babe, who lived on a farm and wanted to become a sheepdog. But the woman was unable to make it through the story without bursting into laughter at several points, which prompted Miller to think that she was not just reading someone else's review of the story, but had actually read the book herself. Her reaction to it intrigued Miller, who noted its title in order to buy it when he arrived in London. When he did, he was absolutely enchanted:

> *I love the story as much for its subtext as for its surface plot. It's about prejudice on a farm where each animal has his preordained place. Into this biased world comes a pig with an unprejudiced heart who takes all the other creatures at face value, and by treating the sheep and all the other animals as equals, he irrevocably changes their lives and becomes world champion sheepdog in the process.*[2]

It had taken King-Smith only three weeks to write the book in 1983, despite his somewhat low-tech approach of writing longhand in pencil in the morning and typing the results out on an ancient portable typewriter with one finger in the afternoon. For twenty years before he took up writing at age fifty-five, King-Smith had been a farmer. The inspiration for *The Sheep Pig* had come during a local village fair, where each year, according to tradition, a small piglet is given away as a prize to the person who most accurately guesses its weight. For King-Smith, this had suggested the idea of somebody winning a pig at such a fair, but then deciding it would not be destined for the deep freeze but for higher things.[3] The resulting book, sold in Great Britain as *The Sheep Pig* and in the United States as *Babe the Gallant Pig,* won a host of awards, including the 1984 Guardian Children's Fiction Award in Great Britain and the Horn Book Award from the *Boston Globe* in 1985.

Within a few months of that British Airways flight, George Miller had contacted Dick King-Smith's agents in London and negotiated an option to buy the worldwide film rights to the book. Because the plot involved many animals talking, there was no competition for the option, and Miller was able to acquire it at a very reasonable price. For a number of reasons, he wanted to avoid making the book into an animated film. For one thing, the animal characters were so realistic that he felt the story would work much better with live animals. Moreover, an animated film would immediately be labeled a children's movie, thus drastically reducing its potential audience. Since Miller believed the story would touch adults as well, he wanted the film to appeal to them, too. However, avoiding animation created a problem, for as he well knew, the computer graphics technology that could make animals appear to speak did not yet exist and, in fact, probably would not exist for another ten years or so. Worse, as Miller found out, most people doubted that it would *ever* exist:

> *Well there it was, 1986 and I had this wonderful book and everybody—I mean everybody—told me it could never be made into a movie. . . . But that little pig, the story of that little guy trying to do something out of the goodness of his heart but being jeered by the prejudiced animals and people who wouldn't let him do dog things, well, the damned spirit of the thing sort of drove me somehow.*[4]

Sensing that the movie, if it were ever to be made with live animals, would need a particularly talented director—someone endowed with vast reserves of patience (more, according to Miller, than he himself possessed) and an eye for detail—Miller got in touch with Chris Noonan, an Australian director he had worked with before. Before long, Noonan also became hooked by the project:

> *I took the book away and read it, and was very moved by the story. I laughed a lot while I was reading it, and when I finished I had tears in my eyes. And that seemed sort of crazy to me: that a whimsical story about a pig should make a grown man cry. I read an average of a script a day, and when you are reading that much material you become quite resistant, and it takes something really getting under your skin for you to treat it seriously. When something does, it stands out quite strongly. So I looked deeper into the story and saw that it was more than just a simple hero's story of success—it had a lot of layers of meaning in it.*
>
> *After talking about the book with George, we discussed the prospects of making a movie from it. He was very much in favor of using digital animation as the only technique, but that was a very fledgling industry at the time. The techniques were rudimentary, and there were no guarantees that the movie could be made with them. We were both very intrigued with the idea of making animals talk for real on the screen and felt that this would really create a stir. Somehow the sheer impossibility of it all made me very attracted to it.*[5]

This was the difficulty that Miller and Noonan faced. The film would not work unless the animals *really* appeared to be speaking and interacting with each other. Another six years would have to pass before the two critical technologies would be in place. The first was *animatronics*, in which real animals are simulated by computer-controlled puppet doubles made of rubber. Animatronics were necessary when the animal characters had to make facial expressions that real animals could not make, for scenes where the camera was pulled back from the animals and their trainers could not get close enough to control them, and for several scenes where real animals might have been hurt or killed. The second technology was *digital photography and image processing*, in which, after a live animal had been filmed, special-effects artists could erase the animal's mouth and digitally create a new one that would speak in time with the actor's voiceover and would be seamlessly "morphed" into the animal's face. The eyes and eyebrows would also be altered to mimic those of humans when they speak.

In 1988, however, the first step for Miller and Noonan was to write a script. At first, they met every day and talked through every aspect of the story and its characters. Two new animal characters were added: Ferdinand the Duck for comic relief, and Rex the Sheepdog to add a little tension. After about three months, the two men had developed a tentative scene-by-scene breakdown of the movie on a big chart on the wall. At this point, Noonan went away and wrote the first draft of a script. When he had finished, he and Miller got back together and worked through it once more, considering carefully what wouldn't work and what would. Then Noonan went away again and wrote the second draft. This process went on continuously for about four years; it took about twenty drafts before he and Miller were satisfied. In mid-1989, the pair began to approach studios for financing. They knew the movie was too expensive for them to find the financing in Australia. It would have to be funded by one of the major American studios. Although all these studios expressed initial interest in the project, their interest declined rapidly during the evaluation process as they discovered just how uncertain a venture such a movie would be. Chris Noonan told us why:

> *It was a pretty radical concept, and an extraordinarily risky project in that it had every ingredient known to go wrong with movies. It had animals, special effects, and all of the shooting was outdoors, and so subject to the weather and the seasons.*[6]

In the end, only Universal Pictures was left. And it almost pulled out just before shooting began.

Even with funding and the appropriate technology, the movie still represented a formidable challenge. Sixty animal trainers were required for the 970 animals involved. The starring role alone was played by not just one pig, but *forty-eight,* each raised from birth by the film's trainers. The reason for this was that today's pigs are bred to grow so fast that they could be filmed only between the ages of sixteen and eighteen weeks. The thirteen-week training regimen for the porcine actresses (the private parts of male pigs proved too visible) began when they were two weeks old. By eighteen weeks, they had outgrown their "cute" stage. Furthermore, each pig had different acting strengths—some were better at sitting still, others at standing or running—so they had to be raised in batches of six, three weeks apart. But in the end, producer George Miller and director Chris Noonan managed to pull off the biggest Australian production ever. By April 1996, the movie had taken in more than $63 million at the box office. *Babe* also won a Golden Globe award for the best comedy, was named the best film of 1995 by the U.S. National Society of Film Critics, and was nominated for seven Academy Awards. Dick King-Smith, who had declined to be involved with the movie because his fear of airplanes effectively precluded travel to Australia, saw the film for the first time at a preview in London in August 1995 with his wife. And both found it convincing:

> *The crux of the whole thing, of course, was to get these animals to open their mouths and speak, or apparently to speak. Although we knew all the facts of the matter, my wife and I hadn't been in our seats more than a few minutes before we were able to persuade ourselves of the surreal idea that as well as teaching all these animals to do all the clever tricks and movements that they did, they had actually taught them to speak as well.*[7]

Nine years before, it had been the laughter and speech inflections of an anonymous reviewer on a British Airways in-flight audio entertainment channel that had caught George Miller's attention. It had alerted him to a story that captured his imagination and set him off on a long and risky journey to produce an unusual movie. The telling question, however, is this. Had another film producer been listening to the same channel on that flight, would the reviewer's voice have had the same effect on him or her?

Thirty-Four Days to Paint a Cadillac?

George Miller was provoked into doing something entirely new. But a stimulus can also be important to a company that already knows what it is looking for, because it can provoke a person into a different and more successful approach to an existing problem.

In the early 1920s, General Motors certainly had a problem—it desperately needed to change the way it painted cars.[8] Actually, all the automobile companies were in the same fix—it took an incredibly long time to paint a car any color other than black. At GM, the average time was three weeks. A Cadillac could take up to thirty-four days. The resulting problems with work-in-process inventory alone were staggering. In his book *My Years with General Motors*, CEO Alfred Sloan wrote that even at the relatively slow rate of production in those days, about a thousand automobiles per day, GM had to maintain some *twenty acres* of covered indoor space for painting.[9] But this bottleneck was actually not the worst of the problems GM had with paint. Even with careful application, its paints would begin to peel off rapidly, sometimes within weeks of leaving the factory. As far as the customer was concerned, a shoddy paint job was just as bad as a poor engine or mechanical problems. Complaints from customers poured in, and it appeared that the company could do nothing about them.

The root cause of the problem was that when automobiles came along, manufacturers simply continued to paint them in exactly the same way in which horse-drawn carriages had always been painted. Unfortunately, what had worked for carriages did not work for cars. The paint could not withstand the changes in temperature caused by the heat of the engine. Moreover, an automobile's paint job took far greater abuse than a carriage's. For the high-volume and cheaper cars, such as the Chevrolet, manufacturers used baked black enamel, the only cheap and moderately durable finish then available. (This fact is what occasioned Henry Ford's famous remark that his customers could have any color car they wanted as long as it was black.) Alfred Sloan was convinced that if General Motors could find a way to paint its automobiles economically with colored paint that would last, customers would line up to buy them. The problem was that such a paint job required the application by hand of five coats over a period of weeks, as well as further touch-ups, also by hand—and even then, the color lacked luster and the paint soon began to peel. Furthermore, Sloan wanted to pursue a very different strategy from Henry Ford's. He wanted a way to release many models of car that were essentially the same, but styled and finished differently, and his strategy depended on the use of color.

As if this were not enough, GM had one more compelling reason to solve its paint problem. Carriages had normally been garaged to protect them from the elements. Many people at GM were coming to realize that a "garageless car" would revolutionize the market. As Pierre du Pont (whose company owned 33 percent of GM at this time) put it to Charles Kettering, GM's head of research and development:

> *A closed car covered with weather proof material . . . could be left at the door at any time, thus proving much more useful to the average owner of a small car than the apparatus which must be carefully housed against the weather.*[10]

To which Kettering answered that the real challenge to manufacturing such a car was "largely a question of paints."

For all these reasons, the pressure was on at GM to find a way to paint vehicles durably and rapidly in various appealing colors. What happened next at GM became one of Charles Kettering's favorite stories about creativity.[11] As he tells it, Kettering called a meeting to which he invited a number of paint suppliers, some paint chemists, and some of GM's own painters. He asked the group what could be done to reduce the time it took to paint an automobile. Very little, was the consensus of the experts, since the paint had to be allowed time to dry.

"Isn't there any way to do the painting more quickly?" asked Kettering.

"Not without ruining the paint." However, after some discussion, the group decided that it might be possible to cut one or two days out of the time.

Someone asked Kettering, "How long do you think it ought to take to paint an automobile?"

His reply stunned the group, "One hour would be about right. . . . Well, why couldn't you?"

"Because the paint won't dry."

"Can't something be done to make the paint dry faster?"

"Not a thing in the world," was the reply. "Nature fixes that."

As Kettering left the meeting he heard someone mutter that he should be put back in the corner where he belonged—and left there. But that didn't stop him. GM had to paint its cars, and Kettering needed to find a way to do it properly.

Not long afterward, Kettering found himself in New York. Having some free time, he went window-shopping on Fifth Avenue. In the window of a jewelry store he saw a small painted pin-tray that had been finished with a new sort of lacquer. He bought one and asked where it had been made. He went to see the person who had made it, and asked him where he had obtained the lacquer. He was given the name and address of someone in New Jersey. Kettering went there and found him making lacquer in a little shed in his backyard. He asked if he could buy a quart of it.

"My goodness, I've never made a quart of lacquer before. What do you want to do with it?"

"I want to paint an automobile door with it."

"You can't do that. This lacquer dries almost instantly. If you put it in one of your spray guns, it will dry and blow away as dust before it ever reaches the car door."

"Can't you do anything to slow it down?" Kettering asked.

"Not a thing in the world," the lacquer maker replied.

And there, as Kettering put it, he had the two extremes. But now, at least, the path was clear. It would take two and a half years of intensive experimentation before GM and Du Pont researchers were able to formulate a lacquer that really worked. This lacquer, called "Duco," quickly came to dominate the market for automobile finishes. In 1925, the first year Du Pont put it on the market, the company sold more than a million gallons at five dollars per gallon. Sales doubled in 1926, yielding Du Pont a profit of $3 million. By 1929, Duco accounted for some 12 percent of the company's profits. In *My Years with General Motors*, Alfred Sloan summed up what the new lacquer had done for his industry:

> *Duco, by reducing the cost of color finishes and increasing enormously the range of color that could be economically applied to cars, made possible the modern era of color and styling. Furthermore, its quick drying removed the most important remaining bottleneck in mass production, and made possible an enormously accelerated rate of production of car bodies.*[12]

For his part, Charles Kettering could not resist the temptation of playing a friendly practical joke on one of the paint suppliers who had been a naysayer at the original meeting. Shortly after Duco had been successfully tested, this man came over to have lunch with Kettering. When he came into the office, Kettering happened to have a color card lying on his desk, with samples of all the different colors available in the prototype Duco.

"Joe," said Kettering, "if you were going to have your car refinished, what color would you pick?" After a moment of thought, the man picked out a color, and he and Kettering went to lunch.

When the pair returned, they talked for a while in Kettering's office. As Joe got up to leave, he glanced out the window. "Somebody's taken my car! It's gone!"

"Nobody took your car," said Kettering. "We just refinished it for you while you were at lunch. You said that was the color you wanted, didn't you?"

When Companies Identify the Stimuli

Many companies have formal programs to bring diverse stimuli to their employees. One company that has done more than most is Hallmark, the largest greeting card company in the world. Much of what Hallmark does is not so unusual and happens at other companies too. For example, the company's Creative Resource Center maintains a library of some twenty thousand books on a wide range of topics and 150 magazines ranging from *Architectural Digest* to *Wired*. Its Visiting Lecture Series brings in an interesting roster of speakers from all walks of life. And a monthly newsletter from the company's Creativity Resource Center keeps Hallmark employees informed about upcoming art shows, exhibits, and new books.

However, Hallmark does other things which set it apart from most companies as far as diverse stimuli are concerned. It offers a program of sabbaticals within its Creative Division, whose staff of more than seven hundred artists and writers create some thirty thousand new cards and related products each year. Sabbaticals are common in colleges and universities, but they are relatively rare in the corporate world. Where they do exist, they are usually meant to give employees time for community service or personal renewal.[13] Sabbaticals at Hallmark, on the other hand, are intended primarily for *creative renewal*. One type of sabbatical gives selected artists and designers the chance to spend four months exploring a new artistic skill. Leaving their regular work behind, the team members relocate to one of several studios in Hallmark's Rice Innovation Center. Whether or not their explorations of new areas such as pottery, papermaking, or computer graphics lead to new products, the participants do return to their regular work not only feeling renewed but with a fresh creative perspective.

Another type of sabbatical is run by the company's Creative Advisory Group. This group's mission is to identify and follow sociological, psychological, and technical trends that might have an impact on the company's future, and to bring these trends to the attention of management and creative staff in as effective a way as possible. Twice a year, the three or four staff members who are selected for this sabbatical program leave their regular work units and join the Creative Advisory Group, where they stay for six months. Here, they work on a group project and a personal one. The group project is to study a particular topic or trend and to make a video on its implications for the company. Ultimately, this video is seen by hundreds of the creative staff as well as top management.

We asked Clar Evans, director of the Creative Advisory Group, how this type of sabbatical got started. She told us that it began in 1990, when she was bedridden for several weeks at home with pneumonia. Out of curiosity, at one point, she turned to MTV, a channel she had never watched before. Maybe a twenty-year-old would not have been startled at what she saw, but Evans wasn't twenty, she was in her late fifties. MTV set her to thinking about Generation X, about its implications for Hallmark's business, and about how she might best communicate this to her company. The answer to this last question, she realized, was obvious—a video. The resulting video on Generation X was very successful and became the first of nine that would be produced between 1991 and 1996. Other topics included angels, long-term illnesses, masculinity, spirituality, and ethnicity, every one of which had implications for the company. As part of the ethnicity project, for example, the four team members read books and articles, interviewed experts, went to folk festivals, and made field trips to ethnic neighborhoods in different cities.

The personal projects on the Creative Advisory Group sabbaticals are selected by the individual team members themselves. For example, one member of the ethnicity group decided to study something she knew little about: African American quilts. Evans told us that she privately had her doubts that this topic would lead anywhere. But when the team member visited collectors, museums, and people who made such quilts, she learned that African American quilts are very different from their more well-known European counterparts, which tend to use tight and highly repetitive patterns. Far from leading nowhere, Evans told us, this project discovered how the use of color and pattern in African American quilts was

> *alive with the inspiration of people who had few resources.*[14]

Both this personal project and the team project on ethnicity had a direct effect on Hallmark's greeting card business. According to one creative writer at the company, the projects clearly indicated that Hallmark did not need

> *a special line for Native Americans, and another for Laotians. Putting a multicultural focus in existing lines—as long as we didn't water it down too much—would do what we wanted.*[15]

These sabbatical projects also led to the introduction of a new product line, "Symbolic Notions" jewelry, based on the ethnic and multicultural symbols discovered by the team during their sabbatical.[16] Clearly, Hallmark can point to some creative outcomes sparked by its sabbatical programs.

Stimuli Arise from the Work Itself

While companies should do all they can to identify and provide diverse stimuli to their employees, they should recognize that such efforts have their limitations. Certainly, programs like those at Hallmark are refreshing and create a positive climate for creativity. However, they have one obvious drawback: there is no way to know in advance how a particular person will respond to a given stimulus. Just because a person is stimulated does not mean that he or she will then do something creative. How can companies possibly guess which stimuli will work? The real challenge is in relating the stimuli to the work of the organization.

While sabbaticals can be effective in developing capacity for change, it is important to recognize that they necessarily have limited reach. Even Hallmark can provide them to only about 10 percent of its workforce—most often people from its creative division. Furthermore, during their sabbaticals, these people are removed from their regular work environment and put into an environment that the company believes will be likely to provide stimuli. But most stimuli that lead to creative acts arise in connection with the work itself—in fact, the nature of work means that it is alive with diverse stimuli. Think back to Roy Plunkett and the way he discovered Teflon. It is likely that the tetrafluoroethylene gas had polymerized in many of his cylinders. Given his alertness, if he hadn't made his discovery with that particular cylinder, he would have made it with another one. He couldn't get *away* from the stimuli that led him to his creative act. But would he have discovered Teflon if he had removed himself from the workplace and sat in front of a blackboard pondering the future of inert materials? The real challenge faced by programs designed to deliver stimuli to employees is to relate those stimuli to actual work in a meaningful way.

We believe that rather than focusing on *devising* and *delivering* stimuli to a select few employees outside of their normal work, it is more important for a company to recognize that most stimuli that lead to creative acts will be found by the employees themselves. And when they are, it is important that employees should have the opportunity to bring these stimuli into the organization and put them to use. Both George Miller and Charles Kettering had clout in their organizations. Given the "right" stimulus, they were clearly in a position to make things happen, and both men did. But most stimuli will be received by front-line employees, who are not so empowered. The real problem for a company is to be open to these stimuli as well, and to exploit them whenever and wherever they occur. Unless stimuli are acted upon, they have no relevance to the company. Employees may receive stimuli from customers or, even if they never see a customer, directly from the work itself. We now turn to examples of these two types of diverse stimuli. It is hard to think how a corporate program of any kind could have provided either one. However, both of the organizations involved had a time and a place where the employee who received the stimulus could bring it up for informal discussion with others and describe the possibilities it suggested.

Banquets at the Imperial

Since it was opened in 1890 to provide luxury Western-style accommodations for foreigners, the Imperial Hotel in Tokyo has become one of the most prestigious hotels in the world. Located next to the Imperial Palace, it has been at the center of a number of historic events. Its second building (designed by Frank Lloyd Wright) opened on September 1, 1923, the day the Great Kanto Earthquake destroyed most of Tokyo. Except, fortunately enough, for the newly opened Imperial Hotel. Reporters from around the world who rushed to Tokyo to cover the earthquake had nowhere else to stay. For the new hotel, this resulted in unparalleled publicity. All the foreign reporters' dispatches had the Imperial Hotel byline, and many of their articles mentioned that the Imperial was "the only place" to stay in Tokyo, which, literally, it was.[17] During the postwar Occupation, General MacArthur's top officials lived in the hotel. Today, when historic events (such as Emperor Hirohito's funeral) bring foreign leaders to Tokyo, they are most likely to stay at the Imperial. And the quality of service at the hotel is largely determined by its roughly two thousand front-line employees. From the front doorman to the chambermaids, these employees interact with customers on a daily basis and are in a unique position to know their needs and desires. Their work is alive with stimuli that can lead to creative acts, and the hotel can never predict which employee will receive one.

One Imperial Hotel waiter serving at a banquet found himself in just that position when he happened to overhear a conversation between two guests, who were talking about an upcoming college reunion. Unlike the United States, where such reunions are held only on major anniversaries (such as at the ten- or twenty-year mark), in Japan, reunions are held annually and are usually very well attended. Overhearing this conversation set the waiter to thinking that such reunions might be a worthwhile new business activity for the Imperial. He had the opportunity to bring up his idea at the regular weekly meeting of his section. Since most reunions are organized by a class volunteer, the problem was to come up with a way to make the process as painless as possible for the organizer. The waiter suggested a clever solution. If the hotel charged nine thousand yen per person (about ninety dollars), it would make the job of the party organizer easy: all that he or she would have to do would be to collect a ten-thousand-yen bill from each attendee, and after paying the Imperial for catering the event, there would be just the right amount left over for incidental expenses. The Imperial Hotel introduced the new service in July 1993, and it was an instant success. In the first two months alone, the response was almost *four times* greater than expected, bringing in some $600,000 in revenue.

The job of the waiter at the Imperial Hotel was to interact with customers, but diverse stimuli can arise in connection with any aspect of work. Consider this example from Johnson Controls' FoaMech plant, the plant described in Chapter Three whose *kaizen* program had 100 percent participation in 1996.

Can We Really Be Wasting All This?

As is common in large American manufacturing operations, FoaMech encouraged its employees to form "employee involvement teams" to work on opportunities for improvement. In October 1995, six third-shift employees in the packing department decided to form their own team: the "Night Owls." The team elected Michelle Johnson as its president, which was fitting in hindsight because she would initiate its first idea. Early one morning in December, as Johnson was sweeping up at the end of her shift, she came across several nuts and bolts lying on the ground next to a machine. These set her to thinking. She knew they were expensive, and that if she hadn't picked them up, they might well have been thrown out later. She realized that many useful things were often left lying around the plant, or were simply thrown away as people left for the day. She began to wonder just how much all these wasted odds and ends were costing her company.

At the first meeting of the Night Owls after the Christmas break, Johnson told her colleagues what she had been thinking. After some discussion, the group decided to conduct a simple experiment. For one month, the Night Owls would collect all the useful abandoned odds and ends they came across in their own department, the restrooms and locker rooms, and the passageways in and out of the plant. As a team, they would track the results and see if the opportunity was worth pursuing any further.

The Night Owls were very surprised at the quantity of material caught in their net. Not only did they fill up their own lockers, but Johnson had to ask the coordinator of FoaMech's employee involvement teams if the team could store the overflow in her office. The team found everything from partially used rolls of tape, permanent markers, nuts and bolts, and single gloves to Exacto knives, C-clamps, brass fittings, and pneumatic hoses. A good example of the pervasive nature of the waste was provided by the "listing wires." Recall that the FoaMech plant makes car seats. Most car seat cushions consist of a skeleton of reinforcing wires baked into polyurethane foam, and listing wires are the bones of these skeletons. Understandably, the FoaMech plant is a big user of them. Listing wires are straight pieces of wire between ten and twelve inches long. FoaMech buys them precut in packs of one hundred, with each pack costing $16.95. One night, on a trip to the bathroom, Michelle Johnson found *sixty-five* of them. It turned out that many employees carried listing wires in their pockets, in order to have them at hand as they worked. But when they went to the bathroom, or changed out of their work clothes at the end of their shift, the listing wires got in the way, so they would take them out and put them aside, or even throw them away.

The items that the Night Owls found during their one-month experiment were only an underestimate of what was actually being lost, because, like the listing wires, many items were simply being thrown away as people left the plant, or else they were being taken out of the plant and not brought back. Employees who happened to walk out of the plant with twelve-inch wires in their pockets, for example, would quickly remember them when they climbed into their cars and got a sharp jab. They would put the wires on the dashboard or the floor and might eventually throw them out or toss them into a box in their garage and forget about them. The employees were not stealing, since none of what was disappearing was being taken intentionally. Cumulatively, however, the daily losses added up.

At the end of the month-long trial period, the team had all the evidence it needed. It sent in the following idea to the FoaMech Kaizen Program: put fluorescent yellow boxes (a color that would not interfere with facility's fire and safety color-coding scheme) around the plant and at the exits, with prominent signs asking employees to check their pockets and empty any useful odds and ends into them. At the end of each shift, team leaders and supervisors would be responsible for emptying the box and returning the items to their proper places. The idea was approved, and savings were estimated at $27,000 per year.

Helping Employees to Find Diverse Stimuli

In addition to providing opportunities for employees to bring stimuli they find into the organization, a company can influence the set of stimuli employees are exposed to, because these depend on which jobs people do. By rotating people into jobs they would not normally do, the company exposes them to more diverse stimuli. One company that has recognized the value of this, for its senior executives at least, is Xerox.

Although Japanese copier companies began to challenge Xerox in the mid-1970s, it was not until 1979 that its management began to wake up to the threat. By the time it did, Xerox was in deep trouble. In 1983, still struggling, it launched the Leadership Through Quality initiative. Putting top management in touch with the company's real problems was central to this effort. One way this was done was through the Customer Care Day program for the top forty Xerox executives, including the CEO. Every day, one of these executives is designated the duty officer and is responsible for answering and resolving any customer complaints that come into headquarters that day. The switchboard operators have a calendar listing the duty officer for each day and are instructed to route all customer complaints directly to that executive, if necessary calling him or her out of a meeting to answer the telephone. With roughly twenty business days per month, this means that each of these top executives spends one day every two months as a duty officer. When the program started, Xerox received a large number of calls each month, and duty officers could look forward to spending their entire day answering one call after another. But over the years, as Xerox's quality initiatives began to take effect, the number of calls dropped off dramatically.

How much of a stimulus can interacting with customers be? Very important, as one Xerox story illustrates. In 1988, not long before he became CEO of Xerox, Paul Allaire issued what he thought was a bold challenge to the company: offer a ninety-day money-back guarantee on all Xerox products. A team was formed to study and develop the idea. This team went to a number of customers to ask their opinion of it. Bad idea, the customers said—everything was wrong with it. First, when they bought Xerox products, they expected them to work for more than ninety days. A guarantee for *nine hundred days* would be more reasonable. Second, if for some reason the product didn't work, the customers wanted Xerox to *fix* the problem, not give them a refund and walk away. Most of them had to go through a laborious purchasing process to buy the equipment in the first place, and none of them wanted to have to redo all the paperwork to order their equipment from another company. They felt that once they had made the decision to go with Xerox, the company should view itself as their partner. Also, the customers wanted the guarantee in plain English, not in language that had to be sent to their legal department for translation. In short, Paul Allaire's challenge would have taken Xerox in the wrong direction. Instead, in 1990, after listening to its customers, Xerox announced an industry first: its Total Satisfaction Guarantee. Essentially it said this:

> *For the first three years that you own a Xerox machine, or for as long as it is financed by Xerox, if for any reason you are unhappy, let us know and we will replace it free of charge.*[18]

Clearly, diverse stimuli are important for all employees, and a company can influence the breadth of their exposure to them.

How to Promote Diverse Stimuli

We believe there are four strategies a company can use to promote diverse stimuli:

1. Identify stimuli and provide them to employees.
2. Rotate employees into every job they are capable of doing.
3. Arrange for employees to interact with those outside the company who are likely to be the source of stimuli.
4. Create opportunities for employees to bring into the organization stimuli they get on their own.

While organizations should do everything they can to identify and provide diverse stimuli to all their employees, it should be recognized that such efforts will have relatively little impact. Programs of visiting lecturers and other special events, extensive libraries, and interesting newsletters may well stimulate new thinking and renewal, and they will certainly create a positive climate for creativity. However, we do not know of a *single* instance where programs such as these actually led to an improvement or an innovation. The problem is that it is impossible to predict how anyone will react to a particular stimulus—what provokes one person may not even be noticed by another. How can a company possibly know what will work? A low "hit rate" is only to be expected. The story is somewhat different for more open-ended kinds of programs like study leaves and sabbaticals. Since employees have a say in what will be explored, they will be more receptive to any stimuli they receive and better able to relate them to their work. Remember the team of Hallmark designers that developed a new line of greeting cards and jewelry as a result of a sabbatical studying ethnicity?

We believe that study leaves and sabbaticals are a good strategy. However, most companies will find it difficult to provide these opportunities for more than a few employees at a time. A different approach is needed to help *every* employee find more stimuli. Such an approach has to be based on the work itself. After all, most of the stimuli that lead to creative acts are already in the workplace, and *everyone* works. To bring the largest number of people in contact with the greatest number of stimuli, an organization should rotate its employees into every job they are capable of doing. And when employees are rotated into other jobs, they often notice stimuli that others before them had not.

Diverse stimuli can also come from customers and all those who work on behalf of an organization: its suppliers, dealers, franchisees, distributors, and anyone who provides independent field service for its products. All these people are close to some aspect of what the company does and represent an excellent source of stimuli. Any opportunities a company can make for its employees to interact with them could well lead to creative acts. Xerox's Customer Care Day is one example of a program that requires senior managers to hear customer complaints for themselves.

But a stimulus has no real relevance for a company until it is acted on. As the head of research at GM, Charles Kettering had no trouble bringing the stimulus he received back to the company and acting on it. But most stimuli are received by employees who are not in powerful positions in their organizations, and they will need help to bring their thoughts to the attention of others. A company has to create regular opportunities for all employees to bring up ideas for informal discussion even when the ideas have no bearing on anything else under consideration. When Michelle Johnson, the third-shift employee at Johnson Controls, started thinking about the leftover nuts and bolts she had found, there was a natural forum for her to bring up her idea: the next meeting of her employee involvement team. At the Imperial Hotel, all it took for management to take advantage of the stimulus the waiter received from a customer was an opportunity in the weekly staff meeting for him to bring up the conversation he had overheard and to describe the possibilities it suggested to him.

MAIN POINTS

A stimulus can either push someone in a completely new direction or give that person fresh insight into what he or she has already set out to do.

Diverse stimuli bumped George Miller, the producer of the movie Babe, *into new activity and led Charles Kettering of General Motors to solve his company's paint problem.*

The majority of stimuli that lead to corporate creativity arise in connection with the work itself.

Overhearing a conversation between two customers led a waiter at the Imperial Hotel to suggest a profitable new line of business for the company.

What serves as a powerful stimulus for one person—for whatever reason—may not even be noticed by someone else.

If a producer other than George Miller had been listening to the audio channel on that British Airways flight, would the reviewer's voice have had the same effect on him or her?

There are four strategies companies can use to promote diverse stimuli:

1. *Identify stimuli and provide them to employees.*
2. *Rotate employees into every job they are capable of doing.*
3. *Arrange for employees to interact with those outside the company who are likely to be the source of stimuli.*
4. *Create opportunities for employees to bring into the organization stimuli they get on their own.*

Chapter Eleven

WITHIN-COMPANY COMMUNICATION

The failure of large organizations in America to innovate is primarily the result of a communication gap, not a decline in ingenuity.

ROBERT ROSENFELD AND JENNY SERVO[1]
Robert Rosenfeld is the founder of Kodak's Office of Innovation.

Many things that seem to happen naturally at smaller companies do not happen so easily at larger ones. One of the most important of these is the sixth element of corporate creativity: *within-company communication*. Every organization carries out activities that are planned and should establish the necessary lines of communication to support them. But these official channels are of limited usefulness for corporate creativity. The majority of creative acts in companies are unplanned and bring together components from unexpected places. If communication occurs only through established channels, the employees who know about these components but who do not normally communicate with each other will never interact. It is precisely these unanticipated exchanges of information—exchanges that allow projects that have not been planned to self-organize—that occur much more easily in smaller companies. The larger the company, the more likely the components of potential creative acts are already present somewhere in it, but the less likely they will be brought together without some help. We believe that a company's creative potential increases rapidly with its size, but that without systems in place to promote unanticipated exchanges of information, this potential will never be realized. Worse, the assumption will continue to be made that creativity can only happen in smaller companies.

Unanticipated exchanges of information can also be important for a creative act that the company *has* targeted, if the right ingredients were not anticipated at the outset. Creativity is often a messy process, even when a company does vaguely anticipate it. Nevertheless, within-company communication can enable an otherwise unwieldy mess to self-organize and move forward. Sometimes, different employees in scattered departments each have a piece of the puzzle, and until they find each other, nothing at all will happen. The story of how Scotchgard was discovered at 3M provides an interesting example of this.

My Shoes Are Ruined

In 1944, Joseph H. Simons, a professor at Pennsylvania State University, approached 3M for funding to continue work on a process he had invented to make fluorochemicals. At the time, these chemicals were brand-new and hardly anything was known about them, except that they had a very unusual property—they were completely incompatible with all known materials. In other words, a fluorochemical would only mix with other fluorochemicals and could only evolve in other fluorochemicals. Both 3M's chairman of the board, William McKnight, and its president, Richard Carlton, were intrigued by these new fluorinated compounds, and after some negotiations, 3M ended up buying the rights to Simons's process. A group was formed in 3M's central research laboratory to see what might come of them. By 1949, the company had committed fully *one-quarter* of its corporate research budget to the new chemicals, an astonishing gamble given that no one was yet able to point to even one potential commercial application for any of them. Top management could be forgiven for occasionally having second thoughts about continuing. However, something about these strange chemicals continued to pique the interest of 3M researchers and management. Even the chemical by-products of Simons's process were studied, but these had no apparent uses either. Worse, they cost about forty dollars per pound to produce, which made them, according to Charles Walton, then 3M's vice president of R&D,

just about the most expensive organic chemicals known to man.[2]

In April 1949, anticipating a board meeting where he expected some tough questions about the company's continuing major commitment to fluorochemicals, Carlton called a meeting of all the researchers in this area. He asked each person to answer three questions:

1. Why are you working on fluorochemicals?
2. Do you feel good about this line of research?
3. What useful products might come out of it?

According to Hugh Bryce, who had joined the company as a young researcher just a few weeks earlier:

Mr. Carlton got an earful about the first two questions, because researchers were enthusiastic about these chemicals. But he didn't learn very much about any useful products 3M might make from them. . . . I don't really think at this point he was trying to figure out whether or not the project would be successful. But he obviously got the idea that we were a bunch of creative people, and that the chemicals we were working on were new and exciting. [3]

At about this time, the fluorochemical research group received a needed boost when it was awarded a contract by the U.S. Air Force to develop a completely new synthetic fluorochemical rubber for use in jet aircraft. The jet engine, which had been invented during World War II, had become a major headache for the Air Force. Each engine required fifteen hundred rubber seals and hoses, and no known rubber could stand up to hot jet fuel for more than about fifty hours of operation. Even though the Air Force used the best rubber then available, the jet fuels would quite literally eat it. After the war, the Air Force pushed hard to make jet aircraft more practical so they could be widely used, possibly even for commercial flights. But unless the problem with seals and hoses could be solved, this vision would never be realized. Tetrafluoroethylene (Teflon), which belonged to the class of fluorochemicals 3M was working with, would have been perfect except that it lacked the elastic properties needed for an effective seal. The Air Force contract was very large; at its peak it supported roughly half of 3M's fluorochemical research effort.

Some 3M researchers were beginning to see another potential application for the new fluorochemicals—as a treatment for paper or fabric to make it oil- and water-repellent. Because these chemicals do not mix with organic solvents and oils, materials impregnated with them might resist oily stains. Their incompatibility with water meant that they could also resist water-based stains, such as those from coffee, tea, or soft drinks. The first product that worked, and worked well for this purpose, was a fluorochemical compound based on chromium. Its only drawback was that it turned everything green. Clearly, it would have a very limited market. 3M would have to do better. By 1952, the company was making serious efforts to eliminate the green color from the chromium compound but was meeting with no success.

However, in mid-July of 1953, nine years after 3M first began experimenting with the exotic and recalcitrant fluorochemicals, a mishap occurred in the laboratory that changed the direction of this research completely.[4] JoAn Mullin was a young research chemist who had joined 3M in 1952, immediately after graduating from college, and had been assigned to the Air Force project. One day she was performing a viscosity test on a very dilute, water-based suspension of fluorochemical rubber particles known as polyperfluorobutyl acrylate, or poly-FBA, for short. As she stood pouring her sample from a beaker into a volumetric flask (to measure its volume), Mullin accidentally spilled three tiny drops onto her brand-new cotton deck shoes. The largest drop was only three-sixteenths of an inch in diameter, and the other two were even smaller. By the time she had finished pouring the beaker into the flask and found a tissue to wipe the spots off, it was too late—they had already sunk into the brand-new cotton. By the end of the day, the spots had dried and disappeared entirely. JoAn Mullin forgot all about them.

Until the weekend, that is. The spill had happened early in the week, and Mullin was in the habit of soaking her shoes in water and laundry soap every Saturday so they would be clean for the following week. This Saturday, however, as she put them in the water, the spots on her shoes *reappeared!* The light blue color of her shoes darkened when the cloth became wet, except for the tiny spots, which remained light blue because they stayed dry. As Mullin observed to us, several things could have kept her from making what would turn out to be a key discovery for 3M:

If I hadn't been standing, the drops wouldn't have fallen on my shoe. They would have fallen on the bench that I had been sitting at. If it hadn't been blue cloth, or a cloth that changed color when it got wet, I don't know whether I would have noticed anything when washing them.[5]

On Monday, July 20, Mullin told her colleagues about what had happened and recorded in her lab notebook that the spots had not come out in the wash. She was aware of work going on elsewhere in the central research laboratories on oil- and water-repellent treatments, knew that it had been stymied so far, and suspected that she had found a possible answer to the problem. In 1953, there was no durable way to treat fabric to make it waterproof, although within a few years silicone would became available to waterproof rainwear. Dry cleaners did offer a paraffin wax treatment that supposedly made rainwear waterproof, but since the wax rubbed off easily and washed out quickly in the rain, the garments did not remain waterproof for long. Mullin's excitement at the possibilities represented by these three tiny drops was certainly justified.

The seven-month period following the spill was difficult for Mullin, as she tried unsuccessfully to get others to pay attention to her idea. Every weekend for a month she washed her shoes, and still the spots remained light blue. Through repeated launderings with a strong household detergent, the drops of poly-FBA lost none of their ability to repel water. She often talked to her colleagues about what she had found, but none of them showed much interest. Her lab notebook for August 17, 1953, a month after the spill, reads, "Spots are still not wetting after five washes and scrubs." A week later, on August 24, her entry read, "Spots are still not wetting," with the sentence completed by her supervisor, George Rathmann, as follows: "as a result of poly-FBA being spilled on her shoes."

According to Mullin, Rathmann was the only member of her group who took her seriously. On his part, Rathmann remembers her coming to him many times about the spots on her shoes. Mullin wanted to have some formal tests done on the poly-FBA, but she felt that it would make a difference if Rathmann, rather than she, requested them. In the week of August 17, he dipped some swatches of blue-jean cloth into the dilute solution of poly-FBA, put them in an envelope, and went downstairs to see Hugh Bryce. He knew that Bryce, by now the head of the fluorochemical applications group in the New Products Division, had been charged with trying to develop commercial fluorochemical products, and that among other things his group was interested in finding a way to treat fabric to make it oil- and water-repellent. Rathmann handed Bryce the envelope of swatches, told him that they might one day prove valuable, and suggested that Bryce's group develop some tests for repellency and use them to test the swatches. Bryce agreed, and as Rathmann left he put the swatches in his desk drawer for safekeeping. Meanwhile, Mullin left a space in her lab notebook to insert the test results when they came back.

But it would still be some time before any tests were done. It turned out that no one in the fluorochemical group was very enthusiastic about testing anything with poly-FBA on it because it had already been tried and found not to work. Sometime afterward, George Rathmann's curiosity led him to go back and try to figure out why researchers in the fluorochemical group had been convinced that poly-FBA wouldn't work, when it so obviously did. It turned out that whoever had done the testing had been so sure that poly-FBA would not stick to fabric that he or she had primed the fabric with a second chemical before applying the poly-FBA to it, in order to make the fabric more receptive. What that person didn't realize, Rathmann discovered, was that the primer actually disrupted the surface characteristics of the fabric so much that it lost its ability to absorb any poly-FBA whatsoever.

For six months after she and Rathmann had handed the envelope over for testing, Mullin continued to wash her shoes every weekend, and still the spots remained as dry and light blue as ever when the fabric was wet. The final entry in her lab notebook on this subject was in February 1954. That month, she asked Rathmann if anything had ever come of the tests on the blue-jean swatches. "Oh, darn," said Rathmann, and immediately called Hugh Bryce to ask if someone would please take a look at the fabric swatches, since poly-FBA was better than anybody in Bryce's group thought it was. At this point, Mullin told us, she became so discouraged because 3M did not seem to be acting on her idea that she switched jobs and played no further role in what would become one of the most successful product lines in the history of the company. The space she left in her notebook for the test results was never filled in.

However, back in the fluorochemical group, George Rathmann's telephone call had had its effect. It so happened that the call came in just as one of Hugh Bryce's researchers, Bill Petersen, was looking for something interesting to work on. Nine months before, when he had returned from active duty as a reserve officer in the Korean War, he had been assigned temporarily to a project in ceramics, which had recently been wrapped up. In March 1954, seven months after the drops had been spilled, Hugh Bryce and Bill Petersen had a conversation in Bryce's office about what Petersen would work on next. Bryce pointed out that while people in the fluorochemical group were already working on oil- and water-repellent treatments for paper, no one was addressing such treatments for fabrics. Petersen was interested by this, and at one point in their talk, Bryce pulled out the envelope containing the blue-jean swatches and handed it over, suggesting that the swatches might be someplace for Petersen to begin.

One of the first problems Petersen faced was to design a test to measure a fabric's oil repellency. At the time, a scientific "spray test" for water repellency did exist, but there was no equivalent test for oil repellency, other than the unsatisfactory one of putting a drop of oil on the fabric and seeing whether or not it was absorbed. An objective and quantitative test for oil repellency was an obvious first step—it would give researchers clear indications of whether their efforts were moving in the right direction. Once Petersen had developed an embryonic oil-repellency test, he used it and the other available tests to evaluate Rathmann's and Mullin's swatches. And when he reported that poly-FBA seemed to have excellent potential as an oil and water repellent, his results shifted the line of 3M's search completely.

Almost overnight, the chromium-based approach that turned everything green was dropped. From now on, instead of ordinary chemical compounds, the company would look to polymers (long chains of molecules) like poly-FBA for its fabric treatments, and this approach would ultimately bring success. Almost a year after Mullin spilled the poly-FBA on her shoes, 3M went into high gear to develop commercially practical treatments for fabrics. Poly-FBA pointed toward the possibility of a treatment that could be applied in water, a far less expensive and more manageable process than the most obvious way to apply fluorochemicals: with exotic fluorochemical solvents. However, once the company began to study the requirements of its real-world customers—the textile mills and the end-use consumers—it quickly became clear that poly-FBA itself was not the answer. Nor, as it turned out, did poly-FBA ever work out as a synthetic rubber in jet engines. It had served a critical enabling role, but now events would leave it behind. As George Rathmann told us, it had been

> *a prototype in hindsight. Certainly an exciting prototype, but in reality, from a commercial standpoint, of virtually no interest at all.*[6]

Once the project became official, the subsequent research effort was intense and long-term, involving many people and hundreds of trial compounds. Two 3M chemists, Patsy Sherman and Samuel Smith, would be inducted into the Carlton Society (the company's elite society of inventors) for their pioneering work in polymer chemistry that ultimately led to the Scotchgard product line. Many formidable challenges had to be met along the way. Some compounds worked well but were too expensive to produce, others repelled oil but not water, and still others would be perfect in all respects but would degrade when laundered. As Patsy Sherman commented:

> *It was a frustrating period. Sometimes it seemed we were never going to be successful. Never going to be able to combine the desired properties in a product that could be priced at what people could afford.*[7]

However, as their understanding of how polymers interact with fibers deepened, Sherman, Smith, and the other 3M researchers began to converge on formulations that met all the criteria. By 1956, they had given 3M a commercial treatment for wool, a far more important fiber at the time than it is today. However, it was clear that treatments would also have to be developed for other fabrics. For the next four years, most Scotchgard went to Australia, and sales stagnated at around $250,000 per year. It would not be until 1960 that the first really practical products would be developed. In the mid-1960s, the advent of permanent-press materials (materials that are given their special properties by pretreating them with a whole host of chemicals) meant that an entirely new line of repellents had to be developed. Sherman and Smith teamed up once more, and in what Bill Petersen called "the most brilliant piece of chemistry to come out of the Scotchgard repeller program," they overcame the tremendous challenges these new materials posed.

Today, Scotchgard is so common that it is taken for granted. But without the unanticipated communication that brought the ingredients together during the unofficial period—JoAn Mullin's persistence, George Rathmann's envelope of swatches, Hugh Bryce's low-key suggestion to a subordinate, and Bill Petersen's interest in working in a new area—the serious science might well never have begun.

Mickey and Minnie in 3-D

During Scotchgard's unofficial period, all of the communication required to bring the essential ingredients together took place between people who either knew each other or were generally aware of each other's activities. Moreover, these people worked in the same building on 3M's campus in St. Paul, Minnesota. As their experience shows, even when people know each other and work relatively near each other, it can be difficult to bring their ideas and expertise together at the right time and in the right way to spark a creative act. However, it is far more difficult when the employees do not know each other. It is precisely through promoting this kind of communication that large companies can take advantage of their huge potential for creativity.

The larger the company, the greater the challenge this presents. A few companies we have studied are aware of the importance of unanticipated communication to creativity and have made attempts to manage it directly. While such efforts can help, they can also be detrimental if they are seen as the "answer" to the communication "problem" and resources are diverted from the actions with real leverage—those which promote self-organized and informal networks within the organization. Much of the unanticipated within-company communication that is so vital for creativity will occur through these networks.

A good example of the role such networks can play in creative acts occurred at Kodak in the late 1980s. With a very light touch, this company's innovation center was able to nurture an informal network of people who had expressed interest in three-dimensional (3-D) images at different times, in different divisions of the company, and in different ways. The result was an entirely unexpected and fantastically successful new product line for Kodak.

With some 50,000 employees in the United States and about 100,000 worldwide, Kodak is one of the largest companies in the world. The principal characters in this story—Bud Taylor, Roland Schindler, and Scott Chase—all worked for Kodak in the Rochester, New York, area where the company is based, but at different locations and in different parts of the company. Although they did not know each other, the three men had something in common. Each had an idea for making 3-D images of some sort, which they had tried to get others at Kodak interested in.

In 1985, no company saw any significant business opportunities in 3-D imaging, which had the unusual disadvantage of being seen as something either too old or too new, depending on whom one talked to. The English scientist Sir Charles Wheatstone had first announced his "stereoscope" a century and a half earlier, in 1838.[8] Within a decade, stereoscopes had became widely available, and between 1850 and 1950, millions of stereo cards were produced. Enthusiasts claimed that viewing photographs in stereo was just like being on the scene in person. By the mid-1980s, however, the stereo cards and cameras, some of which had been made by Kodak, had long since become collectors' items. It seemed that the future of 3-D imaging, if there was any, would lie in the emerging area of holography, not in the rediscovery and reworking of a technology just short of 150 years old.

In 1985, Roy (Bud) Taylor, a Kodak engineer working on his company's ill-fated Disk Camera (in which the film is on a circular disk rather than a roll), took his children to a flea market in Rochester where they happened to come across some antique stereo cards and viewers for sale.[9] They bought a few, and both he and his children became fascinated by them. Taylor started to think of a way that his family could make its own 3-D cards. Using two Disk Cameras he obtained from work, Taylor put together a simple stereo camera that allowed him to snap two pictures simultaneously through lenses sixty-five millimeters apart, the distance between a person's eyes. He then glued each pair of prints onto cardboard cards so they could be looked at through a simple viewer he made that directed one image to each eye. Wondering if Kodak could be persuaded to develop a stereo attachment for the Disk Camera, Taylor took some of his homemade stereo cards into work to show his colleagues. His department head was impressed by them and mentioned to him that Kodak had just started an Office of Innovation. Why not send his idea for a stereo camera system there?

Kodak's innovation center had been created to encourage and develop good ideas that were not directly related to an employee's work, and so did not have a natural home at first. It was hoped that any Kodak employee with an idea for a new product, service, technology, or marketing concept would submit his or her idea to the innovation center. In the spring of 1984, taking the advice of his department head, Taylor did this. His idea described how two of Kodak's Disk Cameras could be mounted in a special frame in such a way that anyone could take stereo photographs. His submission included a few sketches and a stereo picture he took of himself in a mirror.

The innovation center responded by helping Taylor find a seed grant for five thousand dollars to continue experimenting with his idea. But, more important, it alerted him to the fact that there were others in Kodak who were also interested in 3-D imaging. Specifically, the center suggested that he get in touch with Bill Burnham, well known inside the company as an inventor with a passion for stereo photography. Because of Burnham's prominence, seniority, and particular interest in 3-D, he had come to be regarded as a point person for what had turned into an informal network of people who were aware of each other's interest in 3-D. Burnham and the other members of this loosely knit group of people tried to help each other by taking an interest in each other's work and passing along information about any interesting developments. There was enough general awareness of this network within Kodak that whenever someone came up with an idea for 3-D imaging, it was usually forwarded to a member of the network for informal evaluation. And in 1984, another idea that found its way to this informal 3-D community was Roland Schindler's concept for 3-D video.

At the time, Schindler had been with Kodak's School of Engineering and Imaging Science for fifteen years, first as an instructor and later as its manager. Before joining Kodak, Schindler had worked at Motorola as a television designer. He had long been intrigued by the possibility of television in 3-D, which would offer, as he put it, "the excitement of getting images to pop right out of the screen."[10] At Kodak, he began to experiment with the idea and tried to interest others in it. In 1984, Schindler, too, sent his idea in to the innovation center and, with its help, was able to obtain two thousand dollars in funding to continue working on it. The center also suggested that he talk with Bill Burnham and some others in the informal 3-D community.

Meanwhile, in June 1985, Taylor was readying a working prototype of his stereo camera for display at a technology fair organized by the innovation center. This "Techfair," the first of what was to become an annual three-day event, was intended to help ideas find homes by providing the opportunity for managers and engineers from many different divisions to look them over. Taylor was at the Techfair for exactly this reason—he was hoping to find a sponsor for his stereo-camera idea. For three days, no one expressed any serious interest. It was only after the fair's official closing time, just as Taylor was starting to take down his exhibit, he got lucky with the very last person to come by his booth. His visitor, who happened to be the marketing head of Kodak's Consumer Systems Division, was impressed with Taylor's camera and agreed to put up fifteen thousand dollars for a market research study. In this study, customers in shopping malls in two major cities were asked to look at images in both 2-D and 3-D, and to answer questions about them. One finding hinted at what would eventually become the main selling point of the new technology—people looked at the 3-D images about 30 percent longer than the 2-D ones. But overall, the market research study generated no further official interest in 3-D at Kodak, perhaps because its main focus was on finding out whether consumers would be interested in buying a 3-D camera if it came on the market priced at around $400, a proposition in which very few customers expressed any interest. Unfortunately, the market researchers had asked the wrong questions. The future for 3-D looked bleak indeed.

Meanwhile, in yet another division and at a different site, a third Kodak employee was also experimenting with 3-D imaging. Scott Chase, a recent physics and electrical engineering graduate specializing in lasers and holography, was some twenty years younger than Taylor and Schindler. Although his assigned work had to do with optical-disk technology, Chase kept up with developments in holography and had become especially intrigued by so-called multiplex holograms—holograms formed by projecting many narrow holograms together, each of which is a photographic image of the same object taken from a different perspective. Because the images are only one millimeter wide each, when they are projected simultaneously and side by side, a person looking at the multiplexed hologram actually sees four or five different holograms with each eye, a feature that can be used to create the impression of 3-D.

Chase was so intrigued by this idea that he began going into work on weekends and nights to see if he could make some multiplex holograms himself. At one point, he told us, he built an experimental camera capable of generating a multiplex hologram. It had forty lenses and was four feet long—"the world's largest pocket camera," as he called it.[11] Wondering if there wasn't some way to reduce the number of images he needed to photograph to build each multiplex hologram, he sought out a mathematician at Kodak, who alerted him to a way to take pictures from only two or three perspectives, rather than forty, and then to extrapolate the full forty from them. In the spring of 1986, Chase submitted his idea to the innovation center. Roger Kimmel, one of the center's facilitators, came over to see for himself what Chase was up to and helped him to get two thousand dollars for equipment and supplies. Chase continued to work on his idea unofficially for several years, and during that time he submitted two more ideas related to 3-D imaging to the innovation center.

In the meantime, Bud Taylor had received a call from the head of Kodak research in Great Britain, who had found him through the informal 3-D network and who said that he was about to visit Rochester and wanted to alert Taylor to something he thought would be of interest to him. Kodak had an innovation center in London that, in addition to welcoming ideas from employees, welcomed them from the outside as well. Taylor learned that a British inventor, Graham Street, had approached the London center with an idea for "lenticular" 3-D imaging. Not long after, Roger Kimmel (the innovation center facilitator who had visited Scott Chase) happened to be going on a trip to London. He offered to buy one of Street's images while in England and bring it back to Taylor. What Kimmel brought back was a full-color 3-D image of Mickey Mouse that could be viewed directly without a special viewing device. The trick was that the viewing device, or *devices* to be precise—consisting of hundreds of tiny lenses that direct different images from the backing paper to each eye—were built into the surface of the image. When Taylor saw the image, he was stunned. The image seemed to be truly 3-D; some things appeared to be in the foreground, others squarely in the background. However, as he looked more closely into Street's process, he soon realized that it would be almost impossible to commercialize. Nevertheless, the crude image set Taylor to thinking about the possibilities of 3-D imaging without the use of a viewer; now he was more excited than ever about the prospects for 3-D at Kodak.

In August 1990, a small but significant event took place. The innovation center contacted Bud Taylor, Roland Schindler, and Scott Chase and suggested that the three men set up a meeting to explore whether they could make more progress together than they had individually. Although all three were excited about 3-D imaging, this was about as far as their shared interests went—Chase was working on holography, Schindler on video, and Taylor on a still camera. The meeting went well: the three liked each other and decided to work together, even though they had no specific project in mind. The first step, they decided, was to conduct a broad-based study of the possibilities of 3-D imaging, and to do this they would have to find a division that would fund it. With this in mind, the three made the rounds of the company, calling on anyone they thought might be interested, a process that involved many meetings. Unfortunately for them, it was not the best time to be trying to sell a new concept. The company was just entering what would prove to be an eight-year-long period of wrenching restructuring and downsizing. Over the next four years almost a third of Kodak's employees would be laid off or take early retirement as the company refocused on its core businesses. The atmosphere at Kodak in those days was one of general fear and retrenchment, and it is hardly surprising that no one stepped forward to support their new idea.

October 1990 found the three men still looking for support. But they had had enough of fighting the system; they knew that if they were to succeed, they had to get the backing of someone with clout at the company—in other words, a "champion." After careful thought, they settled on Brad Paxton, then the head of Kodak's thermal imaging division. Paxton fit the bill: he was high enough in Kodak to help them, and they were confident that he would pay attention to them since he had been a student in several of Schindler's classes. In December 1990, Schindler and Taylor went to see Paxton. With them to help make their case were two people from the innovation center, Roger Kimmel and Gail Hofferbert. About ten minutes into their presentation, Paxton interrupted and said, "Look. I know you both well, but given the company's cash position and its need to deliver new products, this isn't going to fly. If you think you are going to get money for a year just to sit in a room and gaze at the wallpaper, you're crazy."[12] At this point, wanting to regroup, since the meeting was not going the way they had hoped it would, Schindler and Taylor asked if they could take a break. As the group walked down to the cafeteria to get coffee, Kimmel remembered that he still had Street's 3-D picture of Mickey Mouse in his office and realized that it might help things if he went and got it, which he did.

When the meeting resumed, Taylor held out the image made by Graham Street and asked Paxton, "What do you think of this? We can make something like this using existing Kodak technology."

Paxton looked hard at it before he spoke, "If you can figure out how to do that, I will give you some support. But I can only give you ninety days to show results." So the decision was made: they would pursue the use of lenticular technology that had been pioneered by Kodak in the 1930s and brought to their attention more recently by the work of Graham Street.

Armed with a promise of $100,000 from Paxton, they were able to raise another $50,000 from a Kodak manager in the consumer imaging division. In January 1991, four months after the innovation center had brought Schindler, Taylor, and Chase together and about seven years from the time Taylor had first submitted his idea there, the project was now official. For a brief period of time, Chase, the youngest of the three, tried to keep up his job in optical-disk technology and work on the new project at the same time. But he soon realized that he would have to make a choice and reluctantly opted to end his involvement with the new venture. Taylor and Schindler set up makeshift operations in an empty room of a Kodak building that was being remodeled. They scrounged a few desks and a telephone and set to work.

Many things happened during that crucial three-month period. The two men felt intense pressure to devise a working prototype on schedule, and they did not have much money to do it with. Realistically, even had they wanted to do otherwise, they had no option but to honor their commitment to Paxton and to make use of as many existing Kodak technologies as possible. They used primarily off-the-shelf Kodak software, and to develop equipment that did not already exist, they recruited retired Kodak researchers through the informal 3-D community to help out for relatively little money. Schindler estimated to us that 90 percent of the people who helped them didn't charge anything for their time.

On April 16, 1991, one day after the deadline, the two men succeeded in producing a working prototype of a 3-D imaging system. They used it to make what would prove to be a powerful internal sales tool—an image of Mickey Mouse with Minnie Mouse and Pluto clearly standing behind him. It was powerful in part because Disney has long been one of Kodak's most important customers. And now, armed with this, doors very quickly began to open to them at Kodak. In short order the company found a million dollars to fund their development work. In the fall of 1992, they unveiled the new technology at the world's largest photography show, Photokina, in Cologne, Germany, where it produced an instant sensation. Schindler and Taylor were deluged with telephone calls from radio stations and newspapers around the world. A few months after the trade show, in December 1992, they received their first commercial order. J. C. Penney wanted a 3-D image of precious stones for display in the jewelry sections of its stores. Once word spread around the retail industry that 3-D signs attracted significantly more attention than 2-D ones, Taylor and Schindler's 3-D imaging technology quite literally took off.

Since 1992, in addition to using lenticular technology to create the illusion of depth in their imaging, the two men (with their newly formed project team) went on to make images that would attract even more attention—pictures that move or change as a person walks by them. For example, Kodak can now offer advertisers the ability to make a cork appear to pop out of a champagne bottle, or a model appear to drink a particular beverage, or a can of Coke change into Sprite, as people pass by the images. By 1997, the company's new Dynamic Imaging Division had become a major player in the estimated $15 billion U.S. market for point-of-sale signs. It has proved to be a very profitable new business for the company. And who could have predicted that it would be

Bud Taylor (a person on the verge of taking early retirement), Roland Schindler (who had spent his entire fifteen-year career at Kodak in technical education), and Scott Chase (a recent college graduate)—all in different divisions and areas—who would lead the way?

As far as we are aware, when Kodak set up its Office of Innovation in late 1978, it was the first company in the world to have one. Since that time, a handful of other companies—including Du Pont, Hoechst Celanese, Dow Chemical, and Polaroid—have also established innovation centers. These centers are at their best when, as happened in the case of 3-D imaging at Kodak, they gently reinforce and even nudge along movement in unexpected directions that comes to their attention. A light touch like this can make a big difference to a budding creative act. Roland Schindler told us that it meant a lot to him when Gail Hofferbert, an innovation center facilitator, called every so often to ask him about his idea and offer encouragement. We asked Hofferbert about those telephone calls, and she explained their purpose.

> *In those early days, we wanted to keep the responsibility for the idea with the initiator. Those calls were just a "nudge" to remind them of their idea and let them know we were thinking of it.*[13]

The 3-D imaging story shows an innovation center working at its best. However, innovation centers actually have relatively poor records for promoting creative acts. Under the day-to-day pressures of the business, they are too often tempted to move beyond the "light touch" approach and into managing ideas directly. And when such centers put themselves in the position of choosing winners and losers, rather than trying to find a home within the organization for homeless ideas, they do more harm than good. With a light touch, however, an innovation center can promote some of the essential elements of corporate creativity—self-initiated activity, unofficial activity, diverse stimuli, and the critical communication that allows people who might otherwise never have met to find each other. In the case of 3-D imaging, Kodak's innovation center never wavered from acting as an advocate for the three initiators of the idea and sought every opportunity to bring it to the attention of the company's business units.

Realizing the Creative Potential of Large Companies

Within-company communication is one element of corporate creativity that large Japanese companies have proved to be especially good at. We think this helps to explain something that we and others have noticed about Japanese companies—that *the vast majority of creative acts seem to occur in the larger organizations*—a phenomenon, we hope, that will at some point be more carefully studied and understood. Large Japanese companies do several things that promote the unexpected type of communication so important to their creativity. All new college hires, for example, are put through what has become a standard program of initial training, and for the rest of their careers receive regular rotations to new areas. By doing this, the company ensures that its new employees develop an intimate awareness of the organization's activities and, over time, a network of relationships with other employees throughout the company. As a result, employees are better able to make connections that result in creative acts. And, when they need information, the chances are that they will know the best person to go to, will feel comfortable asking for the information, and will be more likely to get a helpful response.

To illustrate how most large Japanese companies train their new recruits, let us look at the experience of one such person at Japan Railways (JR) East, the largest railway company in the world. Chiharu Watari joined JR East in 1988 after completing his master's degree in engineering at the Tokyo Institute of Technology, one of Japan's most prestigious universities. He began at the company with eight months of full-time new-employee training, just like the other college recruits. For the first three weeks of his training, he learned about the history of the company he had joined. He was introduced to its current business activities, organizational structure, policies, and way of operating. Over the next several months, Watari spent several weeks at each of a number of very different jobs. His first assignment was to punch tickets in one of Tokyo's busiest stations under the watchful eye of the full-timers. He went on to work in the maintenance yard, as an assistant conductor, and on a track-leveling team. He even worked as a platform "pusher," cramming people into rush-hour trains.

Finally, after eight months of education and training, the young engineering graduate was assigned to his first real position—in the New

Business Department, where he did market research for new properties. After eleven months, he was rotated to the personnel department,
where among other things he was assigned to lead the new-employee
orientation that he himself had taken just a few years earlier. Until this
point, his experiences had been very similar to those of the other college graduates JR East had hired with him. What came next, however,
was a little unusual. He was one of a select few chosen to go overseas
on a study leave. In Watari's case, he went to the United States, where
after two years of study he obtained an MBA degree from Carnegie
Mellon University. This, together with the speed of his rotations and
the diversity of his assignments, was an indication that he was highly
thought of. Upon his return to Japan, eight years after he had joined
the company, he found himself assigned to Tokyo Station, JR East's flag-
ship and largest station, as an assistant manager. Although we cannot
know how Watari will use his network of relationships and broad knowledge of company operations in the future, we believe that they will be
valuable to him and JR East throughout his career.

Such new-employee education and training is not the only way that
large Japanese companies work to strengthen within-company communication. Consider the example of Ito-Yokado, one of the three largest
retailers in the world (the other two are Sears, Roebuck & Co. and Wal-
Mart Stores), perhaps best known in the West for its controlling interest in the 7-Eleven chain of convenience stores. For many years
Ito-Yokado has been recognized as a leader in the use of information
technology in retailing. In 1982, 7-Eleven was the first company in
Japan to introduce point-of-sale systems in all its stores, providing in-
stantaneous information about which products are selling and which
are not. By November 1985, Ito-Yokado had installed point-of-sale systems in every one of its stores and was receiving real-time information
about more than six hundred thousand products.[14] Surprisingly, while
Ito-Yokado is a leader in the use of information technology, it puts even
more resources into promoting another kind of within-company communication, the "old-fashioned" kind.

Every Wednesday of every week, the managers of the nearly 160 Ito-
Yokado superstores travel to the company's Tokyo headquarters for an
all-day meeting. In the morning, the entire group assembles in an au-
ditorium to hear directly from the president and top management. In

the afternoon, each manager meets with the other managers in his or her district to exchange information about merchandise, operations, marketing, and sales. Wednesday is a busy day at headquarters, because it is also the day that more than two hundred supervisors selected from Ito-Yokado stores all over Japan come to Tokyo for *their* full-day meeting. This meeting is intended to provide a direct communication link between the sales floor and corporate headquarters. For the first half of the day, the supervisors join the store managers for the session with Ito-Yokado's president and top management. Later in the morning they listen to presentations on merchandise and market trends from the company's buyers. In the afternoon, meeting in groups according to their merchandise sector, they are expected to provide their perspective on market trends.

Tuesday is the day when the top managers of all Ito-Yokado divisions and companies, about 130 people in all, meet with the CEO to talk about current problems and measures to address them. More than six hundred of these weekly "Operational Reform Meetings" have been held since they were first started in 1982. Nor are the Ito-Yokado efforts to promote within-company communication limited to these weekly meetings. In every Ito-Yokado store, the manager of each section meets daily with his or her salespeople to discuss sales information and techniques and the day's goals. Twice a year, some eighty-five hundred managers gather at the Yokohama Arena for a series of presentations about company policy and sales strategies.

All told, Ito-Yokado invests an estimated 3 percent of sales on these daily, weekly, and semiannual gatherings. We asked a senior executive at Ito-Yokado how the company justifies its substantial outlay for promoting within-company communication. His response was interesting. No one at Ito-Yokado had ever tried to justify it, he told us, because so far no one had felt that the expenditure was something that needed justification. Nor has anyone felt it necessary to document any of the creative acts that these meetings may have initiated or furthered.

How to Promote Within-Company Communication

Every company tries to ensure effective communication between employees who depend on each other to do their work. However, most organizations overlook the importance of unanticipated communication between employees who do not normally work together. And these exchanges of information often lead to unexpected creative acts. There are three ways an organization can promote this kind of within-company communication:

1. Provide opportunities for employees who do not normally interact with each other to meet.
2. Ensure that every employee has a sufficient understanding of the organization's activities to be able to tap its resources and expertise.
3. Create a new organizational priority: all employees should know the importance of being responsive to requests for information or help from other employees.

There are several ways a company can bring together employees who would otherwise be unlikely to meet. Once a week, Ito-Yokado managers travel to headquarters from all over Japan. Kodak's Techfairs give employees the opportunity to learn about creative activity elsewhere in the organization, and its Office of Innovation (since renamed the Worldwide Innovation Network) makes connections between employees with common creative interests. A single hit (as in the case of 3-D imaging) will more than pay for a company's efforts in this area.

But like so much else associated with corporate creativity, planned activities can only take a company so far. The real leverage lies in ensuring that every employee has a sufficient understanding of the organization's activities to be able to tap its resources and expertise. The more employees know about their organization, the greater the chances that they will be able to make the connections and get the information they need for a creative act. Earlier in this chapter we looked at the experience of one new hire at JR East, whose intensive initial training and many job rotations gave him a comprehensive understanding of the company. There are a multitude of ways for a company to make it fun, interesting, and worthwhile for employees to learn more about how it works and what it does. It is well worth the effort.

Knowing where to go for information is one thing; actually getting it is another. One more thing is needed to promote effective within-company communication. Create a new organizational priority: all employees should know that it is important to be responsive to a request for information or help from other employees, no matter what level or part of the organization they are from. Because that response might very well be the key to a creative act.

MAIN POINTS

A company's creative potential increases rapidly with its size. The larger the company, the more likely that the components of a creative act are already present, but the less likely that they will be brought together without some help.

The effort that large Japanese companies put into promoting within-company communication is one reason why most corporate creativity in that country seems to occur in larger organizations.

Every organization carries out planned activities, and communication channels are necessary for these activities. But it is the unanticipated exchanges between employees who normally do not communicate with each other which often enable projects that have *not* been planned to self-organize and move forward.

Without the communication between so many different 3M employees, Scotchgard, one of 3M's most successful products, might never have been created.

Innovation centers can help with the unanticipated communication that is often necessary for a creative act. However, once innovation centers succumb to the temptation to manage ideas directly, they do more harm than good.

Kodak's successful new 3-D technology depended on its innovation center bringing together three Kodak employees who normally would not have met each other.

There are three ways a company can promote within-company communication:

1. *Provide opportunities for employees who do not normally interact with each other to meet.*
2. *Ensure that every employee has a sufficient understanding of the organization's activities to be able to tap its resources and expertise.*
3. *Create a new organizational priority: all employees should know the importance of being responsive to requests for information or help from other employees.*

Chapter Twelve

UNLEASHING CORPORATE CREATIVITY: WHERE TO START

History is a record of "effects," the vast majority of which
nobody intended to produce.

JOSEPH A. SCHUMPETER[1]

This book grew out of our journey to discover how creativity happens in companies, how previous attempts to manage it have succeeded and failed, and what can be done to promote it. As we tracked down and detailed instances of creativity, from tiny improvements to spectacular innovations, we learned that creativity in companies does not happen the way most people think it does. As it turns out, most creative acts begin in unexpected ways, and no one can predict what they will be or who will be involved in them. This is the true nature of corporate creativity, and it is where a company's creative potential really lies.

From Our Journey to Yours

Now *your* journey begins. The first step is for you to see for yourself, to realize without a doubt that most of the creative acts in your organization occur unexpectedly. To do this, you will have to dig—as we did—in order to understand how they really happened. In our experience, once a creative act occurs, natural forces in companies inexorably act to substitute simplified accounts of it—stories that often ignore or distort its unexpected beginnings. Even companies that take their creative histories (and futures) very seriously have to work hard to overcome this tendency. Take, for example, the story of 3M's Scotchgard, described in Chapter Eleven. Here is the version of the opening part of the story as it is written in the company's official history, *Our Story So Far: Notes from the First Seventy-Five Years of 3M Company:*

> *One day, a laboratory associate spilled a sample of the material on her tennis shoes. The substance resisted attempts to wash it off with water or hydrocarbon solvents. Furthermore, the affected area of her tennis shoes resisted soiling.*
>
> *The lab associate saw this as a bothersome clean-up problem, but chemists Patsy Sherman and Sam Smith viewed it differently. They saw it as a possible product to make textiles resist water and oil stains.*[2]

In fact, as you now know, Patsy Sherman and Sam Smith were not the only ones who saw the tremendous possibilities of poly-FBA. They were not drawn into the picture until almost a year after JoAn Mullin—the chemist who is the anonymous "laboratory associate" in this account—spilled it on her shoes and first saw its potential. Moreover, she had considerable difficulty in convincing anyone else of it and very nearly failed to do so. Although we did encounter a few 3M employees who were aware of the actual events, the garbled official account reflects how most people, inside and outside 3M, believe things really happened. Why is the period of time when JoAn Mullin tried in vain to interest others in her idea the part of the story that 3M got wrong? This was not the only company we found where time and hearsay had been allowed to downplay the unanticipated origins of creative acts—even acts that changed the very face of the organization. It happened again and again. Unless your company recognizes that the true nature of its creativity is that it will be unexpected, its efforts to promote creativity will not get off the ground.

The fact that most creative acts cannot be anticipated should be seen, not as a source of discomfort, but as a fact of corporate life. While many things can be directly planned for and controlled, creativity cannot. This being the case, when creativity occurs in your company—as it assuredly will—search for its unexpected origins and find them before they are lost. Learn from them.

Criteria for Corporate Creativity

Once you and others in your organization come to recognize the power of the unexpected, implementing the six elements will lead the organization to higher levels of creativity. We suggest that your organization use the following criteria to assess how well it is managing its creativity and to guide and monitor its progress to higher levels of creative performance.

Alignment

Many aspects of your company's performance depend on its alignment—the degree to which the interests and actions of every employee support your organization's key goals—but creativity is the most sensitive to it. To a large extent, your company's alignment will also determine the nature of its creativity. Your organization cannot be consistently creative unless it is strongly aligned. And the most critical step in aligning a company is the first one—recognizing the value of alignment and that it has to be done. Once the commitment is made, it is surprisingly straightforward to get the strong alignment that is needed for creativity.

➤ **Is your organization aligned strongly enough for creativity?**

Are you confident that any employee will recognize and respond positively to a potentially useful idea?

What is your organization aligned for? Are you confident that other employees in your company, regardless of their position, would give the same answer?

How does the nature of your organization's alignment limit its creativity?

Do creative acts come disproportionately from a few parts of your organization? If so, is it because the nature of your alignment puts some employees in a better position than others to be creative?

➤ **Do some policies and rules in your organization cause misalignments that interfere with creativity?**

Can you justify them?

Does your organization have any numerical goals for its creativity? If they weren't there, would your company have any less creativity?

If your company has downsized or taken other major action to cut costs, was the impact on creativity considered beforehand?

Has your company ever laid people off as a result of productivity improvements suggested by employees? If so, how did this affect the willingness of those left behind to propose further ideas?

What formal mechanisms does your organization have in place to seek out misalignment?

➤ **What is your company doing to promote alignment?**

Identify the most significant action of the top executive in your company in the last month. How did this action affect alignment?

Identify the most important recent initiatives that your company has undertaken to promote its key goals.

Within the last year, has your company recognized or rewarded any employees for actions that were consistent with its alignment but had otherwise adverse consequences?

Within the last year, has your company held any employees or managers accountable for actions that were out of alignment?

➤ **Do you know of any organizations that are strongly aligned? Visit them and see how they do it.**

Self-Initiated Activity

If they succeed, planned creative acts almost always take your company where it already expected to go. Most unexpected creative acts come from self-initiated activity. Fortunately, people have a natural desire to be creative. All your organization needs to do is unleash what is already there. The key to company-wide self-initiated activity is an effective system for responding to employee ideas.

➤ Does your organization have an effective system for responding to employee ideas?

Does everyone know how to use it? Is it easy to use?

Does it respond to ideas in a fair and timely manner?

As a percentage of your profits, how much money does your system save your organization each year? How well is this known in your organization?

➤ Is the system based on intrinsic motivation?

Within the last month, have you yourself proposed or initiated at least one creative act that no one asked you to undertake? Did you do it for the reward?

Within the last month, has every employee in your organization proposed or initiated a creative act he or she was not asked to undertake?

Think back to a time in your career when, in good faith, you suggested a bad idea to your manager. How did your manager respond? Did he or she simply reject it? Or was it seen as a learning opportunity?

➤ Does your organization document employee ideas?

Are the quantity and quality of employee ideas tracked?

Are managers evaluated on the quantity and quality of creative acts initiated by the employees they are responsible for?

Is there an easy way for a person in one part of your organization to find out about ideas in a different part?

Does your organization have formal mechanisms to identify notable ideas and publicize them to stimulate the thinking of others?

When an idea occurs in one place, does your company have formal mechanisms for ensuring that it gets to all the places where it might be useful?

Unofficial Activity

Every unexpected creative act begins with unofficial activity, during which an idea is worked on without direct official support. Unofficial activity may last for minutes, or it might go on for years. Unless your organization makes a place for unofficial activity, it will see relatively little creativity. Unofficial status eliminates many of the barriers to creativity. It provides a safe haven for ideas, allows a company to get more from its employees than it could reasonably ask for, makes it easier for creative activity to cross official boundaries, and leads to better decision making about which projects to fund. In the majority of creative acts we looked at, the key aspects of the ideas were arrived at during the unofficial period.

➤ Is unofficial activity legitimate in your organization? That is, when an opportunity arises, are employees encouraged to initiate work on something they have not been assigned to do?

Does your organization have specific policies to legitimize unofficial activity?

Do these policies apply to everyone or are they limited to certain categories of people, namely, those who are expected to be creative?

How would your manager respond if you approached him or her to talk about unofficial work you were doing? If you are a manager, how would you react when those who report to you raised the subject of their unofficial work?

➤ Are you aware of examples of how unofficial activity contributed to a creative act in your organization?

Are you yourself currently involved in unofficial activity? Have you ever been?

Are you aware of the unofficial activity of others you work with?

Think back to the last time your company publicized a creative act. Did the publicity include a description of the unofficial activity involved?

➤ Does your organization have a way for employees' proposals to be independently reviewed by different people at different times and in different ways?

If so, can you think of examples from your company where this process saved an idea that might otherwise have been lost?

If not, can you think of examples from your company of good ideas that were killed because they were reviewed by only one person who did not see their potential?

Serendipity

We believe that serendipity plays a role in every creative act. Unfortunately, the original meaning of serendipity—a fortunate accident that meets with sagacity (keenness of insight)—has been all but lost. Armed with the knowledge of what serendipity means, your organization can do much to promote it. A bias for action, a "just do it" attitude that encourages tinkering and experimentation, will lead to more potentially fortunate accidents. An understanding of the role of serendipity in creative acts helps employees to notice accidents when they do occur. Every accident is an exception to what was expected, so don't overlook exceptions. Beyond this, your organization also has to increase the likelihood of potentially fortunate accidents meeting with sagacity. And this means deliberately creating redundancy—unused human potential for change.

➤ Is every employee in your organization aware that serendipity plays a role in creative acts?

Can you identify fortunate accidents in your organization that have led to creative acts?

Do employees in your organization know that every "exception" is an opportunity that should not be overlooked?

➤ What is your organization doing to increase the frequency of fortunate accidents that might lead to serendipity?

Can you identify specific policies or practices in your company that promote a bias for action and experimentation?

What about policies or practices that work against this bias?

➤ What is your organization doing to increase the likelihood that a potentially fortunate accident will meet with sagacity?

Is every employee in your organization rotated into all of the jobs he or she is qualified for?

Does your organization support opportunities for all employees to develop skills in areas unrelated to their present jobs?

Is there redundant human potential in your organization? Pick one of your colleagues. Make a list of his or her knowledge or skills that are not being put to use in your company. Think about how this unused potential might play a role in a creative act.

Diverse Stimuli

A stimulus either provides fresh insight into something a person has already set out to do or bumps that person into something completely unanticipated. It is impossible to predict how an individual will react to any particular stimulus, and what provokes one person may not even be noticed by another. This being the case, while your company should do all it can to bring diverse stimuli to its employees, it should recognize that most creative acts come as a result of stimuli that arise in the course of work or daily life. It is far more important to help employees find stimuli and then put them to use in the company.

➤ Can you trace examples of creativity in your organization to the stimuli that provoked them?

What were these stimuli, and how did they come about?

Think back to the last time your company publicized a creative act. Did the publicity include a description of the stimuli involved?

➤ Does your organization have programs to bring diverse stimuli to employees?

Can you identify any creative acts that were provoked by these programs?

Are the programs aimed at all employees?

How diverse are the stimuli they offer?

Are some of your programs open-ended? That is, like study leaves and sabbaticals, do they offer employees the freedom to pick an area they think might be a fruitful source of stimuli?

➤ Have any creative acts occurred in your company because employees rotated into another job and noticed a stimulus that others before them had not?

What were the stimuli involved?

What made the employees notice them?

➤ Does your organization make it easy for employees to bring stimuli in and put them to use?

Do all employees have regular opportunities to discuss the potential implications of stimuli with their managers and other employees?

➤ How does your organization help employees get stimuli from customers, suppliers, and others who deal with it?

What is your organization doing to bring employees who do not normally interact with customers or suppliers into contact with them?

Are customer complaints used as a source of stimuli for new activity? Can you trace a creative act in your organization to a complaint?

Within-Company Communication

One of the things that seems to happen naturally at smaller companies but not so easily at larger ones is within-company communication. Every organization carries out planned activities and should establish the necessary channels of communication to support them. But official channels are of limited usefulness for creativity. Since the majority of creative acts in companies are unplanned, they often must bring people and information together in ways that cannot be anticipated. It is precisely these unanticipated exchanges of information—exchanges that allow projects that have not been planned to self-organize—which occur so easily in smaller companies. The larger the company, the more likely it is that the components of potential creative acts will be present within it, but the less likely it is that they will come together without help. There are two ways your company can promote these unanticipated communications. It can provide opportunities for employees who do not normally interact with each other to meet. And it can ensure that all employees have enough understanding of how the company works to be able to tap its resources and expertise.

➤ Can you identify a creative act in your company in which unanticipated within-company communication played a key role?

Did your company help this communication to occur, or did it just happen?

➤ Can you identify the ways in which employees in your company who do not normally interact with each other can come together?

Are you a member of an informal group of employees who have a common interest in a new type of activity?

Do you know of any such informal groups in your organization? Did your company play a role in bringing them together, or did they self-organize?

What does your company do to build or support such networks?

Can you point to some recent instances when a manager in your organization took advantage of an opportunity, however small, to bring together some employees who would not normally interact with each other?

➤ Do all employees in your organization have a sufficient understanding of how the company works to be able to tap its resources and expertise?

Can you identify specific programs that are in place to ensure this?

Are you confident that anyone in your organization is either aware of your special expertise or could easily find out about it?

➤ Is it clear to everyone in your organization that a request for information or help from other employees—no matter what level or part of the organization they are from—should be given a high priority?

Think about the last time you contacted someone from a different part of your organization for information or help. How did that person respond?

How often do others from your organization contact you for information? How do you treat their requests?

We hope that your organization will use these criteria to assess how well it is managing its creativity and to determine what must be done to promote it. Some of these questions, however, ask about you and your colleagues, because our six elements also apply to *your* creativity. If the six elements are implemented in your organization, its overall level of creativity will certainly rise. Use them yourself and you may very well find yourself in the middle of a creative act.

Our criteria also provide a structure that allows your company to examine how other organizations have implemented the six elements, and even to benchmark your company's creative performance. It may seem strange to think about benchmarking creativity. But keep in mind that benchmarking is really about creativity, not about copying or comparing your company to its competitors. It is meant to force people to question their assumptions and realize what might be possible.

Most important of all is for your company to learn from its own creative acts, and for you, yourself, to learn from your personal experiences with creativity. After all, it was a firsthand approach that led us to our six elements and that will now lead you to implement them in the best way for your organization. Our journey led us to *discover* the power of the unexpected. Your journey will lead you to *realize* it.

—*Notes*———

Chapter One

1. Tom Peters, *Crazy Times Call for Crazy Organizations* (New York: Vintage Books, 1994), p. 12.
2. E. Paul Torrance, *Surviving Emergencies and Extreme Conditions: A Summary of Six Years of Research* [Unpublished manuscript prepared for the survival training unit of the Air Force Personnel and Training Research Center] (Washington D.C.: U.S. Air Force, 1959), p. 37.
3. Tomoshige Hori, *Food Engineering Innovation and Reinvention: An Example of Industrial Application* (Tokyo: Snow Brand Milk Products, 1991), p. 9.
4. Tomoshige Hori, "Effect of Rennet Treatment and Water Content on Thermal Conductivity of Skim Milk," *Journal of Food Science,* 48 (1983), 1492–1496.

Chapter Two

1. Frank B. Jewett, "The Promise of Technology," *Science,* 99 (1944), 5.
2. Thomas P. Hughes, *American Genesis: A Century of Invention and Technological Enthusiasm* (New York: Viking Penguin, 1989), p. 13.
3. This memo would later give rise to an amusing incident, because as it was first typed by the typing pool, it had a typographical error in it. Kathy Betts corrected the error and resubmitted it to the typing pool. Unfortunately, her boss, needing the memo in a hurry when the Medicaid commissioner requested a copy, called her at her home (it was on one of the days she wasn't working), found out that the memo was in the typing pool, and went down and pulled it out of the typing queue before the typo had been corrected. This memo, typo and all, became what the governor eventually saw and what was released to the national media. Imagine Kathy Betts's further consternation when, in 1994, she was contacted by an English professor from Pennsylvania State University seeking a copy of the memo to demonstrate to her students the importance of good writing!
4. Kathy Betts, quoted by Bella English in "She Finds Cash, State Finds Hero," *Boston Globe,* June 10, 1991, p. 1 (Metro Region section).
5. Mary B. W. Tabor, "State Worker's Budget Coup: A Windfall for Massachusetts," *New York Times,* June 8, 1991, p.1.

6. English, "She Finds Cash," p. 1.

7. Interview with Kathy Betts, October 18, 1995.

8. For a nice jargon-free summary of attribution theory, see Jean M. Bartunek, "Why Did You Do That? Attribution Theory in Organizations," *Business Horizons*, 24, no. 5 (1981), 66–71.

9. Peter Drucker, *Innovation and Entrepreneurship: Practice and Principles* (New York: HarperCollins, 1985), pp. 26–27.

10. H. Balzer, "Engineers: The Rise and Decline of the Soviet Myth," in Loren Graham, ed., *Science and Soviet Social Order* (Cambridge, Mass.: Harvard University Press, 1990), p. 141.

11. W. Edwards Deming developed his influential "red bead experiment" precisely to illustrate this point: how helpless an individual was in the face of a bad system. See Raphael Aguayo, *Dr. Deming: The American Who Taught the Japanese About Quality* (New York: Simon & Schuster, 1990).

12. Malcolm Cohen, *Labor Shortages: Myth or Reality?* (Ann Arbor: University of Michigan Press, 1995), p. 85.

13. Joseph Juran, personal communication, December 7, 1995.

14. According to Jim Schlatter's lab notebook, on file at the NutraSweet Company of Monsanto.

15. Interview with Jim Schlatter, October 27, 1995.

16. Interview with Robert Mazur, October 26, 1995.

17. Interview with Jim Schlatter, October 27, 1995.

18. Interview with Robert Mazur, October 26, 1995.

19. Interview with John Witt, November 6, 1995.

20. Interview with Robert Mazur, October 26, 1995.

21. C. Hance and R. A. Goldberg, *The NutraSweet Company: Technology to Tailor-Make Foods*, Harvard Business School Case 9-589-050 (Boston: Harvard Business School Publishing Division, 1988).

Chapter Three

1. Emily T. Smith, "Are You Creative?" *Business Week*, September 30, 1985, p. 46.

2. For two different views of the controversy surrounding intelligence testing, see Richard J. Herrnestein and Charles Murray, *The Bell Curve* (New York: Free Press, 1994); and Stephen Jay Gould, *The Mismeasure of Man* (New York: Norton, 1981).

3. J. P. Guilford, "Creativity Research: Past, Present and Future," in Scott G. Isaksen, ed., *Frontiers of Creativity Research* (Buffalo, N.Y.: Bearly Press, 1987), p. 47.

4. J. P. Guilford, "Creativity," *American Psychologist*, 5 (1950), 444.

5. J. W. Getzels and P. W. Jackson, *Creativity and Intelligence: Explorations with Gifted Students* (New York: Wiley, 1962).

6. E. P. Torrance, *Educational Achievement of the Highly Intelligent and the Highly Creative: Eight Partial Replications of the Getzels-Jackson Study*, Research Memorandum BER-60-18 (Minneapolis: Bureau of Education Research, University of Minnesota).

7. Douglas W. MacKinnon, *In Search of Human Effectiveness: Identifying and Developing Creativity* (Buffalo, N.Y.: Creative Education Foundation, 1978), p. 60.
8. Beard himself was remarkably creative early in his life. After the Civil War, while still in his twenties, he was a prolific writer and lecturer on such varied topics as the therapeutic applications of electricity, nervous exhaustion, and the effects of aging on human faculties.
9. George M. Beard, *Legal Responsibility in Old Age* (New York: Russell, 1874).
10. Harvey C. Lehman, *Age and Achievement* (Princeton, N.J.: Princeton University Press, 1953).
11. See, for example, Dean K. Simonton, *Genius, Creativity and Leadership* (Cambridge, Mass.: Harvard University Press, 1984).
12. Henry Ford, *Today and Tomorrow* (reprint, Portland, Oreg.: Productivity Press, 1988), p. 53.
13. Thomas S. Kuhn, *The Structure of Scientific Revolutions* (Chicago: University of Chicago Press, 1970).
14. Herbert A. Simon, "Understanding Creativity and Creative Management," in Robert L. Kuhn, ed., *Handbook for Creative and Innovative Managers* (New York: McGraw-Hill, 1988), p. 16.
15. Roger Schank, *The Creative Attitude* (Old Tappan, N.J.: Macmillan, 1988), p. 59.
16. Margaret Cheney, *Tesla: Man out of Time* (Upper Saddle River, N.J.: Prentice Hall, 1981).
17. Max Nordau, *Degeneration* (New York: Appleton, 1897).
18. Peter F. Drucker, *Innovation and Entrepreneurship: Practice and Principles* (New York: HarperCollins, 1985), p. 139.
19. Jacques Barzun, "The Paradoxes of Creativity," *The American Scholar,* 58 (1989), 347.
20. Graham Wallas, *The Art of Thought* (Orlando, Fla.: Harcourt Brace, 1926).
21. Alex F. Osborn, *Applied Imagination* (New York: Scribner, 1953).
22. Osborn, *Applied Imagination,* p. 151.
23. See, for example, Morris I. Stein, *Stimulating Creativity* (Orlando, Fla.: Academic Press, 1975).
24. David N. Perkins, "The Possibility of Invention," in Robert J. Sternberg, ed., *The Nature of Creativity* (Cambridge: Cambridge University Press, 1988), p. 378.
25. For more information about examples of well-known creativity methods, see Sidney Parnes, *The Magic of Your Mind* (Buffalo, N.Y.: Bearly Press, 1981); William J. Gordon, *Synectics: The Development of Creative Capacity* (New York: HarperCollins, 1961); and Edward deBono, *Six Thinking Hats* (New York: Little, Brown, 1986). For a critical discussion of creativity methods, see Robert W. Weisberg, *Creativity: Beyond the Myth of Genius* (New York: Freeman, 1993); and Morris I. Stein, *Stimulating Creativity,* vols. 1 and 2 (Orlando, Fla.: Academic Press, 1974, 1975).
26. For a discussion of the demise of behaviorism and limits of rewards (including the transcript of an intriguing interview with B. F. Skinner) see Alfie Kohn, *Punished by Rewards* (Boston: Houghton Mifflin, 1993).

27. Edward L. Deci, "Effects of Externally Mediated Rewards on Intrinsic Motivation," *Journal of Personality and Social Psychology,* 18 (1971), 114.

28. Teresa M. Amabile, "The Motivation to Be Creative," in Scott G. Isaksen, ed., *Frontiers of Creativity Research* (Buffalo, N.Y.: Bearly Press, 1987), pp. 229–230.

29. W. Edwards Deming, *The New Economics* (Cambridge, Mass.: MIT Center for Advanced Engineering Study, 1994), pp. 108–109.

30. This example was also written about in an article on FoaMech's *kaizen* system: Robert Rose, "Kentucky Plant Workers Are Cranking Out Good Ideas," *Wall Street Journal,* August 13, 1996.

31. Interview with Kim Darnell, October 18, 1996.

Chapter Four

1. Letter to R. Samuelson, M.P., in Alexander B. Bruce, *The Life of William Denny* (London: Hodder and Stoughton, 1888), p. 82.

2. For a wonderful overview of the Toyota Creative Idea system, see Yuzo Yasuda, *Forty Years, Twenty Million Ideas* (Portland, Oreg.: Productivity Press, 1991).

3. William Denny and Brothers, *Denny Dumbarton* (London: E. J. Burrow, 1932), p. 80.

4. John Ward, "Memoir of the Late William Denny, F.R.S.E., President of the Institution," *Transactions of the Institution of Engineers and Shipbuilders in Scotland,* 30 (1887), 33–286.

5. Alexander B. Bruce, *The Life of William Denny* (London: Hodder and Stoughton, 1888), p. 82.

6. This section is based in part on Dean M. Schroeder and Alan G. Robinson, "America's Most Successful Export to Japan: Continuous Improvement Programs," *Sloan Management Review,* 32, no. 3 (Spring 1991), 67–82.

7. Samuel Crowther, *John H. Patterson—Pioneer in Industrial Welfare* (New York: Doubleday, 1924), p. 196. We are grateful to Mark Bernstein for alerting us to this quote in his book *Grand Eccentrics* (Wilmington, Ohio: Orange Frazer Press, 1996).

8. Alfred A. Thomas, comp., *Asking for Suggestions from Employees at National Cash Register Company: An Exhibit of What the System Is and What It Has Accomplished,* 2nd edition (Dayton, Ohio: NCR, 1905), p. 4.

9. These data are taken from Thomas, *Asking for Suggestions.*

10. I. F. Marcossen, *Wherever Men Trade: The Romance of the Cash Register* (New York: Dodd, Mead, 1945), p. 49.

11. Samuel Crowther, *John H. Patterson—Pioneer in Industrial Welfare* (New York: Doubleday, 1924), p. 73.

12. Thomas Watson, Jr., and Peter Petre, *Father Son and Co.: My Life at IBM and Beyond* (New York: Bantam Books, 1990); and Mark Bernstein, *Grand Eccentrics* (Wilmington, Ohio: Orange Frazer Press, 1996).

13. Although the historical record is clear that NCR's system predated Kodak's system by four years, we often find Kodak's system erroneously cited as the first.

14. The National Cash Register Corporation, *Celebrating the Future,* vol. 1 (Dayton, Ohio: Author, 1984), p. 44.

15. Masaaki Imai, *Kaizen: The Key to Japan's Competitive Success* (New York: Random House, 1986), p. 112.
16. Japan Human Relations Association, *The Idea Book: Improvement Through Total Employee Involvement* (Portland, Oreg.: Productivity Press, 1988).
17. Lawrence K. Rosinger, "What Future for Japan?" *Foreign Policy Reports,* September 1, 1943, p. 144.
18. S. Park, *U.S. Labor Policy in Postwar Japan* (Berlin: EXpress Edition, 1985), p. 95.
19. This and the next section are based on Alan G. Robinson and Dean M. Schroeder, "Training, Continuous Improvement, and Human Relations: The U.S. TWI Programs and the Japanese Management Style," *California Management Review,* 35, no. 2 (1993), 35–57.
20. J. W. Dietz, *Learning by Doing* (Summit, N.J.: J. W. Dietz, 1970).
21. Training Within Industry Service, *The Training Within Industry Report: 1940–1945* (Washington, D.C.: War Manpower Commission Bureau of Training, 1945), p. 94.
22. Interview with Edgar McVoy (a former ESS official), July 29, 1991.
23. Training Within Industry Service, *The Training Within Industry Materials: 1940–1945,* December Bulletin, p. 1.
24. Training Within Industry Service, *The Training Within Industry Materials, JMT Manual* (Washington, D.C.: War Manpower Commission Bureau of Training, 1945), p. 33.
25. N. Noda, "How Japan Absorbed American Management Methods," in *Modern Japanese Management* (London: Management Publications, 1969), p. 53.
26. Japan Human Relations Association, *The Idea Book* (Portland, Oreg.: Productivity Press, 1988), p. 202.
27. Masao Nemoto, *Total Quality Control for Management* (Upper Saddle River, N.J.: Prentice Hall, 1987), p. 4.
28. Interview with H.P.G.H. Thomas, July 30, 1991.
29. F. L. Schodt, *Inside the Robot Kingdom* (Tokyo: Kodansha International, 1988), p. 94.
30. *Management Training Course Conference Outline,* Far East Air Materiel Command (Tachikawa, Japan), 19993-FEC P&PC-11/51–700, pp. 14–22.
31. *Management Training Course Conference Outline,* pp. 14–24.

Chapter Five

1. James C. Collins and Jerry I. Porras, *Built to Last: Successful Habits of Visionary Companies* (New York: HarperBusiness, 1994), pp. 201, 221.
2. Collins and Porras, *Built to Last.*
3. Mark G. Brown, Darcy E. Hitchcock, and Marsha L. Willard, *Why TQM Fails and What to Do About It* (Burr Ridge, Ill.: Irwin, 1994).
4. J. M. Juran, "The Upcoming Century of Quality," *Quality Progress,* August 1994, p. 30.
5. Much of this section on the Soviet Union describes the results of this research project, which is detailed more in Linda Randall, Alan Robinson, and Alexandra N. Tolstaya, "Continuous Improvement: Lessons from the Life and Death

of the Soviet Rationalization Proposal System: 1931–1992," *Proceedings of the 1994 Annual Academy of Management Conference,* Dallas, Texas.

6. Hedrick Smith, *The New Russians* (New York: Avon, 1990), p. 308.

7. Smith, *The New Russians,* p. 308.

8. For an excellent account of this phenomenon, we suggest L. H. Seigelbaum, *Stakhanovism and the Politics of Productivity in the USSR, 1935–1941* (Cambridge: Cambridge University Press, 1990).

9. Training Within Industry Service, *The Training Within Industry Materials, JMT Manual* (Washington, D.C.: War Manpower Commission Bureau of Training, 1945), p. 33.

Chapter Six

1. For the most official version of this story we could get, we have drawn on two books: Dan Reed, *The American Eagle: The Ascent of Bob Crandall and American Airlines* (New York: St. Martin's Press, 1993); and Robert Serling, *Eagle: The Story of American Airlines* (New York: St. Martin's Press, 1985).

2. Our description of the IdeAAs in Action Program is based on many interviews with employees during visits to American's Alliance Maintenance Center and its headquarters in Dallas.

3. Interview with Kathryn Kridel, November 11, 1996.

4. Interview with John Ford, December 8, 1994.

5. Interview with Keith Rapley, January 23, 1995.

Chapter Seven

1. Arthur Koestler, *The Act of Creation* (London: Arkana [Penguin Books], 1964), p. 87.

2. Interviews with Joseph Woodland, October 27, 1995, and July 17, 1996. We were unable to interview Bob Silver, who died at the relatively young age of thirty-eight.

3. Thomas Watson, Jr., and Peter Petre, *Father, Son & Co.: My Life at IBM and Beyond* (New York: Bantam Books, 1990), p. 203.

4. Watson and Petre, *Father, Son & Co.,* p. 195.

5. Interview with Evon Greanias, July 20, 1996.

6. Tony Seidemann, "Bar Codes Sweep the World," in *American Inventions* (Lanham, Md.: Barnes & Noble Books, 1995).

7. Interview with Alec Jablonover, July 27, 1996.

8. "A Standard Labeling Code for Food," *Business Week,* April 7, 1973, p. 72.

9. Interview with Yasunori Kanda, November 9, 1990.

10. F. Dale Robertson, "Chartering a Management Philosophy for the Forest Service," Forest Service memorandum to all employees, December 19, 1989.

11. Interview with Karl Mettke, June 25, 1996.

12. Joseph F. McKenna, "Empowerment Thins a Forest of Bureaucracy," *Industry Week,* April 5, 1993, p. 64.

13. Interview with Bill Millard, July 2, 1996.

14. Ronald E. Yates, "Total Quality Management a Forest Service Resource," *Chicago Tribune,* February 15, 1993, p. 1.
15. Tom Peters, *Crazy Times Call for Crazy Organizations* (New York: Vintage Books, 1994), p. 73.

Chapter Eight

1. Jacques Barzun, "The Paradoxes of Creativity," *The American Scholar,* 58 (1989), 341.
2. Our description of Marker's story is drawn from a variety of sources, including an interview with his son, Russell C. Marker; Bernard Asbell, *The Pill: The Untold Story of the Drug That Changed the World* (New York: Random House, 1995); a nine-page typewritten report by Russell Marker titled *The Early Production of Steroidal Hormones;* and P. A. Lehmann, A. G. Bolivar, and R. R. Quintero, "Russell E. Marker: Pioneer of the Mexican Steroid Industry," *Journal of Chemical Education,* 50 (1973), 195–199.
3. "Russell Marker, Pioneer of the Steroid Hormone Industry, Dies at 92," Obituary, Office of the Dean, Eberly College of Science, March 5, 1995.
4. Marker would not fulfill the University of Maryland's requirements for a doctorate until 1990, more than sixty-five years later. By that time he had satisfied their requirements for an *honorary* doctorate.
5. Interview with Russell C. Marker, November 21, 1995.
6. Stewart H. Holbrook, *The Golden Age of Quackery* (Old Tappan, N.J.: Macmillan, 1959).
7. Marker used his sense of humor in naming the sapogenins he discovered. He called them *pennogenin* for Penn State, *markogenin* for himself, and *rockogenin* for Dean Whitmore, whose nickname was Rocky. One of his names that never appeared in writing was *crapogenin;* Arthur Lamb, editor of the *Journal of the American Chemical Society,* persuaded him to rename it kappogenin.
8. In 1994 Syntex was acquired by the Swiss company Roche for $5.3 billion.
9. P. A. Lehmann, A. G. Bolivar, and R. R. Quintero, "Russell E. Marker: Pioneer of the Mexican Steroid Industry," *Journal of Chemical Education,* 50 (1973), 199.
10. Lord Kelvin, "On a Self-Acting Apparatus for Multiplying and Maintaining Electric Charges, with Applications to Illustrate the Voltaic Theory," *Proceedings of the Royal Society (London),* 16 (1867), 67.
11. Richard G. Sweet, "High Frequency Recording with Electrostatically Deflected Ink Jets," *Review of Scientific Instruments,* 36 (1965), 131–132.
12. Interview with David Donald, July 19, 1996.
13. Thomas P. Hughes, *American Genesis: A Century of Invention and Technological Enthusiasm* (New York: Viking Penguin, 1989), p. 52.
14. Interview with John Meyer, August 14, 1996.
15. Interview with John Vaught, July 11, 1996.
16. Interview with Frank Cloutier, July 26, 1996.
17. Interview with John Meyer, August 14, 1996.

18. Lewis W. Lehr, "Encouraging Innovation and Entrepreneurship in Diversified Corporations," in Robert L. Kuhn, ed., *Handbook for Creative and Innovative Managers* (Old Tappan, N.J.: Macmillan, 1988), p. 215.

Chapter Nine

1. Letter to Horace Mann dated January 28, 1754, in W. S. Lewis, Warren Hunting Smith, and George L. Lam, eds., *The Yale Edition of Horace Walpole's Correspondence*, vol. 20 (New Haven: Yale University Press, 1960), pp. 407–408.
2. Interview with Alan Smith, October 8, 1995.
3. David A. Hounshell and John Kenly Smith, Jr., *Science and Corporate Strategy: Du Pont R&D, 1902–1980* (Cambridge: Cambridge University Press), 1988.
4. R. J. Plunkett, "Monomers and the Man: The Origin of a Legend," *The Journal of Teflon*, 4, no. 3 (1964), 2–7.
5. Lucien Rhodes, "The Un-manager," *Inc. Magazine*, August 1982, p. 36.
6. Actually, the story goes back even further. Armeno himself worked from a popular Persian tale written in 1302 by Amir Khusrau of Delhi, "the greatest Persian poet that India ever produced." Khusrau, in his turn, based his story on one of the classics of the Persian language, a volume of five poems called the *Khamse*, published a hundred years before by the poet Nizami. For more information, see Schuyler V. R. Camann, "Christopher the Armenian and the Three Princes of Serendip," *Comparative Literature Studies*, 4 (1967), 229–258.
7. Letter to Horace Mann dated January 28, 1754, in Lewis, Smith, and Lam, *Yale Edition of Horace Walpole's Correspondence*, pp. 407–408.
8. Theodore G. Remer, ed., *Serendipity and the Three Princes: From the Peregrinaggio of 1557* (Norman: University of Oklahoma Press, 1965), p. 63.
9. Remer, *Serendipity and the Three Princes*, pp. 64–65.
10. Letter to Horace Mann dated January 28, 1754, in Lewis, Smith, and Lam, *Yale Edition of Horace Walpole's Correspondence*, p. 408.
11. Interview with Steven R. Davis, associate professor of chemistry, University of Mississippi, March 20, 1996.
12. Interview with Jason Shih, October 28, 1995. Although Milton Scott could not corroborate the statement that Shih remembers him making, he told us that that was his belief at the time, and that he almost certainly made this emphatically clear to his young postdoctoral fellow (interview, November 10, 1995).
13. M. E. Watanabe, "Thermophilic Biodigestion Yields a Keratinase Enzyme," *Genetic Engineering News*, 12, no. 15 (October 1, 1992).
14. P. W. Barker, *Charles Goodyear: Connecticut Yankee and Rubber Pioneer* (Boston: Godfrey L. Cabot, 1940).
15. Malvin E. Ring, *Dentistry: An Illustrated History* (New York: Abrams, 1986).
16. Interview with Alan Smith, October 8, 1995.
17. Stephen J. Gould, "Creativity in Evolution and Human Innovation," lecture given at the International House of Japan, November 11, 1989. The following paragraph also draws from his talk.
18. Interview with Roger Kimmel, March 20, 1996.

Chapter Ten

1. Jacques Barzun, "The Paradoxes of Creativity," *The American Scholar,* 58 (1989), 350.
2. George Miller, quoted on Kennedy-Miller Productions' home page, November 1995. [http:\\www.movieweb.com\movie\babe\babe.txt]
3. Interview with Dick King-Smith, October 26, 1995.
4. George Miller, quoted in Peter Stack, "Producer's Pet Project Is a 'Babe,'" *San Francisco Chronicle,* July 31, 1995, p. C-1.
5. Interview with Chris Noonan, August 12, 1996.
6. Interview with Chris Noonan, August 12, 1996.
7. Interview with Dick King-Smith, October 26, 1995.
8. This story has been compiled from a number of sources, including Alfred P. Sloan, *My Years with General Motors* (New York: Doubleday, 1963); T. A. Boyd, ed., *Prophet of Progress: Selections from the Speeches of Charles F. Kettering* (New York: NAL/Dutton, 1961); T. A. Boyd, *Professional Amateur* (New York: NAL/Dutton, 1957); Stuart W. Leslie, *Boss Kettering* (New York: Columbia University Press, 1983); Mark Bernstein, *Grand Eccentrics* (Wilmington, Ohio: Orange Frazer Press, 1996); David A. Hounshell and John Kenly Smith, Jr., *Science and Corporate Strategy: Du Pont R&D, 1902–1980* (Cambridge: Cambridge University Press, 1988); and our own transcript of a taped speech about the paint story by Charles Kettering.
9. Sloan, *My Years with General Motors.*
10. Leslie, *Boss Kettering,* p. 191.
11. Bernstein, *Grand Eccentrics.*
12. Sloan, *My Years with General Motors,* p. 236.
13. Helen Axel, *Redefining Corporate Sabbaticals for the 1990s* (New York: The Conference Board, 1992).
14. Interview with Clar Evans, November 21, 1996.
15. Charles Fishman, "At Hallmark, Sabbaticals Are Serious Business," *Fast Company,* October 1996, p. 44.
16. Interview with Clar Evans, November 21, 1996.
17. Nan and Ivan Lyons, *Imperial Taste: A Century of Elegance at Tokyo's Imperial Hotel* (Tokyo: Kodansha International, 1990), p. 31.
18. Interview with Sam Malone, director, quality services at Xerox, November 22, 1996.

Chapter Eleven

1. Robert Rosenfeld and Jenny C. Servo, "Business and Creativity," *The Futurist,* August 1984, pp. 21–26.
2. 3M Company, *Our Story So Far: Notes from the First Seventy-Five Years of 3M Company* (St. Paul: Minnesota Mining and Manufacturing Company, 1977), p. 107.
3. Interview with Hugh Bryce, July 23, 1996.
4. Interview with JoAn Mullin, September 18, 1996. JoAn Mullin's lab notes were unclear as to whether the day in question was July 14 or 15.

5. Interview with JoAn Mullin, July 17, 1996.

6. Interview with George Rathmann, July 2, 1996.

7. 3M Company, *A Chemical History of 3M, 1933–1990* (St. Paul: Minnesota Mining and Manufacturing Company, 1990), p. 73.

8. The idea of stereoscopy preceded stereo photography. In his talk on binocular vision, Wheatstone proposed a device that could represent solid objects. He suggested that it be called a "stereoscope." It would be another decade, however, before the first stereoscope was made.

9. Interview with Bud Taylor, September 19, 1996.

10. Interview with Roland Schindler, July 31, 1996.

11. Interview with Scott Chase, September 19, 1996.

12. Interview with Bud Taylor, September 19, 1996.

13. Interview with Gail Hofferbert, October 14, 1996.

14. For more on this subject, see, for example, Taiichi Ohno and Setsuo Mito, *Just-in-Time for Today and Tomorrow* (Portland, Oreg.: Productivity Press, 1988).

Chapter Twelve

1. Joseph A. Schumpeter, *Business Cycles: A Theoretical, Historical and Statistical Analysis of the Capitalist Process,* vol. 2 (New York: McGraw-Hill, 1939), p. 1045.

2. 3M Company, *Our Story So Far: Notes from the First Seventy-Five Years of 3M Company* (St. Paul: Minnesota Mining and Manufacturing Company, 1977), p. 107.

—Index—

The Authors

Alan G. Robinson, professor of management at the Isenberg School of Management, University of Massachusetts, graduated from Cambridge University in mathematics and received his Ph.D. in operations research from the Johns Hopkins University. His research on corporate creativity has taken him to several hundred companies around the world, including the United States, Japan, Canada, Mexico, Great Britain, China, India, Brazil, Greece, Jamaica, and Russia.

Robinson has been a consultant to more than fifty companies (large and small) in eight countries on how to improve their creative performance and is one of relatively few professors to have been invited to serve on the Board of Examiners of the United States Malcolm Baldrige National Quality Award. He is a frequent public speaker on the subject of creativity in companies. He lives in Amherst, Massachusetts, with his wife and two girls.

Sam Stern is professor of education at Oregon State University, where his research and writing are concerned with creativity and its connection with business and education. He has also taught in the Department of Economics at Harvard University, the MBA Program at the Athens Laboratory of Business Administration in Greece, and in the Department of Systems Science at Tokyo Institute of Technology.

While in Japan from 1990 through 1992, Stern served as the Japan Management Association (JMA) Professor of Creativity Development and led a research team in a multiyear study of creativity in some two hundred companies. He is one of the few non-Japanese to have held an endowed professorship in Japan. Stern has served as an adviser on creativity to organizations in the United States, Japan, and other countries, including Hewlett-Packard, NASA, NEC, Polaroid, and Seiko-Epson. He lives in Corvallis, Oregon, with his wife and two boys.

Berrett-Koehler Publishers

Berrett-Koehler is an independent publisher of books, periodicals, and other publications at the leading edge of new thinking and innovative practice on work, business, management, leadership, stewardship, career development, human resources, entrepreneurship, and global sustainability.

Since the company's founding in 1992, we have been committed to supporting the movement toward a more enlightened world of work by publishing books, periodicals, and other publications that help us to integrate our values with our work and work lives, and to create more humane and effective organizations.

We have chosen to focus on the areas of work, business, and organizations, because these are central elements in many people's lives today. Furthermore, the work world is going through tumultuous changes, from the decline of job security to the rise of new structures for organizing people and work. We believe that change is needed at all levels—individual, organizational, community, and global—and our publications address each of these levels.

We seek to create new lenses for understanding organizations, to legitimize topics that people care deeply about but that current business orthodoxy censors or considers secondary to bottom-line concerns, and to uncover new meaning, means, and ends for our work and work lives.

See next page for other books from Berrett-Koehler Publishers

Other leading-edge business books
from Berrett-Koehler Publishers

How to Get Ideas

Jack Foster, Illustrated by Larry Corby

JACK FOSTER draws on three decades of experience as an advertising writer and creative director to take the mystery and anxiety out of getting ideas. Describing eight ways to condition your mind to produce ideas and five subsequent steps for creating and implementing ideas on command, he makes it easy and fun.

Paperback, 150 pages, 11/96 • ISBN 1-57675-006-X CIP
Item no. 5006X-248 $14.95

301 Ways to Have Fun at Work

Dave Hemsath and Leslie Yerkes

Illustrated by Dan McQuillen

IN THIS ENTERTAINING and comprehensive guide, Hemsath and Yerkes show readers how to have fun at work—everyday. Written for anyone who works in any type of organization, *301 Ways to Have Fun at Work* provides ideas for creating a dynamic, fun-filled work environment.

Paperback, 300 pages, 6/97 • ISBN 1-57675-019-1 CIP
Item no. 50191-1248 $14.95

Artful Work

Awakening Joy, Meaning, and Commitment in the Workplace

Dick Richards

RICHARDS APPLIES the assumptions of artists about work and life to the challenges facing people and organizations today. Readers will learn to take an inspired approach to their work, renewing their experience of it as a creative, participative, and purposeful endeavor.

Hardcover, 144 pages, 3/95 • ISBN 1-881052-63-X CIP
Item no. 5263X-248 $25.00

Available at your favorite bookstore, or call (800) 929-2929

Put the leading-edge business practices you read about to use in your work and in your organization

D O YOU EVER WISH there was a forum in your organization for discussing the newest trends and ideas in the business world? Do you wish you could explore the leading-edge business practices you read about with others in your company? Do you wish you could set aside a few hours every month to connect with like-minded coworkers or to get to know others in your business community?

If you answered yes to any of these questions, then the answer is simple: Start a business book reading group in your organization or business community. For step-by-step advice on how to do just that, visit the Berrett-Koehler website at <www.bkpub.com> and click on "Business Literacy 2000." There you'll find specific guidelines to help in all aspects of creating a successful reading group—from locating interested participants to selecting books, and facilitating discussions.

The website is part of the Business Literacy 2000 program launched by the Consortium for Business Literacy—a group of 19 business book publishers whose primary goal has been to promote the formation of business reading groups within corporations and business communities.

Business Literacy 2000 is dedicated to providing you with tools to help you build a dialog with others in your company or business community, share ideas, build lasting relationships, and bring new ideas and knowledge to bear in your work and organizations. On our website, you'll find guidelines for starting and running a reading group, suggested readings, study guides, and activities to help ensure lively and useful discussions.

For more information on Business Literacy 2000, guidelines for starting a business book reading group, or copies of any of our study guides, please visit our website at: <www.bkpub.com>.

If you do not have Internet access, you may request information by contacting us at:

Berrett-Koehler Publishers
450 Sansome St., Suite 1200
San Francisco, CA 94111
Fax: (415) 362-2512
Email: bkpub@bkpub.com

Please be sure to include your name, address, phone number, email address, and the information you would like to receive.

I F YOU LIKE THE IDEAS in *Corporate Creativity* and would like to explore them with others, please fill out the form below and mail, fax, or email the information to:

Berrett-Koehler Publishers
450 Sansome St., Suite 1200
San Francisco, CA 94111
Fax: (415) 362-2512
Email: bkpub@bkpub.com

Name _____

Title _____

Company _____

Address _____

_____

Telephone _____

Fax_ _____

Email _____

Where did you buy this book? _____

_____

Please be sure to include complete information.